Fast Data Processing with Spark 2

Third Edition

Learn how to use Spark to process big data at speed and scale for sharper analytics. Put the principles into practice for faster, slicker big data projects.

Krishna Sankar

BIRMINGHAM - MUMBAI

Fast Data Processing with Spark 2

Third Edition

First published: October 2013

Second edition: March 2015

Third edition: October 2016

Production reference: 1141016

Published by Packt Publishing Ltd.

Livery Place

35 Livery Street

Birmingham B3 2PB, UK.

ISBN 978-1-78588-927-1

www.packtpub.com

Credits

Author

Krishna Sankar

Reviewers

Sumit Pal

Alexis Roos

Commissioning Editor

Akram Hussain

Acquisition Editor

Tushar Gupta

Content Development Editor

Nikhil Borkar

Technical Editor

Madhunikita Sunil Chindarkar

Copy Editor

Safis Editing

Project Coordinator

Suzzane Coutinho

Proofreader

Safis Editing

Indexer

Tejal Daruwale Soni

Graphics

Kirk D'Penha

Production Coordinator

Melwyn D'sa

About the Author

Krishna Sankar is a Senior Specialist—AI Data Scientist with Volvo Cars focusing on Autonomous Vehicles. His earlier stints include Chief Data Scientist at http://cadenttech .tv/, Principal Architect/Data Scientist at Tata America Intl. Corp., Director of Data Science at a bioinformatics startup, and as a Distinguished Engineer at Cisco. He has been speaking at various conferences including ML tutorials at Strata SJC and London 2016, Spark Summit [goo.gl/ab30lD], Strata-Spark Camp, OSCON, PyCon, and PyData, writes about Robots Rules of Order [goo.gl/5yyRv6], Big Data Analytics—Best of the Worst [goo.gl/ImWCaz], predicting NFL, Spark [http://goo.gl/E4kqMD], Data Science [http://goo.gl/9pyJMH], Machine Learning [http://goo.gl/SXF53n], Social Media Analysis [http://goo.gl/D9YpV Q] as well as has been a guest lecturer at the Naval Postgraduate School. His occasional blogs can be found at https://doubleclix.wordpress.com/. His other passion is flying drones (working towards Drone Pilot License (FAA UAS Pilot) and Lego Robotics—you will find him at the St.Louis FLL World Competition as Robots Design Judge.

My first thanks goes to you, the reader, who is taking time to understand the technologies that Apache Spark brings to computation and to the developers of the Spark platform. The book reviewers Sumit and Alexis did a wonderful and thorough job morphing my rough materials into correct readable prose. This book is the result of dedicated work by many at Packt, notably Nikhil Borkar, the Content Development Editor, who deserves all the credit. Madhunikita, as always, has been the guiding force behind the hard work to bring the materials together, in more than one way. On a personal note, my bosses at Volvo viz. Petter Horling, Vedad Cajic, Andreas Wallin, and Mats Gustafsson are a constant source of guidance and insights. And of course, my spouse Usha and son Kaushik always have an encouraging word; special thanks to Usha's father Mr.Natarajan, whose wisdom we all rely upon, and my late mom for her kindness.

About the Reviewers

Sumit Pal has more than 22 years of experience in the software industry in various roles spanning companies from startups to enterprises. He is a big data, visualization, and data science consultant and a software architect and big data enthusiast and builds end-to-end data-driven analytic systems. He has worked for Microsoft (SQL server development team), Oracle (OLAP development team), and Verizon (big data analytics team) in a career spanning 22 years. Currently, he works for multiple clients, advising them on their data architectures and big data solutions and does hands on coding with Spark, Scala, Java, and Python. He has extensive experience in building scalable systems across the stack from middle tier, data tier to visualization for analytics applications, using big data and NoSQL databases.

Sumit has deep expertise in DataBase Internals, Data Warehouses, Dimensional Modeling, and Data Science with Java and Python and SQL. Sumit started his career being part of SQL Server development team at Microsoft in 1996-97 and then as a Core Server Engineer for Oracle at their OLAP development team in Burlington, MA. Sumit has also worked at Verizon as an Associate Director for big data architecture, where he strategized, managed, architected, and developed platforms and solutions for analytics and machine learning applications. He has also served as Chief Architect at ModelN/LeapfrogRX (2006-2013) where he architected the middle tier core Analytics Platform with open source OLAP engine (Mondrian) on J2EE and solved some complex Dimensional ETL, modeling, and performance optimization problems. Sumit has MS and BS in computer science.

Alexis Roos (@alexisroos) has over 20 years of software engineering experience with strong expertise in data science, big data, and application infrastructure. Currently an engineering manager at Salesforce, Alexis is managing a team of backend engineers building entry level Salesforce CRM (SalesforceIQ). Prior Alexis designed a comprehensive US business graph built from billion of records using Spark, GraphX, MLLib, and Scala at Radius Intelligence.

Alexis also worked for Couchbase, Concurrent Inc startups, and Sun Microsystems/Oracle for over 13 years and several large SIs over in Europe where he built and supported dozens of architectures of distributed applications across a range of verticals including telecommunications, healthcare, finance, and government. Alexis holds a master's degree in computer science with a focus on cognitive science. He has spoken at dozens of conferences worldwide (including Spark summit, Scala by the Bay, Hadoop Summit, and Java One) as well as delivered university courses and participated in industry panels.

www.PacktPub.com

For support files and downloads related to your book, please visit www.PacktPub.com.

Did you know that Packt offers eBook versions of every book published, with PDF and ePub files available? You can upgrade to the eBook version at www.PacktPub.comand as a print book customer, you are entitled to a discount on the eBook copy. Get in touch with us at service@packtpub.com for more details.

At www.PacktPub.com, you can also read a collection of free technical articles, sign up for a range of free newsletters and receive exclusive discounts and offers on Packt books and eBooks.

https://www.packtpub.com/mapt

Get the most in-demand software skills with Mapt. Mapt gives you full access to all Packt books and video courses, as well as industry-leading tools to help you plan your personal development and advance your career.

Why subscribe?

- Fully searchable across every book published by Packt
- Copy and paste, print, and bookmark content
- On demand and accessible via a web browser

Table of Contents

Preface

Apache Spark has captured the imagination of the analytics and big data developers, rightfully so. In a nutshell, Spark enables distributed computing at scale in the lab or in production. Until now, the collect-store-transform pipeline was distinct from the data science Reason-Model pipeline , which was again distinct from the deployment of the analytics and machine learning models. Now with Spark and technologies such as Kafka, we can seamlessly span the data management and data science pipelines. Moreover, now we can build data science models on larger datasets and need not just sample data. And whatever models we build can be deployed into production (with added work from engineering on the "ilities", of course). It is our hope that this book will enable a data engineer to get familiar with the fundamentals of the Spark platform as well as provide hands-on experience of some of the advanced capabilities.

What this book covers

Chapter 1, *Installing Spark and Setting Up Your Cluster,* details some common methods for setting up Spark.

Chapter 2, *Using the Spark Shell,* introduces the command line for Spark. The shell is good for trying out quick program snippets or just figuring out the syntax of a call interactively.

Chapter 3, *Building and Running a Spark Application,* covers the ways for compiling Spark applications.

Chapter 4, *Creating a SparkSession Object,* describe the programming aspects of the connection to a spark server regarding the Spark session and the enclosed spark context.

Chapter 5, *Loading and Saving Data in Spark,* deals with how we can get data in and out of a spark environment.

Chapter 6, *Manipulating Your RDD,* describes how to program Resilient Distributed Datasets, which is the fundamental data abstraction layer in Spark that makes all the magic possible.

Chapter 7, *Spark 2.0 Concepts,* is a short, interesting chapter that discusses the evolution of Spark and the concepts underpinning the Spark 2.0 release, which is a major milestone.

Chapter 8 , *Spark SQL,* deals with the SQL interface in Spark. Spark SQL probably is the most widely used feature.

Chapter 9, *Foundations of Datasets/DataFrames – The Proverbial Workhorse for DataScientists,* is another interesting chapter, which introduces the Datasets/DataFrames that are added in the Spark 2.0 release.

Chapter 10, *Spark with Big Data,* describes the interfaces with Parquet and HBase.

Chapter 11, *Machine Learning with Spark ML Pipelines,* is my favorite chapter. We talk about regression, classification, clustering, and recommendation in this chapter. This is probably the largest chapter in this book. If you are stranded in a remote island and could take only one chapter with you, this should be the one!

Chapter 12, *GraphX,* talks about an important capability, processing graphs at scale, and also discusses interesting algorithms such as PageRank.

What you need for this book

Like any development platform, learning to develop systems with Spark takes trial and error. Writing programs, encountering errors, and agonizing over pesky bugs are all part of the process. We assume a basic level of programming – Python or Java and experience in working with operating system commands. We have kept the examples simple and to the point. In terms of resources, we do not assume any esoteric equipment for running the examples and developing code. A normal development machine is enough.

Who this book is for

Data scientists and data engineers who are new to Spark will benefit from this book. Our goal in developing this book is to give an in-depth, hands-on, end-to-end knowledge of Apache Spark 2. We have kept it simple and short so that one can get a good introduction in a short period of time. Folks who have an exposure to big data and analytics will recognize the patterns and the pragmas. Having said that, anyone who wants to understand distributed programming will benefit from working through the examples and reading the book.

Conventions

In this book, you will find a number of text styles that distinguish between different kinds of information. Here are some examples of these styles and an explanation of their meaning.

Code words in text, database table names, folder names, filenames, file extensions, pathnames, dummy URLs, user input, and Twitter handles are shown as follows: "The hallmark of a `MapReduce` system is this: `map` and `reduce`, the two primitives."

A block of code is set as follows:

```
<dependency>
  <groupId>junit</groupId>
  <artifactId>junit</artifactId>
  <version>4.11</version>
  <scope>test</scope>
</dependency>
```

Any command-line input or output is written as follows:

```
./ec2/spark-ec2 -i ~/spark-keypair.pem launch myfirstsparkcluster --resume
```

New terms and **important words** are shown in bold. Words that you see on the screen, for example, in menus or dialog boxes, appear in the text like this: "From Spark 2.0.0 onwards, they have changed the packaging, so we have to include `spark-2.0.0/assembly/target/scala-2.11/jars` in **Add External Jars....**"

Warnings or important notes appear in a box like this.

Tips and tricks appear like this.

Reader feedback

Feedback from our readers is always welcome. Let us know what you think about this book-what you liked or disliked. Reader feedback is important for us as it helps us develop titles that you will really get the most out of. To send us general feedback, simply e-mail `feedback@packtpub.com`, and mention the book's title in the subject of your message. If there is a topic that you have expertise in and you are interested in either writing or contributing to a book, see our author guide at `www.packtpub.com/authors`.

Customer support

Now that you are the proud owner of a Packt book, we have a number of things to help you to get the most from your purchase.

Downloading the example code

You can download the example code files for this book from your account at `http://www.p acktpub.com`. If you purchased this book elsewhere, you can visit `http://www.packtpub.c om/support` and register to have the files e-mailed directly to you.

You can download the code files by following these steps:

1. Log in or register to our website using your e-mail address and password.
2. Hover the mouse pointer on the **SUPPORT** tab at the top.
3. Click on **Code Downloads & Errata**.
4. Enter the name of the book in the **Search** box.
5. Select the book for which you're looking to download the code files.
6. Choose from the drop-down menu where you purchased this book from.
7. Click on **Code Download**.

Once the file is downloaded, please make sure that you unzip or extract the folder using the latest version of:

- WinRAR / 7-Zip for Windows
- Zipeg / iZip / UnRarX for Mac
- 7-Zip / PeaZip for Linux

The code bundle for the book is also hosted on GitHub at `https://github.com/PacktPubl ishing/Fast-Data-Processing-with-Spark-2`. We also have other code bundles from our rich catalog of books and videos available at `https://github.com/PacktPublishing/`. Check them out!

Errata

Although we have taken every care to ensure the accuracy of our content, mistakes do happen. If you find a mistake in one of our books-maybe a mistake in the text or the code—we would be grateful if you could report this to us. By doing so, you can save other readers from frustration and help us improve subsequent versions of this book. If you find any errata, please report them by visiting http://www.packtpub.com/submit-errata, selecting your book, clicking on the **Errata Submission Form** link, and entering the details of your errata. Once your errata are verified, your submission will be accepted and the errata will be uploaded to our website or added to any list of existing errata under the Errata section of that title.

To view the previously submitted errata, go to https://www.packtpub.com/books/content/support and enter the name of the book in the search field. The required information will appear under the **Errata** section.

Piracy

Piracy of copyrighted material on the Internet is an ongoing problem across all media. At Packt, we take the protection of our copyright and licenses very seriously. If you come across any illegal copies of our works in any form on the Internet, please provide us with the location address or website name immediately so that we can pursue a remedy.

Please contact us at copyright@packtpub.com with a link to the suspected pirated material.

We appreciate your help in protecting our authors and our ability to bring you valuable content.

Questions

If you have a problem with any aspect of this book, you can contact us at questions@packtpub.com, and we will do our best to address the problem.

1
Installing Spark and Setting Up Your Cluster

This chapter will detail some common methods to set up Spark. Spark on a single machine is excellent for testing or exploring small Datasets, but here you will also learn to use Spark's built-in deployment scripts with a dedicated cluster via **Secure Shell** (**SSH**). For Cloud deployments of Spark, this chapter will look at EC2 (both traditional and Elastic Map reduce). Feel free to skip this chapter if you already have your local Spark instance installed and want to get straight to programming. The best way to navigate through installation is to use this chapter as a guide and refer to the Spark installation documentation at `http://s park.apache.org/docs/latest/cluster-overview.html`.

Regardless of how you are going to deploy Spark, you will want to get the latest version of Spark from `https://spark.apache.org/downloads.html` (Version 2.0.0 as of this writing). Spark currently releases every 90 days. For coders who want to work with the latest builds, try cloning the code directly from the repository at `https://github.com/apache/spark`. The building instructions are available at `https://spark.apache.org/docs/latest/build ing-spark.html`. Both source code and prebuilt binaries are available at this link. To interact with **Hadoop Distributed File System** (**HDFS**), you need to use Spark, which is built against the same version of Hadoop as your cluster. For Version 2.0.0 of Spark, the prebuilt package is built against the available Hadoop Versions 2.3, 2.4, 2.6, and 2.7. If you are up for the challenge, it's recommended that you build against the source as it gives you the flexibility of choosing the HDFS version that you want to support as well as apply patches with. In this chapter, we will do both.

As you explore the latest version of Spark, an essential task is to read the release notes and especially what has been changed and deprecated. For 2.0.0, the list is slightly long and is available at `https://spark.apache.or` `g/releases/spark-release-2--.html#removals-behavior-changes-an` `d-deprecations`. For example, the note talks about where the EC2 scripts have moved to and support for Hadoop 2.1 and earlier.

To compile the Spark source, you will need the appropriate version of Scala and the matching JDK. The Spark source `tar` utility includes the required Scala components. The following discussion is only for information there is no need to install Scala.

The Spark developers have done a good job of managing the dependencies. Refer to the `htt` `ps://spark.apache.org/docs/latest/building-spark.html` web page for the latest information on this. The website states that:

"Building Spark using Maven requires Maven 3.3.9 or newer and Java 7+."

Scala gets pulled down as a dependency by Maven (currently Scala 2.11.8). Scala does not need to be installed separately; it is just a bundled dependency.

Just as a note, Spark 2.0.0 by default runs with Scala 2.11.8, but can be compiled to run with Scala 2.10. I have just seen e-mails in the Spark users' group on this.

This brings up another interesting point about the Spark community. The two essential mailing lists are `user@spark.apache.org` and `dev@spark.apache.org`. More details about the Spark community are available at `https://spark.apache.org/community.html`.

Directory organization and convention

One convention that would be handy is to download and install software in the `/opt` directory. Also, have a generic soft link to Spark that points to the current version. For example, `/opt/spark` points to `/opt/spark-2.0.0` with the following command:

```
sudo ln -f -s spark-2.0.0 spark
```

Downloading the example code

You can download the example code files for all of the Packt books you have purchased from your account at `http://www.packtpub.com`. If you purchased this book elsewhere, you can visit `http://www.packtpub.com/` `support` and register to have the files e-mailed directly to you.

Later, if you upgrade, say to Spark 2.1, you can change the soft link.

However, remember to copy any configuration changes and old logs when you change to a new distribution. A more flexible way is to change the configuration directory to `/etc/opt/spark` and the log files to `/var/log/spark/`. In this way, these files will stay independent of the distribution updates. More details are available at `https://spark.apac he.org/docs/latest/configuration.html#overriding-configuration-directory` and `https://spark.apache.org/docs/latest/configuration.html#configuring-logging`.

Installing the prebuilt distribution

Let's download prebuilt Spark and install it. Later, we will also compile a version and build from the source. The download is straightforward. The download page is at `http://spark. apache.org/downloads.html`. Select the options as shown in the following screenshot:

We will use `wget` from the command line. You can do a direct download as well:

```
cd /opt
sudo wget
http://www-us.apache.org/dist/spark/spark-2.0.0/spark-2.0.0-bin-hadoop2.7.t
gz
```

We are downloading the prebuilt version for Apache Hadoop 2.7 from one of the possible mirrors. We could have easily downloaded other prebuilt versions as well, as shown in the following screenshot:

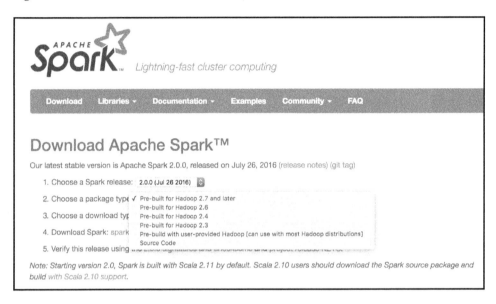

To uncompress it, execute the following command:

```
sudo tar xvf spark-2.0.0-bin-hadoop2.7.tgz
```

To test the installation, run the following command:

```
/opt/spark-2.0.0-bin-hadoop2.7/bin/run-example SparkPi 10
```

It will fire up the Spark stack and calculate the value of Pi. The result will be as shown in the following screenshot:

```
USS-Defiant:opt ksankar$ /opt/spark-2.0.0-bin-hadoop2.7/bin/run-example SparkPi 10
Using Spark's default log4j profile: org/apache/spark/log4j-defaults.properties
16/10/13 17:59:19 INFO SparkContext: Running Spark version 2.0.0
[..]
16/10/13 17:59:20 INFO Utils: Successfully started service 'sparkDriver' on port 50557.
[..]
16/10/13 17:59:20 INFO MemoryStore: MemoryStore started with capacity 366.3 MB
[..]
16/10/13 17:59:22 INFO DAGScheduler: Job 0 finished: reduce at SparkPi.scala:38, took 0.932408 s
Pi is roughly 3.1413151413151414
[..]
```

Building Spark from source

Let's compile Spark on a new AWS instance. In this way, you can clearly understand what all the requirements are to get a Spark stack compiled and installed. I am using the Amazon Linux AMI, which has Java and other base stacks installed by default. As this is a book on Spark, we can safely assume that you would have the base configurations covered. We will cover the incremental installs for the Spark stack here.

> The latest instructions for building from the source are available at `http:/ /spark.apache.org/docs/latest/building-spark.html`.

Downloading the source

The first order of business is to download the latest source from `https://spark.apache.or g/downloads.html`. Select **Source Code** from option **2**. Choose a package type and either download directly or select a mirror. The download page is shown in the following screenshot:

We can either download from the web page or use `wget`.

We will use `wget` from the first mirror shown in the preceding screenshot and download it to the `opt` subdirectory, as shown in the following command:

```
cd /opt
sudo wget http://www-eu.apache.org/dist/spark/spark-2.0.0/spark-2.0.0.tgz
sudo tar -xzf spark-2.0.0.tgz
```

 The latest development source is in GitHub, which is available at `https:/ /github.com/apache/spark`. The latest version can be checked out by the Git clone at `https://github.com/apache/spark.git`. This should be done only when you want to see the developments for the next version or when you are contributing to the source.

Compiling the source with Maven

Compilation by nature is uneventful, but a lot of information gets displayed on the screen:

```
cd /opt/spark-2.0.0
export MAVEN_OPTS="-Xmx2g -XX:MaxPermSize=512M -
XX:ReservedCodeCacheSize=512m"
sudo mvn clean package -Pyarn -Phadoop-2.7 -DskipTests
```

In order for the preceding snippet to work, we will need Maven installed on our system. Check by typing `mvn -v`. You will see the output as shown in the following screenshot:

```
USS-Defiant:spark-2.0.0 ksankar$ mvn -v
Apache Maven 3.3.9 (bb52d8502b132ec0a5a3f4c09453c07478323dc5; 2015-11-10T08:41:47-08:00)
Maven home: /usr/local/apache-maven-3.3.3
Java version: 1.7.0_60, vendor: Oracle Corporation
Java home: /Library/Java/JavaVirtualMachines/jdk1.7.0_60.jdk/Contents/Home/jre
Default locale: en_US, platform encoding: UTF-8
OS name: "mac os x", version: "10.11.5", arch: "x86_64", family: "mac"
USS-Defiant:spark-2.0.0 ksankar$
```

In case Maven is not installed in your system, the commands to install the latest version of Maven are given here:

```
wget
http://mirror.cc.columbia.edu/pub/software/apache/maven/maven-3/3.3.9/binar
ies/apache-maven-3.3.9-bin.tar.gz
sudo tar -xzf apache-maven-3.3.9-bin.tar.gz
sudo ln -f -s apache-maven-3.3.9 maven
export M2_HOME=/opt/maven
export PATH=${M2_HOME}/bin:${PATH}
```

Detailed Maven installation instructions are available at `http://maven.ap ache.org/download.cgi#Installation`.

Sometimes, you will have to debug Maven using the `-X` switch. When I ran Maven, the Amazon Linux AMI didn't have the Java compiler! I had to install `javac` for Amazon Linux AMI using the following command:
```
sudo yum install java-1.7.0-openjdk-devel
```

The compilation time varies. On my Mac, it took approximately 28 minutes. The Amazon Linux on a `t2-medium` instance took 38 minutes. The times could vary, depending on the Internet connection, what libraries are cached, and so forth.

In the end, you will see a build success message like the one shown in the following screenshot:

```
[INFO] Spark Project External Flume Assembly .............. SUCCESS [  2.405 s]
[INFO] Spark Integration for Kafka 0.8 .................... SUCCESS [ 36.764 s]
[INFO] Spark Project Examples ............................. SUCCESS [ 51.358 s]
[INFO] Spark Project External Kafka Assembly .............. SUCCESS [  4.443 s]
[INFO] Spark Integration for Kafka 0.10 ................... SUCCESS [ 41.691 s]
[INFO] Spark Integration for Kafka 0.10 Assembly .......... SUCCESS [  3.720 s]
[INFO] ------------------------------------------------------------------------
[INFO] BUILD SUCCESS
[INFO] ------------------------------------------------------------------------
[INFO] Total time: 24:26 min
[INFO] Finished at: 2016-08-13T22:16:33-07:00
[INFO] Final Memory: 101M/1126M
[INFO] ------------------------------------------------------------------------
USS-Defiant:spark-2.0.0 ksankar$
```

Compilation switches

As an example, the switches for the compilation of -Pyarn -Phadoop-2.7 -DskipTests are explained in https://spark.apache.org/docs/latest/building-spark.html#specifying-the-hadoop-version. The -D instance defines a system property and -P defines a profile.

 You can also compile the source code in IDEA, and then upload the built version to your cluster.

Testing the installation

A quick way to test the installation is by calculating Pi:

```
/opt/spark/bin/run-example SparkPi 10
```

The result will be a few debug messages, and then the value of Pi, as shown in the following screenshot:

```
USS-Defiant:spark-2.0.0 ksankar$ bin/run-example SparkPi 10
Using Spark's default log4j profile: org/apache/spark/log4j-defaults.properties
16/08/13 22:20:45 INFO SparkContext: Running Spark version 2.0.0
[..]
16/08/13 22:20:48 INFO Executor: Starting executor ID driver on host localhost
[..]
16/08/13 22:20:50 INFO DAGScheduler: Job 0 finished: reduce at SparkPi.scala:38, took 1.096171 s
Pi is roughly 3.142163142163142
[..]
USS-Defiant:spark-2.0.0 ksankar$
```

Spark topology

This is a good time to talk about the basic mechanics and mechanisms of Spark. We will progressively dig deeper, but for now let's take a quick look at the top level.

Essentially, Spark provides a framework to process the vast amounts of data, be it in gigabytes, terabytes, and occasionally petabytes. The two main ingredients are computation and scale. The size and effectiveness of the problems that we can solve depends on these two factors, that is, the ability to apply complex computations over large amounts of data in a timely fashion. If our monthly runs take 40 days, we have a problem.

The key, of course, is parallelism, massive parallelism to be exact. We can make our computational algorithm tasks work in parallel, that is, instead of doing the steps one after another, we can perform many steps at the same time, or carry out data parallelism. This means that we run the same algorithms over a partitioned Dataset in parallel. In my humble opinion, Spark is extremely effective in applying data parallelism in an elegant framework. As you will see in the rest of this book, the two components are **Resilient Distributed Dataset** (**RDD**) and cluster manager. The cluster manager distributes the code and manages the data that is represented in RDDs. RDDs with transformations and actions are the main programming abstractions and present parallelized collections. Behind the scenes, a cluster manager controls the distribution and interaction with RDDs, distributes code, and manages fault-tolerant execution. As you will see later in the book, Spark has more abstractions on RDDs, namely **DataFrames** and **Datasets**. These layers make it extremely efficient for a data engineer or a data scientist to work on distributed data. Spark works with three types of cluster managers-standalone, Apache Mesos, and Hadoop YARN. The Spark page at `http://spark.apache.org/docs/latest/cluster-overview.html` has a lot more details on this. I just gave you a quick introduction here.

> If you have installed Hadoop 2.0, it is recommended to install Spark on YARN. If you have installed Hadoop 1.0, the standalone version is recommended. If you want to try Mesos, you can choose to install Spark on Mesos. Users are not recommended to install both YARN and Mesos.

Refer to the following diagram:

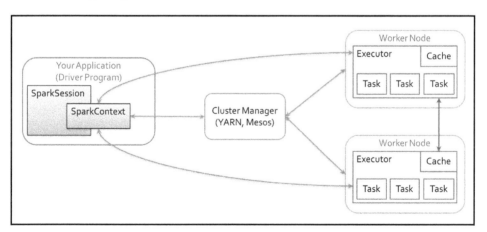

The Spark driver program takes the program classes and hands them over to a cluster manager. The cluster manager, in turn, starts executors in multiple worker nodes, each having a set of tasks. When we ran the example program earlier, all these actions happened transparently on your machine! Later, when we install in a cluster, the examples will run, again transparently, across multiple machines in the cluster. This is the magic of Spark and distributed computing!

A single machine

A single machine is the simplest use case for Spark. It is also a great way to sanity check your build. In spark/bin, there is a shell script called run-example, which can be used to launch a Spark job. The run-example script takes the name of a Spark class and some arguments. Earlier, we used the run-example script from the /bin directory to calculate the value of Pi. There is a collection of the sample Spark jobs in examples/src/main/scala/org/apache/spark/examples/.

All of the sample programs take the parameter, master (the cluster manager), which can be the URL of a distributed cluster or local[N], where N is the number of threads.

Going back to our run-example script, it invokes the more general bin/spark-submit script. For now, let's stick with the run-example script.

To run GroupByTest locally, try running the following command:

```
bin/run-example GroupByTest
```

This line will produce an output like this given here:

```
14/11/15 06:28:40 INFO SparkContext: Job finished: count at
GroupByTest.scala:51, took 0.494519333 s
2000
```

All the examples in this book can be run on a Spark installation on a local machine. So you can read through the rest of the chapter for additional information after you have gotten some hands-on exposure to Spark running on your local machine.

Running Spark on EC2

Till Spark 2.0.0, the `ec2` directory contained the script to run a Spark cluster in EC2. From 2.0.0, the `ec2` scripts have been moved to an external repository hosted by the UC Berkeley AMPLab. These scripts can be used to run multiple Spark clusters and even run on-the-spot instances. Spark can also be run on **Elastic MapReduce** (**Amazon EMR**), which is Amazon's solution for MapReduce cluster management, and it gives you more flexibility around scaling instances. The UCB AMPLab page at `https://github.com/amplab/spark-ec2` has the latest onrunning Spark on EC2.

> The Stack Overflow page at `http://stackoverflow.com/questions/386 11573/how-to-launch-spark-2--on-ec2` is a must-read before attempting to run Spark on EC2. The blog at `https://medium.com/@eyald ahari/how-to-set-apache-spark-cluster-on-amazon-ec2-in-a-few-s imple-steps-d29fd6f1a81#.8wfa4vqbl` also has some good tips for running Spark in EC2.

Downloading EC-scripts

There are many ways you can get the scripts. The best way is to download the `.zip` file from the AMPLab GitHub, unzip it, and move it from the `ec2` directory to the `spark-2.0.0` directory. In this way, things will work as before and are contained in the `spark` directory.

> Remember to repeat this, that is, download the `.zip` file, and then move the `ec2` directory, when you download newer versions of spark, say `spark-2.1.0`.

You can download a `.zip` file from GitHub, as shown here:

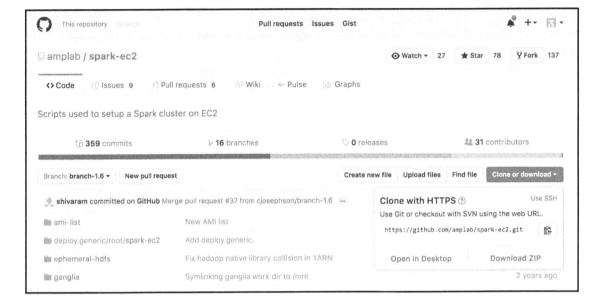

Perform the following steps:

1. Download the `.zip` file from GitHub to, say `~/Downloads` (or another equivalent directory).

2. Run this command to unzip the files:

    ```
    unzip spark-ec2-branch-1.6.zip
    ```

3. Rename the subdirectory:

    ```
    mv spark-ec2-branch-1.6 ec2
    ```

4. Move the directory under `spark-2.0.0`:

    ```
    mv ~/Downloads/ec2 /opt/spark-2.0.0/
    ```

5. Viola! It is as if the `ec2` directory was there all along!

Running Spark on EC2 with the scripts

To get started, you should make sure you have EC2 enabled on your account by signing up at https://portal.aws.amazon.com/gp/aws/manageYourAccount. Then it is a good idea to generate a separate access key pair for your Spark cluster, which you can do at https://portal.aws.amazon.com/gp/aws/securityCredentials. You will also need to create an EC2 key pair so that the Spark script can SSH to the launched machines, which can be done at https://console.aws.amazon.com/ec2/home by selecting **Key Pairs** under **NETWORK & SECURITY**. Remember that key pairs are created per region and so you need to make sure that you create your key pair in the same region as you intend to run your Spark instances. Make sure to give it a name that you can remember as you will need it for the scripts (this chapter will use spark-keypair as its example key pair name.). You can also choose to upload your public SSH key instead of generating a new key. These are sensitive; so make sure that you keep them private. You also need to set AWS_ACCESS_KEY and AWS_SECRET_KEY as environment variables for the Amazon EC2 scripts:

```
chmod 400 spark-keypair.pem
export AWS_ACCESS_KEY=AWSACcessKeyId
export AWS_SECRET_KEY=AWSSecretKey
```

You will find it useful to download the EC2 scripts provided by Amazon from http://docs.aws.amazon.com/AWSEC2/latest/CommandLineReference/set-up-ec2-cli-linux.html. Once you unzip the resulting .zip file, you can add bin to PATH in a manner similar to the way you did with the Spark bin instance:

```
wget http://s3.amazonaws.com/ec2-downloads/ec2-api-tools.zip
unzip ec2-api-tools.zip
cd ec2-api-tools-*
export EC2_HOME='pwd'
export PATH=$PATH:'pwd'/bin
```

In order to test whether this works, try the following command:

```
$ec2-describe-regions
```

This command will display the output shown in the following screenshot:

```
USS-Defiant:ec2 ksankar$ export EC2_HOME=~/aws/ec2-api-tools-1.7.5.1
USS-Defiant:ec2 ksankar$ ~/aws/ec2-api-tools-1.7.5.1/bin/ec2-describe-regions
REGION  eu-west-1       ec2.eu-west-1.amazonaws.com
REGION  ap-southeast-1  ec2.ap-southeast-1.amazonaws.com
REGION  ap-southeast-2  ec2.ap-southeast-2.amazonaws.com
REGION  eu-central-1    ec2.eu-central-1.amazonaws.com
REGION  ap-northeast-1  ec2.ap-northeast-1.amazonaws.com
REGION  us-east-1       ec2.us-east-1.amazonaws.com
REGION  sa-east-1       ec2.sa-east-1.amazonaws.com
REGION  us-west-1       ec2.us-west-1.amazonaws.com
REGION  us-west-2       ec2.us-west-2.amazonaws.com
```

Finally, you can refer to the EC2 command-line tool reference page at `http://docs.aws.am azon.com/AWSEC2/latest/CommandLineReference/set-up-ec2-cli-linux.html` as it has all the gory details.

The Spark EC2 script automatically creates a separate security group and firewall rules for running the Spark cluster. By default, your Spark cluster will be universally accessible on port `8080`, which is somewhat poor. Sadly, the `spark_ec2.py` script does not currently provide an easy way to restrict access to just your host. If you have a static IP address, I strongly recommend limiting access in `spark_ec2.py`; simply replace all instances of `0.0.0.0/0` with `[yourip]/32`. This will not affect intra-cluster communication as all machines within a security group can talk to each other by default.

Next, try to launch a cluster on EC2:

```
./ec2/spark-ec2 -k spark-keypair -i pk-[....].pem -s 1 launch
myfirstcluster
```

If you get an error message, such as `The requested Availability Zone is currently constrained and...`, you can specify a different zone by passing in the `--zone` flag.

The `-i` parameter (in the preceding command line) is provided for specifying the private key to log into the instance; `-i pk-[....].pem` represents the path to the private key.

If you get an error about not being able to SSH to the master, make sure that only you have the permission to read the private key, otherwise SSH will refuse to use it.

You may also encounter this error due to a race condition, when the hosts report themselves as alive but the `spark-ec2` script cannot yet SSH to them. A fix for this issue is pending in `https://github.com/mesos/spark/pull/555`. For now, a temporary workaround until the fix is available in the version of Spark you are using is to simply sleep an extra 100 seconds at the start of `setup_cluster` using the `-w` parameter. The current script has 120 seconds of delay built in.

If you do get a transient error while launching a cluster, you can finish the launch process using the `resume` feature by running the following command:

```
./ec2/spark-ec2 -i ~/spark-keypair.pem launch myfirstsparkcluster  --resume
```

Refer to the following screenshot:

```
USS-Defiant:ec2 ksankar$ ./spark-ec2 -i ~/aws/SparkKeys.pem launch myCluster --resume
Searching for existing cluster myCluster in region us-east-1...
Found 1 master, 1 slave.
Waiting for cluster to enter 'ssh-ready' state....
```

It will go through a bunch of scripts, thus setting up Spark, Hadoop, and so forth. If everything goes well, you will see something like the following screenshot:

```
ec2-54-172-122-248.compute-1.amazonaws.com: Killed 0 processes
ec2-54-165-102-78.compute-1.amazonaws.com: Killed 0 processes
Starting master @ ec2-54-172-249-0.compute-1.amazonaws.com
ec2-54-172-122-248.compute-1.amazonaws.com: TACHYON_LOGS_DIR: /root/tachyon/libexec/../logs
ec2-54-165-102-78.compute-1.amazonaws.com: TACHYON_LOGS_DIR: /root/tachyon/libexec/../logs
ec2-54-172-122-248.compute-1.amazonaws.com: Formatting RamFS: /mnt/ramdisk (6154mb)
ec2-54-165-102-78.compute-1.amazonaws.com: Formatting RamFS: /mnt/ramdisk (6154mb)
ec2-54-172-122-248.compute-1.amazonaws.com: Starting worker @ ip-172-31-44-34.ec2.internal
ec2-54-165-102-78.compute-1.amazonaws.com: Starting worker @ ip-172-31-44-33.ec2.internal
Setting up ganglia
RSYNC'ing /etc/ganglia to slaves...
ec2-54-172-122-248.compute-1.amazonaws.com
ec2-54-165-102-78.compute-1.amazonaws.com
Shutting down GANGLIA gmond:                    [FAILED]
Starting GANGLIA gmond:                         [  OK  ]
Shutting down GANGLIA gmond:                    [FAILED]
Starting GANGLIA gmond:                         [  OK  ]
Connection to ec2-54-172-122-248.compute-1.amazonaws.com closed.
Shutting down GANGLIA gmond:                    [FAILED]
Starting GANGLIA gmond:                         [  OK  ]
Connection to ec2-54-165-102-78.compute-1.amazonaws.com closed.
Shutting down GANGLIA gmetad:                   [FAILED]
Starting GANGLIA gmetad:                        [  OK  ]
Stopping httpd:                                 [FAILED]
Starting httpd:                                 [  OK  ]
Connection to ec2-54-172-249-0.compute-1.amazonaws.com closed.
Spark standalone cluster started at http://ec2-54-172-249-0.compute-1.amazonaws.com:8080
Ganglia started at http://ec2-54-172-249-0.compute-1.amazonaws.com:5080/ganglia
Done!
USS-Defiant:spark ksankar$
```

This will give you a barebones cluster with one master and one worker with all of the defaults on the default machine instance size. Next, verify that it started up and your firewall rules were applied by going to the master on port 8080. You can see in the preceding screenshot that the UI for the master is the output at the end of the script with port at 8080 and ganglia at 5080.

Your AWS EC2 dashboard will show the instances as follows:

The ganglia dashboard shown in the following screenshot is a good place to monitor the instances:

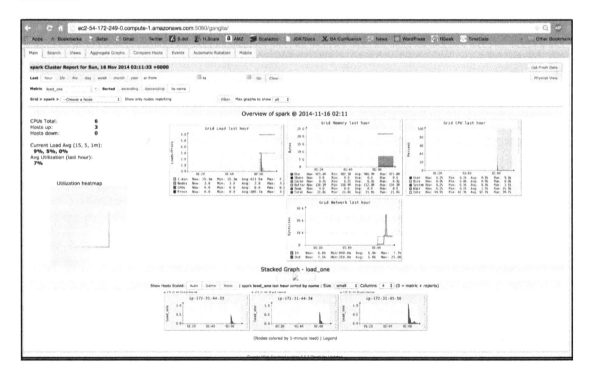

Try running one of the example jobs on your new cluster to make sure everything is okay, as shown in the following screenshot:

```
USS-Defiant:spark ksankar$ ssh -i ~/aws/SparkKeys.pem root@ec2-54-172-249-0.compute-1.amazonaws.com
Last login: Sun Nov 16 01:57:54 2014 from c-98-234-120-205.hsd1.ca.comcast.net


       __|  __|_  )
       _|  (     /   Amazon Linux AMI
      ___|\___|___|

https://aws.amazon.com/amazon-linux-ami/2013.03-release-notes/
There are 67 security update(s) out of 275 total update(s) available
Run "sudo yum update" to apply all updates.
Amazon Linux version 2014.09 is available.
root@ip-172-31-45-56 ~]$ ls -la
total 104
drwxr-xr-x 19 root root 4096 Nov 16 01:59 .
dr-xr-xr-x 27 root root 4096 Nov 16 01:59 ..
-rw-------  1 root root   65 Feb  2 2014 .bash_history
-rw-r--r--  1 root root   18 Jan 15 2011 .bash_logout
-rwxr-xr-x  1 root root  188 Nov 16 01:59 .bash_profile
-rw-r--r--  1 root root  100 Jan 15 2011 .cshrc
drwxr-xr-x 14 root root 4096 Oct  3 2012 ephemeral-hdfs
drwxr-xr-x  2 root root 4096 Jun 26 2013 hadoop-native
drwxr-xr-x  3 root root 4096 Aug 21 2013 .ipython
drwxr-xr-x  4 root root 4096 Apr 18 2013 .ivy2
drwxr-xr-x  3 root root 4096 Apr 18 2013 .m2
drwxr-xr-x  3 root root 4096 Nov 16 01:59 mapreduce
drwxr-xr-x  2 root root 4096 Aug 21 2013 .matplotlib
drwxr-xr-x 14 root root 4096 Oct  3 2012 persistent-hdfs
drwxr-----  3 root root 4096 Nov 16 01:57 .pki
drwxr-xr-x  4 root root 4096 Apr 18 2013 .sbt
drwxrwxr-x  9 2000 2000 4096 Sep 27 2013 scala
drwxr-xr-x  3 root root 4096 Nov 16 01:59 shark
drwxr-xr-x  3 root root 4096 Nov 16 01:59 spark
drwxr-xr-x 14 root root 4096 Nov 16 01:59 spark-ec2
drwx------  2 root root 4096 Nov 16 01:58 .ssh
drwxr-xr-x 10 1000 1000 4096 Nov 16 02:00 tachyon
-rw-r--r--  1 root root  129 Jan 15 2011 .tcshrc
drwxrwxr-x  6 root root 4096 Aug 21 2013 .vim
-rw-------  1 root root  512 Aug 21 2013 .viminfo
-rw-r--r--  1 root root   94 Aug 21 2013 .vimrc
root@ip-172-31-45-56 ~]$ ls
ephemeral-hdfs  hadoop-native  mapreduce  persistent-hdfs  scala  shark  spark  spark-ec2  tachyon
root@ip-172-31-45-56 ~]$ 
```

The JPS should show this:

```
root@ip-172-31-45-56 ~]$ jps
1904 NameNode
2856 Jps
2426 Master
2078 SecondaryNameNode
```

The script has started the Spark master, the Hadoop name node, and data nodes (in slaves).

Let's run the two programs that we ran earlier on our local machine:

```
cd spark
bin/run-example GroupByTest
bin/run-example SparkPi 10
```

The ease with which one can spin up a few nodes in the Cloud, install the Spark stack, and run the program in a distributed manner is interesting.

The `ec2/spark-ec2 destroy <cluster name>` command will terminate the instances.

```
USS-Defiant:ec2 ksankar$ ./spark-ec2 destroy myCluster
Searching for existing cluster myCluster in region us-east-1...
Found 1 master, 1 slave.
The following instances will be terminated:
> ec2-52-91-112-189.compute-1.amazonaws.com
> ec2-52-90-123-113.compute-1.amazonaws.com
ALL DATA ON ALL NODES WILL BE LOST!!
Are you sure you want to destroy the cluster myCluster? (y/N) y
Terminating master...
Terminating slaves...
```

If you have a problem with the key pairs, I found the command, `~/aws/ec2-api-tools-1.7.5.1/bin/ec2-describe-keypairs` helpful to troubleshoot.

Now that you've run a simple job on our EC2 cluster, it's time to configure your EC2 cluster for our Spark jobs. There are a number of options you can use to configure with the `spark-ec2` script.

The `ec2/ spark-ec2 -help` command will display all the options available.

First, consider what instance types you may need. EC2 offers an ever-growing collection of instance types and you can choose a different instance type for the master and the workers. The instance type has the most obvious impact on the performance of your Spark cluster. If your work needs a lot of RAM, you should choose an instance with more RAM. You can specify the instance type with `--instance-type= (name of instance type)`. By default, the same instance type will be used for both the master and the workers; this can be wasteful if your computations are particularly intensive and the master isn't being heavily utilized. You can specify a different master instance type with `--master-instance-type= (name of instance)`.

Spark's EC2 scripts use **Amazon Machine Images** (**AMI**) provided by the Spark team. Usually, they are current and sufficient for most of the applications. You might need your own AMI in certain circumstances, such as custom patches (for example, using a different version of HDFS) for Spark, as they will not be included in the machine image.

Deploying Spark on Elastic MapReduce

In addition to the Amazon basic EC2 machine offering, Amazon offers a hosted MapReduce solution called **Elastic MapReduce** (**EMR**). The blog at `http://blogs.aws.amazon.com/bi gdata/post/Tx6J5RM2WPG5V/Building-a-Recommendation-Engine-with-Spark-ML-on-A mazon-EMR-using-Zeppelin` has lots of interesting details on how to start Spark in EMR.

Deploying a Spark-based EMR has become very easy, Spark is a first class entity in EMR. When you create an EMR cluster, you have the option to select Spark. The following screenshot shows the **Create Cluster-Quick Options** of EMR:

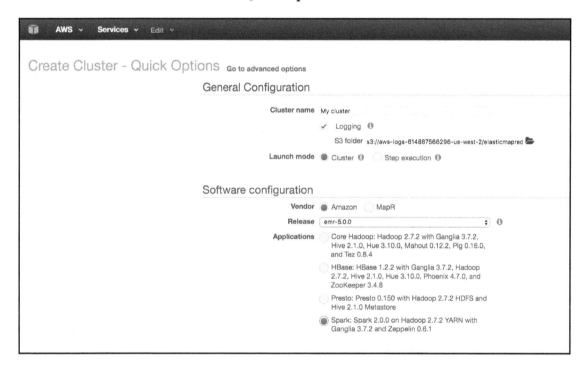

The advanced option has Spark as well as other stacks.

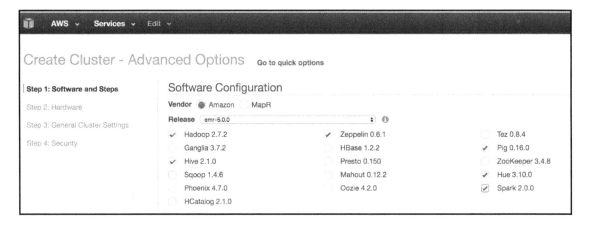

Deploying Spark with Chef (Opscode)

Chef is an open source automation platform that has become increasingly popular for deploying and managing both small and large clusters of machines. Chef can be used to control a traditional static fleet of machines and can also be used with EC2 and other cloud providers. Chef uses cookbooks as the basic building blocks of configuration and can either be generic or site-specific. If you have not used Chef before, a good tutorial for getting started with Chef can be found at `https://learnchef.opscode.com/`. You can use a generic Spark cookbook as the basis for setting up your cluster.

To get Spark working, you need to create a role for both the master and the workers as well as configure the workers to connect to the master. Start by getting the cookbook from `https://github.com/holdenk/chef-cookbook-spark`. The bare minimum requirements are to set the master host name (as master) to enable worker nodes to connect, and the username so that Chef can be installed in the correct place. You will also need to either accept Sun's Java license or switch to an alternative JDK. Most of the settings that are available in `spark-env.sh` are also exposed through the cookbook settings. You can see an explanation of the settings in the *Configuring multiple hosts over SSH* section. The settings can be set as per role or you can modify the global defaults.

Create a role for the master with a knife role; create `spark_master_role -e [editor]`. This will bring up a template role file that you can edit. For a simple master, set it to this code:

```
{
  "name": "spark_master_role", "description": "", "json_class":
"Chef::Role",   "default_attributes": {   }, "override_attributes": {
    "username":"spark", "group":"spark", "home":"/home/spark/sparkhome",
"master_ip":"10.0.2.15", }, "chef_type": "role", "run_list": [
"recipe[spark::server]", "recipe[chef-client]", ], "env_run_lists": {
  }
}
```

Then, create a role for the client in the same manner except that instead of `spark::server`, you need to use the `spark::client` recipe. Deploy the roles to different hosts:

```
knife node run_list add master role[spark_master_role]
knife node run_list add worker role[spark_worker_role]
```

Then, run `chef-client` on your nodes to update. Congrats, you now have a Spark cluster running!

Deploying Spark on Mesos

Mesos is a cluster management platform for running multiple distributed applications or frameworks on a cluster. Mesos can intelligently schedule and run Spark, Hadoop, and other frameworks concurrently on the same cluster. Spark can be run on Mesos either by scheduling individual jobs as separate Mesos tasks or running all of the Spark code as a single Mesos task. Mesos can quickly scale up to handle large clusters beyond the size of which you would want to manage with the plain old SSH scripts. Mesos, written in C++, was originally created at UC Berkley as a research project; it is currently undergoing Apache incubation and is actively used by Twitter.

The Spark web page, `http://spark.apache.org/docs/latest/running-on-mesos.html`, has detailed instructions on installing and running Spark on Mesos.

Spark on YARN

YARN is Apache Hadoop's NextGen Resource Manager. The Spark project provides an easy way to schedule jobs on YARN once you have a Spark assembly built. The Spark web page, `http://spark.apache.org/docs/latest/running-on-yarn.html`, has the configuration details for YARN, which we had built earlier for compiling with the `-Pyarn` switch.

Spark standalone mode

If you have a set of machines without any existing cluster management software, you can deploy Spark over SSH with some handy scripts. This method is known as **standalone mode** in the Spark documentation at http://spark.apache.org/docs/latest/spark-sta ndalone.html. An individual master and worker can be started by sbin/start-master.sh and sbin/start-slaves.sh, respectively. The default port for the master is 8080. As you likely don't want to go to each of your machines and run these commands by hand, there are a number of helper scripts in bin/ to help you run your servers.

A prerequisite for using any of the scripts is having password less SSH access set up from the master to all of the worker machines. You probably want to create a new user for running Spark on the machines and lock it down. This book uses the username sparkuser. On your master, you can run ssh-keygen to generate the SSH keys and make sure that you do not set a password. Once you have generated the key, add the public one (if you generated an RSA key, it would be stored in ~/.ssh/id_rsa.pub by default) to ~/.ssh/authorized_keys2 on each of the hosts.

> The Spark administration scripts require that your usernames match. If this isn't the case, you can configure an alternative username in your ~/.ssh/config.

Now that you have the SSH access to the machines set up, it is time to configure Spark. There is a simple template in [filepath]conf/spark-env.sh.template[/filepath], which you should copy to [filepath]conf/spark-env.sh[/filepath].

You may also find it useful to set some (or all) of the environment variables shown in the following table:

Name	Purpose	Default
MESOS_NATIVE_LIBRARY	This variable is used to point to math where Mesos lives.	None
SCALA_HOME	This variable is used to point to where you extracted Scala.	None, must be set
SPARK_MASTER_IP	This variable states the IP address for the master to listen on and the IP address for the workers to connect to.	The result of running hostname

`SPARK_MASTER_PORT`	This variable states the port # for the Spark master to listen on.	`7077`
`SPARK_MASTER_WEBUI_PORT`	This variable states the port # of the WEB UI on the master.	`8080`
`SPARK_WORKER_CORES`	This variable states the number of cores to use.	All of them
`SPARK_WORKER_MEMORY`	This variable states how much memory to use.	Max of (system memory-1 GB, 512 MB)
`SPARK_WORKER_PORT`	This variable states what port # the worker runs on.	`Rand`
`SPARK_WEBUI_PORT`	This variable states what port # the worker WEB UI runs on.	`8081`
`SPARK_WORKER_DIR`	This variable states where to store files from the worker.	`SPARK_HOME/work_dir`

Once you have completed your configuration, it's time to get your cluster up and running. You will want to copy the version of Spark and the configuration you have built to all of your machines. You may find it useful to install pssh, a set of parallel SSH tools, including pscp. The pscp tool makes it easy to scp to a number of target hosts, although it will take a while, as shown here:

```
pscp -v -r -h conf/slaves -l sparkuser ../opt/spark ~/
```

If you end up changing the configuration, you need to distribute the configuration to all of the workers, as shown here:

```
pscp -v -r -h conf/slaves -l sparkuser conf/spark-env.sh
/opt/spark/conf/spark-env.sh
```

If you use a shared NFS on your cluster, while by default Spark names log files and similar with shared names, you should configure a separate worker directory; otherwise, they will be configured to write to the same place. If you want to have your worker directories on the shared NFS, consider adding `'hostname'`, for example `SPARK_WORKER_DIR=~/work-'hostname'`.

You should also consider having your log files go to a scratch directory for performance.

Now you are ready to start the cluster and you can use the `sbin/start-all.sh`, `sbin/start-master.sh`, and `sbin/start-slaves.sh` scripts. It is important to note that `start-all.sh` and `start-master.sh` both assume that they are being run on the node, which is the master for the cluster. The start scripts all daemonize, and so you don't have to worry about running them on a screen.

```
ssh master bin/start-all.sh
```

If you get a class not found error stating `java.lang.NoClassDefFoundError: scala/ScalaObject`, check to make sure that you have Scala installed on that worker host and that the `SCALA_HOME` is set correctly.

The Spark scripts assume that your master has Spark installed in the same directory as your workers. If this is not the case, you should edit `bin/spark-config.sh` and set it to the appropriate directories.

The commands provided by Spark to help you administer your cluster are given in the following table. More details are available on the Spark website at `http://spark.apache.org/docs/latest/spark-standalone.html#cluster-launch-scripts`.

Command	Use
`bin/slaves.sh <command>`	This command runs the provided command on all of the worker hosts. For example, `bin/slave.sh uptime` will show how long each of the worker hosts have been up.
`bin/start-all.sh`	This command starts the master and all of the worker hosts. This command must be run on the master.
`bin/start-master.sh`	This command starts the master host. This command must be run on the master.
`bin/start-slaves.sh`	This command starts the worker hosts.
`bin/start-slave.sh`	This command starts a specific worker.

`bin/stop-all.sh`	This command stops master and workers.
`bin/stop-master.sh`	This command stops the master.
`bin/stop-slaves.sh`	This command stops all the workers.

You now have a running Spark cluster. There is a handy Web UI on the master running on port 8080 you should go and visit, and on all of the workers on port 8081. The Web UI contains helpful information such as the current workers, and current and past jobs.

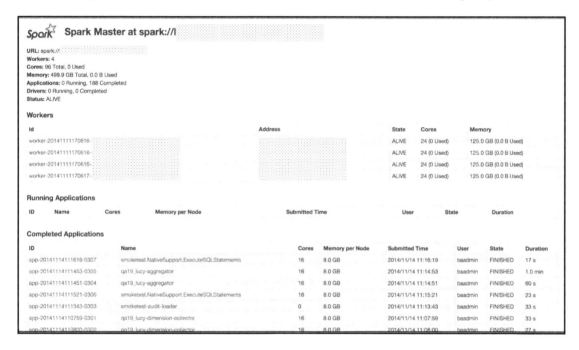

Now that you have a cluster up and running, let's actually do something with it. As with the single host example, you can use the provided run script to run the Spark commands. All of the examples listed in `examples/src/main/scala/spark/org/apache/spark/examples/` take a parameter, `master`, which points them to the master. Assuming that you are on the master host, you could run them with this command:

```
./run-example GroupByTest spark://'hostname':7077
```

> If you run into an issue with
> `java.lang.UnsupportedClassVersionError`, you may need to update
> your JDK or recompile Spark if you grabbed the binary version. Version
> 1.1.0 was compiled with JDK 1.7 as the target. You can check the version of
> the JRE targeted by Spark with the following commands:
> ```
> java -verbose -classpath ./core/target/scala-
> 2.9.2/classes/
> spark.SparkFiles |head -n 20
> ```
> Version 49 is JDK1.5, Version 50 is JDK1.6, and Version 60 is JDK1.7.

If you can't connect to `localhost`, make sure that you've configured your master
(`spark.driver.port`) to listen to all of the IP addresses (or if you don't want to replace
`localhost` with the IP address configured to listen to). More port configurations are listed
at `http://spark.apache.org/docs/latest/configuration.html#networking`.

If everything has worked correctly, you will see the following log messages output to
`stdout`:

```
13/03/28 06:35:31 INFO spark.SparkContext: Job finished: count at
GroupByTest.scala:35, took 2.482816756 s
2000
```

References

The references are listed here:

- http://archive9.linux.com/feature/15134
- http://spark-project.org/docs/latest/spark-standalone.html
- http://bickson.blogspot.com/212/1/deploying-graphlabsparkmesos-cluster-on.html
- http://www.ibm.com/developerworks/library/os-spark/
- http://mesos.apache.org/
- http://aws.amazon.com/articles/Elastic-MapReduce/4926593393724923
- http://spark-project.org/docs/latest/ec2-scripts.html
- http://spark.apache.org/docs/latest/cluster-overview.html

- https://www.cs.berkeley.edu/~matei/papers/212/nsdi_spark.pdf
- http://research.google.com/pubs/pub41378.html
- http://aws.amazon.com/articles/4926593393724923
- http://docs.aws.amazon.com/ElasticMapReduce/latest/DeveloperGuide/emr-cli-install.html

Summary

In this chapter, we have installed Spark on our machine for local development and set it up on our cluster, and so we are ready to run the applications that we write. While installing and maintaining a cluster is a good option, Spark is also available as a service option from Databricks. Databricks' Databricks Cloud for Spark, available at http://databricks.com/product, is a very convenient offering for anyone who does not want to deal with the set up/maintenance of the cluster. They have the concept of a big data pipeline from ETL to analytics. This looks truly interesting to explore!

In the next chapter, you will learn to use the Spark shell.

2
Using the Spark Shell

In this chapter, we will cover the following topics related to the Spark shell:

- Running the Spark shell
- Loading a simple text file
- Interactively loading data from S3
- Running the Spark shell in Python

The Spark shell

The Spark shell is an excellent tool for rapid prototyping with Spark. It works with Scala and Python. It allows you to interact with the Spark cluster and as a result of which, the full API is under your command. It can be great for debugging, just trying things out, or interactively exploring new Datasets or approaches.

The previous chapter should have gotten you to the point of having a Spark instance running; now all you need to do is start your Spark shell and point it at your running instance with the command given in the table we're soon going to check out.

For local mode, Spark will start an instance when you invoke the Spark shell or start a Spark program from an IDE. So, a local installation on a Mac or Linux PC/laptop is sufficient to start exploring the Spark shell. Not having to spin up a real cluster to do the prototyping is an important and useful feature of Spark. The **Quick Start** guide at `http://s park.apache.org/docs/latest/quick-start.html` is a good reference.

Assuming that you have installed Spark in the `/opt` directory and also have a soft link to Spark, run the commands shown in the following table:

	Let Spark shell start a Spark Instance	Start Spark shell on an already running instance (local or a Spark cluster)
scala	**cd /opt/spark bin/spark-shell**	**cd /opt/spark export MASTER= spark://'hostname':7077 bin/spark-shell**
python	**cd /opt/spark bin/pyspark**	**cd /opt/spark export MASTER= spark://'hostname':7077 bin/pyspark**

The documentation link `http://spark.apache.org/docs/latest/progr` `amming-guide.html#using-the-shell` has a list of Spark shell options. For example, `Bin/spark-shell -master local[2]` will start the Spark with two threads.

You will see the shell prompt as shown in the following screenshot:

```
USS-Defiant:spark-2.0.0 ksankar$ cd ~/Downloads/spark-2.0.0/
USS-Defiant:spark-2.0.0 ksankar$ bin/spark-shell
16/08/14 12:35:35 WARN NativeCodeLoader: Unable to load native-hadoop library for your platform... using builtin-java classes where applicable
16/08/14 12:35:36 WARN SparkContext: Use an existing SparkContext, some configuration may not take effect.
Spark context Web UI available at http://10.0.1.2:4040
Spark context available as 'sc' (master = local[*], app id = local-1471203336278).
Spark session available as 'spark'.
Welcome to
      ____              __
     / __/__  ___ _____/ /__
    _\ \/ _ \/ _ `/ __/  '_/
   /___/ .__/\_,_/_/ /_/\_\   version 2.0.0
      /_/

Using Scala version 2.11.8 (Java HotSpot(TM) 64-Bit Server VM, Java 1.7.0_60)
Type in expressions to have them evaluated.
Type :help for more information.

scala>
```

I have downloaded and compiled Spark in `~/Downloads/spark-2.0.0` and it is running in local mode.

A few points of interest are as follows:

- The shell has instantiated a connection object (`SparkSession`) to the Spark instance in the `spark` variable. This is new to Spark 2.0.0. Earlier versions had `SparkContext`, `sqlContext`, and `hiveContext`. From Version 2.0.0 onward, all these subcontexts are consolidated under `SparkSession`, but are available from the `SparkSession` object. We will explore all these concepts in later chapters.

- The Spark monitor UI can be accessed at port 4040, as shown in the following screenshot:

Exiting out of the shell

When we start any program, the first thing we should know is how to exit. Exiting the shell is easy: use the `:quit` command and you will be dropped out of the `spark-shell` command.

Using Spark shell to run the book code

As a convention that makes it easy to navigate directories, let's start the Spark shell from the directory in which you have downloaded the code and data for this book, which means from either the GitHub, `https://github.com/xsankar/fdps-v3`, or the Packt support site.

Assuming the book code/data is at `~/fdps-v3` and Spark at `~/Downloads/spark-2.0.0`, start the Spark shell as follows:

```
cd ~/fdps-v3
~/Downloads/spark-2.0.0/bin/spark-shell
```

If you have used a different directory structure, please adjust accordingly, that is, change the directory to `fdps-v3` and start `spark-shell` from there.
The `fdps-v3/code` has the code and `fdps-v3/data` has the data.

Loading a simple text file

Let's download a Dataset and do some experimentation. One of the (if not the best) books for machine learning is *The Elements of Statistical Learning, Trevor Hastie, Jerome H. Friedman, Robert Tibshirani, Springer*. The book site has an interesting set of Datasets. Let's grab the spam Dataset using the following command:

```
wget http://www-stat.stanford.edu/~tibs/ElemStatLearn/ datasets/spam.data
```

Alternatively, you can find the spam Dataset from the GitHub link at https://github.com /xsankar/fdps-v3.

All the examples assume that you have downloaded the repository in the `fdps-v3` directory in your home folder, that is, `~/fdps-v3/`. Please adjust the directory name if you have downloaded them somewhere else.

Now, load it as a text file into Spark with the following commands inside your Spark shell:

```
scala> val inFile = sc.textFile("data/spam.data")
scala> inFile.count()
```

This loads the `spam.data` file into Spark with each line being a separate entry in the **Resilient Distributed Datasets** (**RDDs**). You will learn about RDDs in the later chapters; however, RDD, in brief, is the basic data structure that Spark relies on. They are very versatile in terms of scaling, computation capabilities, and transformations.

Spark uses the paradigm of lazy evaluation. The `sc.textFile` operation is a lazy operation in Spark, so it doesn't load anything until an action is invoked on the RDD. For example, `count()` is an action. So the command `sc.textfile` would succeed even when the user enters a bogus file directory; the RDD will still be created. However, when you type in the `action` command, it will fail.

The `sc` command in the command line is the Spark context. While applications would create a Spark context explicitly, the Spark shell creates something called `sc` for you and this is what we normally use.

You will see the result as follows:

```
USS-Defiant:spark-2.0.0 ksankar$ cd ~/fdps-v3
USS-Defiant:fdps-v3 ksankar$ ~/Downloads/spark-2.0.0/bin/spark-shell
16/08/14 12:53:36 WARN NativeCodeLoader: Unable to load native-hadoop library for your platform... using builtin-java classes where applicable
16/08/14 12:53:37 WARN SparkContext: Use an existing SparkContext, some configuration may not take effect.
Spark context Web UI available at http://10.0.1.2:4040
Spark context available as 'sc' (master = local[*], app id = local-1471204417489).
Spark session available as 'spark'.
Welcome to
      ____              __
     / __/__  ___ _____/ /__
    _\ \/ _ \/ _ `/ __/  '_/
   /___/ .__/\_,_/_/ /_/\_\   version 2.0.0
      /_/

Using Scala version 2.11.8 (Java HotSpot(TM) 64-Bit Server VM, Java 1.7.0_60)
Type in expressions to have them evaluated.
Type :help for more information.

scala> val inFile = sc.textFile("data/spam.data")
inFile: org.apache.spark.rdd.RDD[String] = data/spam.data MapPartitionsRDD[1] at textFile at <console>:24

scala> inFile.count()
res0: Long = 4601
```

The `count()` function gives the number of lines in a file.

Now, let's look at the first line. Type in the following command:

scala> inFile.first()
And you will see a string like the screen shot below ! Excellent, you have
written your first scala code !

Refer to the following screenshot:

```
scala> val inFile = sc.textFile("data/spam.data")
inFile: org.apache.spark.rdd.RDD[String] = data/spam.data MapPartitionsRDD[1] at textFile at <console>:24

scala> inFile.count()
res0: Long = 4601

scala> inFile.first()
res1: String = 0 0.64 0.64 0 0.32 0 0 0 0 0 0 0.64 0 0 0 0.32 0 1.29 1.93 0 0.96 0 0 0 0 0 0 0 0 0 0 0 0 0
 61 278 1
```

Note that if you're connected to a Spark master, it's possible that it will attempt to load the file on any one of the different machines in the cluster, so make sure that it can be accessed by all the worker nodes in a cluster. In general, you will need to put your data in HDFS, S3, or similar distributed file systems to avoid this problem. In local mode, you can just load the file directly (for example, `sc.textFile([filepath])`). You can also use the `addFile` function on the Spark context to make a file available across all of the machines like this:

```scala
scala> import org.apache.spark.SparkFiles
scala> val file = sc.addFile("data/spam.data")
scala> val inFile = sc.textFile(SparkFiles.get("spam.data"))
```

 Like most shells, the Spark shell has a command history; you can press the up arrow key to get to the previous commands. Are you getting tired of typing or not being sure about what method you want to call on an object? Press *Tab* and the Spark shell will autocomplete the line of code in the best way it can.

For this example, the RDD with each line as an individual string isn't super useful as our input data is actually space-separated numerical information. We can use the `map()` operation to iterate over the elements of the RDD and quickly convert it to a usable format. Note that `_.toDouble` is the Scala syntactic sugar for `x => x.toDouble`. The numbers are separated by the space. We use a map operation to convert the line to a set of numbers in string format (split the line using the space character) and then convert each of the numbers to a double, as shown next:

```scala
scala> val nums = inFile.map(line => line.split(' ').map(_.toDouble))
```

Verify that this is what we want by inspecting some elements in the `nums` RDD and comparing them against the original string RDD. Take a look at the first element of each of these by calling `.first()` on the RDDs:

 Most of the output that will follow these commands will be extraneous `INFO` messages. No doubt, it will be informative to see what Spark does under the covers. However, if you want to keep the detailed messages out, you can copy `conf/log4j.properties.template` as `conf/log4j.properties` and set `log4j.logger.org.apache.spark.repl.Main=WARN` instead of `INFO`. Once this is done, none of these messages will appear, and it will be possible for you to concentrate only on the commands and the output.

The screenshot is shown as follows:

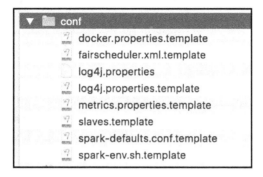

```
cp log4j.properties.template log4j.properties
```

Then, edit the `log4j.properties` file and change
`log4j.logger.org.apache.spark.repl.Main` to `WARN`, as shown in the following
screenshot:

```
# Set the default spark-shell log level to WARN. When running the spark-shell, the
# log level for this class is used to overwrite the root logger's log level, so that
# the user can have different defaults for the shell and regular Spark apps.
log4j.logger.org.apache.spark.repl.Main=WARN
```

We inspect the first line with the `first()` method:

```
scala> inFile.first()
res1: String = 0 0.64 0.64 0 0.32 0 0 0 0 0 0.64 0 0 0 0.32 0 1.29 1.93 0
0.96 0 0 0 0 0 0 0 0 0 0 0 0 0 0 0 0 0 0 0 0 0 0 0 0 0 0 0 0 0.778 0 0
3.756 61 278 1
scala> nums.first()
res2: Array[Double] = Array(0.0, 0.64, 0.64, 0.0, 0.32, 0.0, 0.0, 0.0, 0.0,
0.0, 0.0, 0.64, 0.0, 0.0, 0.0, 0.32, 0.0, 1.29, 1.93, 0.0, 0.96, 0.0, 0.0,
0.0, 0.0, 0.0, 0.0, 0.0, 0.0, 0.0, 0.0, 0.0, 0.0, 0.0, 0.0, 0.0, 0.0, 0.0,
0.0, 0.0, 0.0, 0.0, 0.0, 0.0, 0.0, 0.0, 0.0, 0.0, 0.0, 0.0, 0.0, 0.778,
0.0, 0.0, 3.756, 61.0, 278.0, 1.0)
```

When you run a command and do not specify the left-hand side of the assignment (that is,
leaving out the `val x` value of `val x = y`), the Spark shell will assign a default name (that
is, `res[number]`) to the value.

Operators in Spark are divided into transformations and actions. Transformations are evaluated lazily. Spark just creates the RDDs' lineage graph when you call a transformation, such as a map. No actual work is done until an action is invoked on the RDD. Creating the RDD and the map functions are transformations. The `.first()` function is an action that forces the execution.

So, when we created `inFile`, it really didn't do anything except create a variable and set up the pointers. Only when we call an action, such as `.first()`, does Spark evaluate the transformations. As a result, even if we point `inFile` to a nonexistent directory, Spark will take it. However, when we call `inFile.first()`, it will throw the `Input path does not exist:` error.

As you can see, the Spark shell is quite powerful. Much of the power comes from it being based on the Scala REPL (the Scala interactive shell) and so it inherits all of the power of the Scala REPL. That being said, most of the time you will probably prefer to work with more traditionally compiled code rather than in the REPL.

Interactively loading data from S3

Now let's try another exercise with the Spark shell. As part of Amazon's EMR Spark support, they have handily provided some sample data of Wikipedia traffic statistics in S3, in the format that Spark can use. To access the data, you first need to set your AWS access credentials as shell params. For instructions on signing up for EC2 and setting up the shell parameters, see the *Running Spark on EC2 with the scripts* section in `Chapter 1`, *Installing Spark and Setting Up Your Cluster* (S3 access requires additional keys such as `fs.s3n.awsAccessKeyId/awsSecretAccessKey` or the use of the `s3n://user:pw@` syntax). You can also set the shell parameters as `AWS_ACCESS_KEY_ID` and `AWS_SECRET_ACCESS_KEY`. We will leave the AWS configuration out of this discussion, but it needs to be completed.

This is a slightly advanced topic and needs a few S3 configurations (which we won't cover here). The Stack Overflow has two good links on this, namely `http://stackoverflow.com/questions/3385981/how-to-acces s-s3a-files-from-apache-spark` and `http://stackoverflow.com/ques tions/2829134/how-can-i-access-s3-s3n-from-a-local-hadoop-2-6-installation`.

Once this is done, load the S3 data and take a look at the first line:

```
scala> val file = sc.textFile("s3n://bigdatademo/sample/wiki/")
14/11/16 00:02:43 INFO MemoryStore: ensureFreeSpace(34070) called with
curMem=512470, maxMem=278302556
14/11/16 00:02:43 INFO MemoryStore: Block broadcast_105 stored as values in
memory (estimated size 33.3 KB, free 264.9 MB)
file: org.apache.spark.rdd.RDD[String] = s3n://bigdatademo/sample/wiki/
MappedRDD[105] at textFile at <console>:17
scala> file.first()
14/11/16 00:02:58 INFO BlockManager: Removing broadcast 104
14/11/16 00:02:58 INFO BlockManager: Removing block broadcast_104
[..]
14/11/16 00:03:00 INFO SparkContext: Job finished: first at <console>:20,
took 0.442788 s
res6: String = aa.b Pecial:Listusers/sysop 1 4695
scala> file.take(1)
14/11/16 00:05:06 INFO SparkContext: Starting job: take at <console>:20
14/11/16 00:05:06 INFO DAGScheduler: Got job 105 (take at <console>:20)
with 1 output partitions (allowLocal=true)
14/11/16 00:05:06 INFO DAGScheduler: Final stage: Stage 105(take at
<console>:20)
[...]
14/11/16 00:05:07 INFO SparkContext: Job finished: take at <console>:20,
took 0.777104 s
res7: Array[String] = Array(aa.b Pecial:Listusers/sysop 1 4695)
```

You don't need to set your AWS credentials as shell params; the general form of the S3 path is `s3n://<AWS ACCESS ID>:<AWS SECRET>@bucket/path`.

It is important to take a look at the first line of the data; the reason for this is that due to lazy evaluation, Spark won't actually bother to load the data unless we force it to materialize something with it. It is useful to note that Amazon has provided a small sample Dataset to get started with. This data is pulled from a much larger set available at `http://aws.amazon .com/datasets/4182`. This practice can be quite useful when developing in interactive mode as in this mode, you would want to receive fast feedback of the jobs that are getting completed quickly. If your sample data is too big and your runs are taking too long, you could quickly slim down the RDD by using the `sample` functionality built into the Spark shell:

```
scala> val seed  = (100*math.random).toInt
seed: Int = 8
scala> val sample = file.sample(false,1/10.,seed)
res10: spark.RDD[String] = SampledRDD[4] at sample at <console>:17
```

If you want to rerun on the sampled data later, you could write it back to S3:

```
scala> sample.saveAsTextFile("s3n://mysparkbucket/test")
13/04/21 22:46:18 INFO spark.PairRDDFunctions: Saving as hadoop file  of
type (NullWritable, Text)
....
13/04/21 22:47:46 INFO spark.SparkContext: Job finished:  saveAsTextFile at
<console>:19, took 87.462236222 s
```

Now that you have the data loaded, you'll need to find the most popular articles in a sample. First, parse the data by separating it into the name and count fields. Then, reduce the count using the key function, as there can be multiple entries with the same name. Finally, swap the key/value pair so that when we sort by key, we get back the highest count item:

```
scala> val parsed = file.sample(false,1/10.,seed).map(x => x.split("
")).map(x => (x(1), x(2).toInt))
parsed: spark.RDD[(java.lang.String, Int)] = MappedRDD[5] at map at
<console>:16
scala> val reduced = parsed.reduceByKey(_+_)
13/04/21 23:21:49 WARN util.NativeCodeLoader: Unable to load native- hadoop
library for your platform... using builtin-java classes where  applicable
13/04/21 23:21:49 WARN snappy.LoadSnappy: Snappy native library not  loaded
13/04/21 23:21:50 INFO mapred.FileInputFormat: Total input paths to
process : 1
reduced: spark.RDD[(java.lang.String, Int)] = MapPartitionsRDD[8] at
reduceByKey at <console>:18
scala> val countThenTitle = reduced.map(x => (x._2, x._1))
countThenTitle: spark.RDD[(Int, java.lang.String)] = MappedRDD[9] at  map
at <console>:20
scala> countThenTitle.sortByKey(false).take(10)
13/04/21 23:22:08 INFO spark.SparkContext: Starting job: take at
<console>:23
....
13/04/21 23:23:15 INFO spark.SparkContext: Job finished: take at
<console>:23, took 66.815676564 s
res1: Array[(Int, java.lang.String)] = Array((213652,Main_Page),
(14851,Special:Search), (9528,Special:Export/Can_You_Hear_Me),
(6454,Wikipedia:Hauptseite), (4189,Special:Watchlist),
(3520,%E7%89%B9%E5%88%A5:%E3%81%8A%E3%81%BE%E3%81%8B%E3%81%9B%E8%A1%A
8%E7%A4%BA), (2857,Special:AutoLogin), (2416,P%C3%A1gina_principal),
(1990,Survivor_(TV_series)), (1953,Asperger_syndrome))
```

Running the Spark shell in Python

If you are more comfortable with Python than Scala, you can work with Spark interactively in Python by running [cmd].`/pyspark`[/cmd]. In order to start working in the Python shell, let's perform the commands in quick start, as shown at `http://spark.apache.org/d ocs/latest/quick-start.html`. This is just a simple exercise. We will see more of Python in `Chapter 9`, *Foundations of Datasets/DataFrames – The Proverbial Workhorse for DataScientists*:

```
USS-Defiant:fdps-v3 ksankar$ ~/Downloads/spark-2.0.0/bin/pyspark
Python 2.7.12 |Continuum Analytics, Inc.| (default, Jun 29 2016, 11:09:23)
[GCC 4.2.1 (Based on Apple Inc. build 5658) (LLVM build 2336.11.00)] on darwin
Type "help", "copyright", "credits" or "license" for more information.
Anaconda is brought to you by Continuum Analytics.
Please check out: http://continuum.io/thanks and https://anaconda.org
16/08/14 13:44:55 WARN NativeCodeLoader: Unable to load native-hadoop library for your platform.
Welcome to
      ____              __
     / __/__  ___ _____/ /__
    _\ \/ _ \/ _ `/ __/  '_/
   /__ / .__/\_,_/_/ /_/\_\   version 2.0.0
      /_/

Using Python version 2.7.12 (default, Jun 29 2016 11:09:23)
SparkSession available as 'spark'.
>>>
```

The Spark community has done a good job of mapping the APIs so the Scala and Python APIs are very congruent, except when it comes to accommodating language differences. Therefore, if you have done the programming in this book with Scala, you can transfer the skills to Python very easily.

```
Using Python version 2.7.12 (default, Jun 29 2016 11:09:23)
SparkSession available as 'spark'.
>>> textFile = sc.textFile("README.md")
>>> textFile.count()
2
>>> textFile.first()
u'# fdps-v3'
>>> exit()
USS-Defiant:fdps-v3 ksankar$
```

Creating text files, `count()`, and `first()` all work in the same manner.

Type `exit()` to exit the session.

As you can see, Python operations are very similar to those in Scala.

Summary

In this chapter, you learned how to start the Spark shell (Scala and Python) and load data.

Now that you've seen how Spark's interactive console works, it's time to see how to build Spark jobs in a more traditional and persistent environment in the subsequent chapters.

3
Building and Running a Spark Application

This chapter focuses on the mechanics of building Spark applications. There are many tool chains and IDEs with their own details for compiling and building applications. This chapter gives you a quick overview.

If you are a Spark beginner, all the programs in this book can be run from the Spark shell and you can skip this chapter.

Building Spark applications

Using Spark in an interactive mode with the Spark shell is very good for quick prototyping; however for developing applications, we need an IDE. The choices for the Spark IDE have come a long way since the days of Spark 1.0. One can use an array of the Spark IDEs for developing algorithms, data wrangling (that is, exploring data), and modeling analytics applications. As a general rule of thumb, iPython and Zeppelin are used for data exploration IDEs. The language of choice for iPython is Python and Scala/Java for Zeppelin. This is a general observation; all of them can handle the major languages; Scala, Java, Python, and SQL. For developing Scala and Java, the preferred IDE is Eclipse and IntelliJ. We will mostly use the Spark shell (and occasionally iPython) in this book, as our focus is data wrangling and understanding the Spark APIs. Of course, deploying Spark applications require compiling for Java and Scala.

Building the Spark jobs is a bit trickier than building a normal application as all dependencies have to be available on all the machines that are in your cluster.

In this chapter, we will first look at iPython and Eclipse, and then cover the process of building a Java and Scala Spark job with Maven, and learn to build the Spark jobs with a non-Maven aware build system. A reference website for building Spark is at `http://spark .apache.org/docs/latest/building-spark.html`.

Data wrangling with iPython

I found iPython to be the best way to learn Spark. It is also a very good choice for data scientists and data engineers to explore, model, and reason with data.

- The exploration step includes understanding the data, experimenting with multiple transformations, extracting features for aggregation, and machine learning as well as ETL strategies
- The modeling and reason (of relationships and distributions between the variables) steps require fast iteration over the data and extracted features with different algorithms, experimenting with different parameters and arriving at a set of ML algorithms to develop an analytics app

The iPython installation for your system (depending on OS, CPU, and so on) is best described at the iPython site, `http://ipython.org/install.html` and `https://ipython.r eadthedocs.org/en/stable/install/install.html`. The iPython command shell requires the Jupyter notebook system, and then the iPython libraries. Of course, you also would need to have Python installed in your system.

Once iPython is working, starting the Spark development with iPython is very easy. The iPython IDE hooks up to `pyspark` and the interface is via the web browser as follows:

- Use `cd` into the directory where your notebooks are; for example, assuming that you have downloaded GitHub's `fdps-v3` into your home directory, enter as follows:

```
cd ~/fdps-v3
PYSPARK_DRIVER_PYTHON=ipython
PYSPARK_DRIVER_PYTHON_OPTS="notebook"
~/Downloads/spark-2.0.0-preview/bin/pyspark
```

- I have `spark` in my `Downloads` directory. If you have `spark` in your `/opt` directory, the command would be as follows:

  ```
  PYSPARK_DRIVER_PYTHON=ipython PYSPARK_DRIVER_PYTHON_OPTS="notebook"
  /opt/spark/bin/pyspark
  ```

- What you are doing is invoking `pyspark` via the iPython IDE.
- You will see the IDE on the browser as shown in the following screenshot:

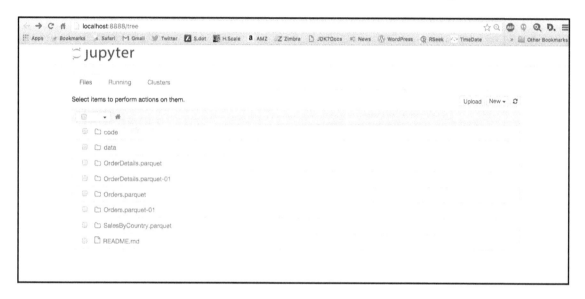

Developing Spark with Eclipse

Eclipse is the IDE of choice for Java developers. The best way is to install the Scala version (2.11.8) of Eclipse from `http://scala-ide.org/`. This will enable one to develop the Scala and Java programs.

Let's first create a Scala project like so:

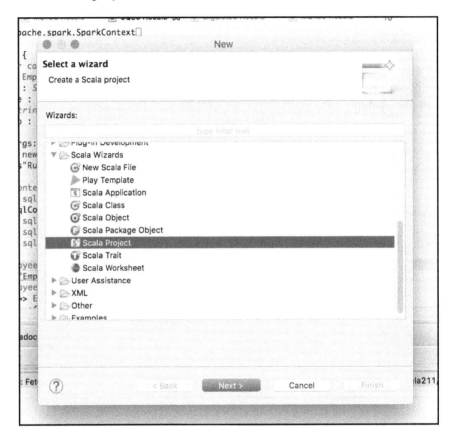

From Spark 2.0.0 onwards, they have changed the packaging, so we have to include `spark-2.0.0/assembly/target/scala-2.11/jars` in **Add External Jars...** as shown in the following screenshot:

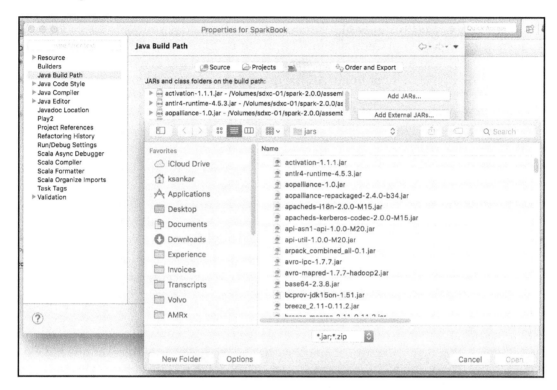

Developing Spark with other IDEs

IntelliJ is a very popular IDE, which a lot of engineers use for developing Spark applications. I also like the Zeppelin IDE, which is very interactive, with good visualization capabilities, and supports Python, Scala, Java, and SQL.

To keep it simple and focused on our goals of working with Spark, we will use the Spark shell most of the time in this book.

We want to make sure you understand the essentials of Spark and get to work with all its features and not worry about IDEs. Once you are familiar with Spark, you can use your favorite language and IDE.

Building your Spark job with Maven

Maven is an open source Apache project that builds the Spark jobs in Java or Scala. As of Version 2.0.0, the building Spark site states that Maven is the official recommendation for packaging Spark and is the "build of reference" too. As with `sbt`, you can include the Spark dependency through Maven Central, simplifying our build process. Also, similar to `sbt` is the ability of Spark and all of our dependencies to put everything in a single JAR file using a plugin or build Spark as a monolithic JAR file using the `sbt/sbt` assembly for inclusion.

To illustrate the build process for the Spark jobs with Maven, this section will use Java as an example, as Maven is more commonly used to build the Java tasks. As a first step, let's take a Spark job that already works and go through the process of creating a build file for it. We can start by copying the `GroupByTest` example into a new directory and generating the Maven template, as shown here:

```
mkdir example-java-build/; cd example-java-build
mvn archetype:generate \
  -DarchetypeGroupId=org.apache.maven.archetypes \
  -DgroupId=spark.examples \
  -DartifactId=JavaWordCount \
  -Dfilter=org.apache.maven.archetypes:maven-archetype-quickstart
  cp ../examples/src/main/java/spark/examples/JavaWordCount.java
  JavaWordCount/src/main/java/spark/examples/JavaWordCount.java
```

Next, update your Maven `example-java-build/JavaWordCount/pom.xml` path to include information on the version of Spark we are using. Also, since the example file we are working with requires a JDK version greater than 1.5, we will need to update the Java version that Maven is configured to use; the current version is 1.3. In between the project tags, we will need to add the following code:

```
<dependencies>
  <dependency>
    <groupId>junit</groupId>
    <artifactId>junit</artifactId>
    <version>4.11</version>
    <scope>test</scope>
  </dependency>
  <dependency>
    <groupId>org.spark-project</groupId>
    <artifactId>spark-core_2.11</artifactId>
    <version>2.0.0</version>
  </dependency>
</dependencies>
<build>
  <plugins>
```

```
    <plugin>
      <groupId>org.apache.maven.plugins</groupId>
      <artifactId>maven-compiler-plugin</artifactId>
      <configuration>
        <source>1.7</source>
        <target>1.7</target>
      </configuration>
    </plugin>
  </plugins>
</build>
```

We can now build our JAR file with the mvn package, run the following command:

```
SPARK_HOME="../"  SPARK_EXAMPLES_JAR="./target/JavaWordCount-1.0-
SNAPSHOT.jar"  java -cp ./target/JavaWordCount-1.0-
SNAPSHOT.jar:../../core/target/spark-core-assembly-1.5.2.jar
spark.examples.JavaWordCount local[1] ../../README
```

We can use a plugin to include all of the dependencies in our JAR file. Between the <plugins> tags, add the following code:

```
<plugin>
  <groupId>org.apache.maven.plugins</groupId>
  <artifactId>maven-shade-plugin</artifactId>
  <version>2.3</version>
  <configuration>
    <!-- This transform is used so that merging of akka
configuration files works -->
    <transformers>
      <transformer
implementation="org.apache.maven.plugins.shade.resource.
ApacheLicenseResourceTransformer">
      </transformer>
      <transformer
implementation="org.apache.maven.plugins.shade.resource.
AppendingTransformer">
        <resource>reference.conf</resource>
      </transformer>
    </transformers>
  </configuration>
  <executions>
    <execution>
      <phase>package</phase>
      <goals>
        <goal>shade</goal>
      </goals>
    </execution>
  </executions>
```

```
</plugin>
```

Then, run the `mvn` assembly and the resulting JAR file can be run as shown in the preceding section; however, leave out the Spark assembly JAR file from the class path.

Building your Spark job with something else

If neither `sbt` nor Maven suits your needs, you may decide to use another build system. Thankfully, Spark supports building a fat JAR file with all its dependencies, which makes it easy to include in the build system of your choice. Simply, run the `sbt/sbt` assembly in the Spark directory and copy the resulting assembly JAR file at `core/target/spark-core-assembly-1.5.2.jar` to your build dependencies, and you are good to go. It is more common to use the `spark-assembly-1.5.2-hadoop2.6.0.jar` file. These files exist in `$SPARK_HOME$/lib` (if users use a prebuilt version) or in `$SPARK_HOME$/assembly/target/scala-2.10/` (if users build the source code with Maven or `sbt`).

No matter what your build system is, you may find yourself wanting to use a patched version of the Spark libraries. In this case, you can deploy your Spark library locally. I recommend giving it a different version number to ensure that `sbt`/Maven picks up the modified version. You can change the version by editing `project/SparkBuild.scala` and changing the `version:=` part according to the version you have installed. If you are using `sbt`, you should run the `sbt/sbt` update in the project that is importing the custom version. For other build systems, you just need to ensure that you use the new assembly JAR file as part of your build.

References

The references are listed here:

- http://spark.apache.org/docs/latest/building-spark.html
- http://www.scala-sbt.org/
- https://github.com/sbt/sbt-assembly

- http://spark-project.org/docs/latest/scala-programming-guide.html
- http://maven.apache.org/guides/getting-started/
- http://maven.apache.org/plugins/maven-compiler-plugin/examples/set-compiler-source-and-target.html
- http://maven.apache.org/plugins/maven-dependency-plugin/

Summary

So now you can wrangle with data using iPython and Eclipse, as well as build your Spark jobs with Maven or a build system of your choice. It's time to jump in and start learning how to do more fun and exciting things, such as learning how to create a Spark session in the subsequent chapter. For this book, you can use the Spark shell and all the code will work. We also have the iPython notebooks for machine learning and DataFrames.

4
Creating a SparkSession Object

This chapter will cover how to create a `SparkSession` object in your cluster. A `SparkSession` object represents the connection to a Spark cluster (local or remote) and provides the entry point to interact with Spark. We need to create `SparkSession` so that we can interact with Spark and distribute our jobs. In Chapter 2, *Using the Spark Shell*, we interacted with Spark through the Spark shell which helped us create a `SparkSession` object and a `SparkContext` object. Now you can create RDDs, broadcast variables, and counters, and actually do fun things with your data. The Spark shell serves as an example of how to interact with the Spark cluster through the `SparkSession` and `SparkContext` object.

For a client to establish a connection to the Spark cluster, the `SparkSession` object needs some basic information, which is given here:

- **Master URL**: This URL can be `local[n]` for local mode, `Spark://[sparkip]` for the Spark server, or `mesos://path` for a Mesos cluster
- **Application name**: This information is a human-readable application name
- **Spark home**: This information is the path to Spark on the master/workers
- **JARs**: This information is the path to the JARs required for your job

SparkSession versus SparkContext

You would have noticed that we are using `SparkSession` and `SparkContext`, and this is not an error. Let's revisit the annals of Spark history for a perspective. It is important to understand where we came from, as you will hear about these connection objects for some time to come.

Prior to Spark 2.0.0, the three main connection objects were `SparkContext`, `SqlContext`, and `HiveContext`. The `SparkContext` object was the connection to a Spark execution environment and created RDDs and others, `SQLContext` worked with SparkSQL in the background of `SparkContext`, and `HiveContext` interacted with the `Hive` stores.

Spark 2.0.0 introduced Datasets/DataFrames as the main distributed data abstraction interface and the `SparkSession` object as the entry point to a Spark execution environment. Appropriately, the `SparkSession` object is found in the namespace, `org.apache.spark.sql.SparkSession` (Scala), or `pyspark.sql.sparkSession`. A few points to note are as follows:

- In Scala and Java, Datasets form the main data abstraction as typed data; however, for Python and R (which do not have compile time type checking), the data abstraction is DataFrame. For all practical API purposes, the Datasets in Scala/Java are the same as DataFrames in Python/R.
- While Datasets/DataFrames are top-level interfaces, RDDs have not disappeared. In fact, the underlying structures are still RRDs. (You will see more on RDDs in `Chapter 6`, *Manipulating Your RDD*.) Also, to interact with RDDs, we still need a `SparkContext` object and we can get one from the `SparkSession` object.
- The `SparkSession` object encapsulates the `SparkContext` object. As of version 2.0.0, `SparkContext` is still the conduit to a Spark cluster (local or remote); therefore, you will need `SparkCLuster` for doing execution environment operations, such as accumulators, `addFile`, `addJars`, and so on.

  However, for operations such as reading and creating Datasets, use the `SparkSession` object.

The chapters in this book will deal with this evolutionary influence. The first few chapters will cover `SparkContext` and RDDs, and we'll then move on to `SparkSession`, Datasets, and DataFrames.

 Coincidently, as I was doing the author review for this chapter, Jules Damji of Databricks wrote a very relevant blog, *How to use SparkSession in Spark 2.0.0* available at `https://databricks.com/blog/216/8/15/how-to -use-sparksession-in-apache-spark-2-.html`.

Building a SparkSession object

In the Scala and Python programs, you build a `SparkSession` object with the following build pattern:

```
val sparkSession = new
SparkSession.builder.master(master_path).appName("application
name").config("optional configuration parameters").getOrCreate()
```

While you can hardcode all these values, it's better to read them from the environment with reasonable defaults. This approach provides maximum flexibility to run the code in a changing environment without having to recompile. Using `local` as the default value for the master makes it easy to launch your application in a test environment locally. By carefully selecting the defaults, you can avoid having to overspecify this.

The `spark-shell/pyspark` creates the `SparkSession` object automatically and assigns to the `spark` variable.

The `SparkSession` object has the `SparkContext` object, which you can access with `spark.sparkContext`.

As we will see later, the `SparkSession` object unifies more than the context; it also unifies the process of reading data in different formats and creating Datasets/DataFrames as well as views to execute SQL statements.

So, in short, the rules are as follows:

- Build a `SparkSession` object (or using the one created in the case of `spark-shell/pyspark`)
- Use the `SparkSession` object for reads, creating views for SQL statements, and creating Datasets and DataFrames
- Get the `SparkContext` object from `SparkSession` for things such as accumulators, distributing cache files, and working with RDD.

Now you understand why we have been talking about `SparkSession` and `SparkContext` as if they are the same.

SparkContext – metadata

The `SparkContext` object has a set of metadata that I found useful. The version number, application name, and memory available are useful pieces of information. At the start of a Spark program, I usually display/log the version number.

Value	Use
appName	This value is the application name. If you have established a convention, this field can be useful at runtime.
getConf	This value returns configuration information.
getExecutorMemoryStatus	This value retrieves memory details. It could be useful if you want to check memory details. As Spark is distributed, the values do not mean that you are out of memory.
Master	This value is the name of the master.
Version	I found this value very useful, especially while testing with different versions.

Execute the following command from the shell:

```
cd ~/Downloads/spark-2.0.0   ( Or to wherever you have your spark installed)
bin/spark-shell
```

Refer to the following screenshot:

```
USS-Defiant:fdps-v3 ksankar$ ~/Downloads/spark-2.0.0/bin/spark-shell
16/08/14 16:28:30 WARN NativeCodeLoader: Unable to load native-hadoop library for your platform... using builtin-java classes where applicable
16/08/14 16:28:31 WARN SparkContext: Use an existing SparkContext, some configuration may not take effect.
Spark context Web UI available at http://10.0.1.2:4040
Spark context available as 'sc' (master = local[*], app id = local-1471217311152).
Spark session available as 'spark'.
Welcome to
      ____              __
     / __/__  ___ _____/ /__
    _\ \/ _ \/ _ `/ __/  '_/
   /___/ .__/\_,_/_/ /_/\_\   version 2.0.0
      /_/

Using Scala version 2.11.8 (Java HotSpot(TM) 64-Bit Server VM, Java 1.7.0_60)
Type in expressions to have them evaluated.
Type :help for more information.

scala> spark.version
res0: String = 2.0.0

scala> sc.appName
res1: String = Spark shell

scala> sc.version
res2: String = 2.0.0

scala>
```

```
scala> spark.version
res0: String = 2.0.0
```

```
scala> sc.appName
res1: String = Spark shell
scala> sc.version
res2: String = 2.0.0
scala> spark.
```

Press the *Tab* key and you will see the commands as shown in the following screenshot:

```
scala> spark.
baseRelationToDataFrame   createDataFrame   emptyDataset    listenerManager   read          sql          streams   version
catalog                   createDataset     experimental    newSession        readStream    sqlContext   table
conf                      emptyDataFrame    implicits       range             sparkContext  stop         udf
```

```
scala>sc.
```

Press the *Tab* key and you will see a bigger list of commands, as shown in the following screenshot:

```
scala> sc.
accumulable               broadcast             files                    hadoopConfiguration   makeRDD            sequenceFile          submitJob
accumulableCollection     cancelAllJobs         getAllPools              hadoopFile            master             setCallSite           textFile
accumulator               cancelJobGroup        getCheckpointDir         hadoopRDD             newAPIHadoopFile   setCheckpointDir      uiWebUrl
addFile                   clearCallSite         getConf                  isLocal               newAPIHadoopRDD    setJobDescription     union
addJar                    clearJobGroup         getExecutorMemoryStatus  isStopped             objectFile         setJobGroup           version
addSparkListener          collectionAccumulator getExecutorStorageStatus jars                  parallelize        setLocalProperty      wholeTextFiles
appName                   defaultMinPartitions  getLocalProperty         killExecutor          range              setLogLevel
applicationAttemptId      defaultParallelism    getPersistentRDDs        killExecutors         register           sparkUser
applicationId             deployMode            getPoolForName           listFiles             requestExecutors   startTime
binaryFiles               doubleAccumulator     getRDDStorageInfo        listJars              runApproximateJob  statusTracker
binaryRecords             emptyRDD              getSchedulingMode        longAccumulator       runJob             stop
```

```
scala> sc.getExecutorMemoryStatus
res3: scala.collection.Map[String,(Long, Long)] = Map(10.0.1.2:54783 ->
(384093388,384093388))
```

The `localhost:54783` value is the address and the port number of the machine. The first value represents the maximum amount of memory allocated for the block manager (to buffer the intermediate data or cache RDDs), while the second value represents the amount of remaining memory:

```
scala> sc.getConf
res5: org.apache.spark.SparkConf = org.apache.spark.SparkConf@7bc17541
scala> sc.getConf.toString()
res6: String = org.apache.spark.SparkConf@48acaa84
scala>
```

A more informative call of this is given here:

```
scala> sc.getConf.toDebugString
res5: String = hive.metastore.warehouse.dir=file:/Users/ksankar/fdps-
v3/spark-warehouse
spark.app.id=local-1471217311152
```

```
spark.app.name=Spark shell
spark.driver.host=10.0.1.2
spark.driver.port=54782
spark.executor.id=driver
spark.home=/Users/ksankar/Downloads/spark-2.0.0
spark.jars= spark.master=local[*]
spark.repl.class.outputDir=/private/var/folders/gq/70vnnyfj6913b6lms_td7gb4
0000gn/T/spark-63174a71-e33f-4265-a427-bdc140553210/repl-35c5c348-
cd19-482c-af47-3aff08a7fa42
spark.repl.class.uri=spark://10.0.1.2:54782/classes
spark.sql.catalogImplementation=in-memory
spark.submit.deployMode=client.
scala> :quit (To exit the shell)
```

Shared Java and Scala APIs

Once you have a SparkSession object created, it will serve as your main entry point. In the next chapter, you will learn how to use the SparkSession object to load and save data. You can also use SparkSession.SparkContext to launch more Spark jobs and add or remove dependencies. Some of the non-data-driven methods you can use on the SparkSession.SparkContext object are shown here:

Method	Use
addJar(path)	This method adds the JAR file for all the future jobs that would run through the SparkContext object.
addFile(path)	This method downloads the file to all the nodes on the cluster.
listFiles/listJars	This method shows the list of all the currently added files/JARs.
stop()	This method shuts down SparkContext.
clearFiles()	This method removes the files so that new nodes will not download them.
clearJars()	This method removes the JARs from being required for future jobs.

This appears straightforward.

Python

The Python `SparkSession` object behaves in the same way as Scala. We can almost run the same commands as shown in the previous section, within the constraints of language semantics:

```
bin/pyspark
```

Refer to the following screenshot:

```
USS-Defiant:fdps-v3 ksankar$ ~/Downloads/spark-2.0.0/bin/pyspark
Python 2.7.12 |Continuum Analytics, Inc.| (default, Jun 29 2016, 11:09:23)
[GCC 4.2.1 (Based on Apple Inc. build 5658) (LLVM build 2336.11.00)] on darwin
Type "help", "copyright", "credits" or "license" for more information.
Anaconda is brought to you by Continuum Analytics.
Please check out: http://continuum.io/thanks and https://anaconda.org
16/08/14 16:43:03 WARN NativeCodeLoader: Unable to load native-hadoop library for your
Welcome to
      ____              __
     / __/__  ___ _____/ /__
    _\ \/ _ \/ _ `/ __/  '_/
   /__ / .__/\_,_/_/ /_/\_\   version 2.0.0
      /_/

Using Python version 2.7.12 (default, Jun 29 2016 11:09:23)
SparkSession available as 'spark'.
```

```
>>> spark.version
    u'2.0.0'
>>> sc.version
    u'2.0.0'
>>> sc.appName
    u'PySparkShell'
>>> sc.master
    u'local[*]'
>>> sc.getMemoryStatus
    Traceback (most recent call last):
      File "<stdin>", line 1, in <module>
    AttributeError: 'SparkContext' object has no attribute
'getMemoryStatus'
>>> from pyspark.conf import SparkConf
>>> conf = SparkConf()
>>> conf.toDebugString()
u'spark.app.name=PySparkShell\nspark.master=local[*]\nspark.submit.deployMo
de=client'
>>>
>>> exit()  (To exit the pyspark shell)
```

The `PySpark` instance does not have the `getExecutorMemoryStatus` call yet, but we can get some information with the `.toDebugString` call.

iPython

Finally, let's fire up iPython and interact with the `SparkContext` object. As mentioned in `Chapter 3`, *Building and Running a Spark Application*, refer to the iPython site (`http://jupyt er.readthedocs.org/en/latest/install.html`) for installing the Jupyter and iPython system.

First, change the directory to `fdps-v3`, where you would have downloaded the code and data for this book:

```
cd ~/fdps-v3
```

The command to start iPython is as follows:

```
PYSPARK_DRIVER_PYTHON=ipython PYSPARK_DRIVER_PYTHON_OPTS="notebook"
~/Downloads/spark-2.0.0/bin/pyspark
```

The iPython notebook will be launched in the web browser, as shown in the following screenshot, and you will see a list of iPython notebooks:

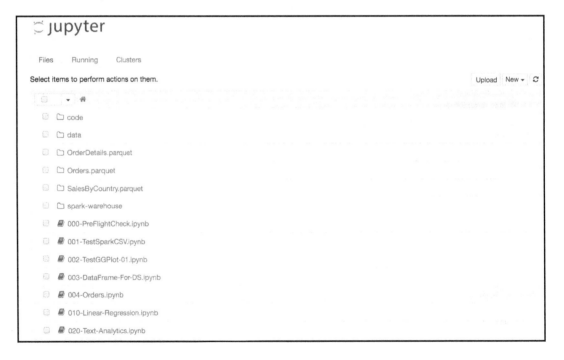

Click on the `000-PreFlightCheck.ipynb` notebook:

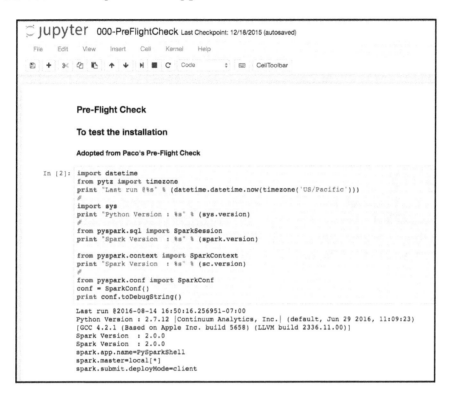

Run the first cell using *Shift + Enter*. You will see the results, including the Python version, Spark version, and so on, as shown in the preceding screenshot. The notebook has more cells, which we will see in the next few chapters.

Now that you are able to create a connection with your Spark cluster, it's time to start loading data into Spark, which we will see in the next chapter.

Reference

The references are listed here:

- https://databricks-prod-cloudfront.cloud.databricks.com/public/427ec 92e239c93eaaa8714f173bcfc/612296529858466/43155438669884/4814681571 89561/latest.html
- http://spark-project.org/docs/latest/quick-start.html
- http://www-stat.stanford.edu/~tibs/ElemStatLearn/data.html

- https://github.com/mesos/spark/blob/master/repl/src/main/scala/spark
  /repl/SparkILoop.scala
- http://spark.apache.org/docs/latest/api/python/pyspark.html#pyspark.
  SparkContext
- http://www.scala-lang.org/api/current/index.html#scala.util.Properti
  es$
- http://spark.apache.org/docs/latest/api/java/org/apache/spark/SparkC
  ontext.html

Summary

In this chapter, we covered how to connect to our Spark cluster using a `SparkSession` and `SparkContext` object. We saw how the APIs are uniform across all the languages, such as Scala and Python. We also learned a bit about the interactive shell and iPython. Using this knowledge, we will look at the different data sources we can use to load data into Spark in the next chapter.

5
Loading and Saving Data in Spark

Until now, you have experimented with the Spark shell, figured out how to create a connection with the Spark cluster, and build jobs for deployment. Now to make these jobs useful, you will need to learn how to load and save data in Spark, which we'll do in this chapter.

Before we dive into data, we have a couple of background tasks to do. First we need to get a view of Spark abstractions, and second, have a quick discussion about the different modalities of data.

Spark abstractions

The goal of this book is that you get a good understanding of Spark via hands-on programming. The best way to understand Spark is to work through operations iteratively. As we are still in the initial chapters, some of the things might not be very clear, but they should be clear enough for the current context. As you write code and read further chapters, you will gather more information and insight. With this in mind, let's move to a quick discussion on Spark abstractions. We will revisit the abstractions in more detail in the following chapters.

The main features of Apache Spark are distributed data representation and computation, thus achieving massive scaling of data operations. Spark's primary unit for representation of data is RDD, which allows for easy parallel operations on the data. Until 2.0.0, everyone worked with RDDs. However, they are low-level raw structures, which can be optimized for performance and scalability.

This is where Datasets/DataFrames come into the picture. Datasets/DataFrames are API-level abstractions, that is, the main programming interface. They provide most of the RDD operations but are layered over RDDs via optimized query plans. So, the underlying representation is still an RDD but accessed via the Dataset/DataFrame APIs.

> RDDs can be viewed as arrays of arrays with primitive data types, such as integers, floats, and strings. Datasets/DataFrames, on the other hand, are similar to a table or a spreadsheet with column headings-such as name, title, order number, order date, and movie rating-and the associated data types.
>
> The best part is that there are a few patterns that are recommended with respect to Datasets.
>
> Wherever possible, use Datasets and DataFrames. Use `SparkSession`. However, if you need low-level manipulations to implement complex operations or algorithms, use RDDs. Use the `sparkcontext` object encapsulated by `SparkSession`.
>
> Datasets/DataFrames and RDDs can be converted back and forth using `dataset.rdd()` and `SparkSession.createDataset(rdd)/SparkSession.createDataFrame(rdd)`.

RDDs

Now let's quickly discuss RDDs. Later, we have individual chapters dedicated to Datasets/DataFrames as well as one chapter on RDD operations. Spark RDDs can be created from any supported Hadoop source. Native collections in Scala, Java, and Python can also serve as the basis for an RDD. Creating RDDs from a native collection is especially useful for testing.

As an RDD follows the principle of lazy evaluation, it evaluates an expression only when it is needed, that is, when an action is called for. This means that when you try to access the data in an RDD, it could fail. The computation to create the data in an RDD is only done when the data is referenced by caching or writing out the RDD. This also means that you can chain a large number of operations and will not have to worry about excessive blocking in a computational thread. It's important to note during application development that you can write code, compile it, and even run your job; however, unless you materialize the RDD, your code would not even try to load the original data.

Each time you materialize an RDD, it is recomputed; therefore, if we are going to use something frequently, performance improvement can be achieved by caching the RDD.

Data modalities

From a modality perspective, all data can be grouped into three categories: structured, semi-structured, and unstructured. The modality is independent of the data source, organization, or storage technologies. In fact, different representations, organizations, and storage technologies perform well with, at the most, one modality. It is very difficult to efficiently support more than one modality.

- Structured data is usually stored in databases, Oracle, HBase, Cassandra, and so on. Relational tables are the most commonly used organization and storage mechanism. Usually, structured data formats, data types, and sizes are fixed and well known.
- Semi-structured data, as the name implies, has enough structure; however, there is also variability in its size, type, and format. The most common semi-structured formats are `csv`, `json`, and `parquet`.
- Unstructured data, of course, is about 85 percent of the data we encounter. Images, audio files, and social media data all are unstructured. A lot of the data that we eventually process starts out as unstructured, which is structured via ETL, transformations, and other techniques.

Data modalities and Datasets/DataFrames/RDDs

Now let's tie together the modalities with the Spark abstractions and see how we can read and write data. Before 2.0.0, things were conceptually simpler-we only needed to read data into RDDs and use `map()` to transform the data as required. However, data wrangling was harder. With Dataset/DataFrame, we have the ability to read directly into a table with headings, associate data types with domain semantics, and start working with data more effectively.

As a general rule of thumb, perform the following steps:

1. Use `SparkContext` and RDDs to handle unstructured data.

2. Use `SparkSession` and Datasets/DataFrames for semi-structured and structured data. As you will see in the later chapters, `SparkSession` has unified the read from various formats, such as the `.csv`, `.json`, `.parquet`, `.jdbc`, `.orc`, and `.text` files. Moreover, there is a pluggable architecture called DataSource API to access any type of structured data.

Loading data into an RDD

In this chapter, we will examine the different sources you can use for your RDD. If you decide to run it through the examples in the Spark shell, you can call `.cache()` or `.first()` on the RDDs you generate to check whether it can be loaded. In `Chapter 2`, *Using the Spark Shell*, you learned how to load data text from a file and from S3. In this chapter, we will look at the different formats of data (text file and CSV) and the different sources (filesystem and HDFS) supported.

One of the easiest ways to create an RDD is taking an existing Scala collection and converting it into an RDD. The `SparkContext` object provides a function called `parallelize` that takes a Scala collection and converts it into an RDD of the same type as the input collection, as shown here.

As mentioned in the previous chapters, `cd` to the `fdps-v3` directory and run `spark-shell` or `pyspark`.

For Scala, refer to the following screenshot:

```
USS-Defiant:fdps-v3 ksankar$ ~/Downloads/spark-2.0.0/bin/spark-shell
16/08/15 13:56:26 WARN NativeCodeLoader: Unable to load native-hadoop library for your platform...
16/08/15 13:56:28 WARN SparkContext: Use an existing SparkContext, some configuration may not take
Spark context Web UI available at http://10.106.168.196:4040
Spark context available as 'sc' (master = local[*], app id = local-1471294587837).
Spark session available as 'spark'.
Welcome to
      ____              __
     / __/__  ___ _____/ /__
    _\ \/ _ \/ _ `/ __/  '_/
   /___/ .__/\_,_/_/ /_/\_\   version 2.0.0
      /_/

Using Scala version 2.11.8 (Java HotSpot(TM) 64-Bit Server VM, Java 1.7.0_60)
Type in expressions to have them evaluated.
Type :help for more information.

scala> val dataRDD = sc.parallelize(List(1,2,4))
dataRDD: org.apache.spark.rdd.RDD[Int] = ParallelCollectionRDD[0] at parallelize at <console>:24

scala> dataRDD.take(3)
res0: Array[Int] = Array(1, 2, 4)

scala>
```

For Java, refer to the following code:

```java
import java.util.Arrays;
import org.apache.spark.SparkConf;
import org.apache.spark.api.java.*;
import org.apache.spark.api.java.function.Function;

public class LDSV01 {

  public static void main(String[] args) {
    SparkConf conf = new SparkConf().setAppName("Chapter
05").setMaster("local");
    JavaSparkContext ctx = new JavaSparkContext(conf);
    JavaRDD<Integer> dataRDD = ctx.parallelize(Arrays.asList(1,2,4));
    System.out.println(dataRDD.count());
    System.out.println(dataRDD.take(3));
  }

}
Using Spark's default log4j profile:org/apache/spark/log4j-
defaults.properties
16/01/03 08:55:25 INFO SparkContext: Running Spark version 2.0.0
[..]
16/01/03 08:55:28 INFO DAGScheduler: Job 0 finished: count at
LDSV01.java:13, took 0.380508 s
3
16/01/03 08:55:28 INFO SparkContext: Starting job: take at LDSV01.java:14
[..]
16/01/03 08:55:29 INFO DAGScheduler: Job 1 finished: take at
LDSV01.java:14, took 0.020155 s
[1, 2, 4]
16/01/03 08:55:29 INFO SparkContext: Invoking stop() from shutdown hook
```

The reason for a full program in Java is that you can use the Scala and Python shell;
however, for Java, you need to compile and run the program.

For Python, refer to the following screenshot:

```
USS-Defiant:fdps-v3 ksankar$ ~/Downloads/spark-2.0.0/bin/pyspark
Python 2.7.12 |Continuum Analytics, Inc.| (default, Jun 29 2016, 11:09:23)
[GCC 4.2.1 (Based on Apple Inc. build 5658) (LLVM build 2336.11.00)] on darwin
Type "help", "copyright", "credits" or "license" for more information.
Anaconda is brought to you by Continuum Analytics.
Please check out: http://continuum.io/thanks and https://anaconda.org
16/08/15 13:58:07 WARN NativeCodeLoader: Unable to load native-hadoop library for your platform
Welcome to
      ____              __
     / __/__  ___ _____/ /__
    _\ \/ _ \/ _ `/ __/  '_/
   /__ / .__/\_,_/_/ /_/\_\   version 2.0.0
      /_/

Using Python version 2.7.12 (default, Jun 29 2016 11:09:23)
SparkSession available as 'spark'.
>>> rdd = sc.parallelize([1,2,3])
>>> rdd.take(3)
[1, 2, 3]
>>>
```

The simplest method to load external data is loading the text from a file. This has a requirement that the file should be available on all the nodes in the cluster, which isn't much of a problem for local mode. When you're in distributed mode, you will want to use the addFile functionality of Spark to copy the file to all the machines in your cluster. Assuming that your SparkContext object is called sc, we could load the text data from a file that we downloaded in Chapter 2, *Using the Spark Shell*.

The data and code are available on GitHub at https://github.com/xsank ar/fdps-v3, which you can download into ~/fdps-v3.

For Scala, refer to the following code:

```
import org.apache.spark.SparkFiles;
...
sc.addFile("data/spam.data")
val inFile = sc.textFile(SparkFiles.get("spam.data"))
inFile.first()
```

Here's a screenshot of this:

```
USS-Defiant:fdps-v3 ksankar$ ~/Downloads/spark-2.0.0/bin/spark-shell
16/08/15 14:04:37 WARN NativeCodeLoader: Unable to load native-hadoop library for your platform...
16/08/15 14:04:38 WARN SparkContext: Use an existing SparkContext, some configuration may not take
Spark context Web UI available at http://10.106.168.196:4040
Spark context available as 'sc' (master = local[*], app id = local-1471295078635).
Spark session available as 'spark'.
Welcome to
      ____              __
     / __/__  ___ _____/ /__
    _\ \/ _ \/ _ `/ __/  '_/
   /___/ .__/\_,_/_/ /_/\_\   version 2.0.0
      /_/

Using Scala version 2.11.8 (Java HotSpot(TM) 64-Bit Server VM, Java 1.7.0_60)
Type in expressions to have them evaluated.
Type :help for more information.

scala> import org.apache.spark.SparkFiles;
import org.apache.spark.SparkFiles

scala> sc.addFile("data/spam.data")

scala> val inFile = sc.textFile(SparkFiles.get("spam.data"))
inFile: org.apache.spark.rdd.RDD[String] = /private/var/folders/gq/70vnnyfj6913b6lms_td7gb40000gn/
69a24-96d5-49dd-af6d-a03c58b566de/spam.data MapPartitionsRDD[1] at textFile at <console>:25

scala> inFile.first()
res1: String = 0 0.64 0.64 0 0.32 0 0 0 0 0 0.64 0 0 0 0.32 0 1.29 1.93 0 0.96 0 0 0 0 0 0 0 0
 61 278 1

scala> █
```

For Java, refer to the following code:

```java
import org.apache.spark.SparkConf;
import org.apache.spark.api.java.*;
import org.apache.spark.SparkFiles;;

public class LDSV02 {

  public static void main(String[] args) {
    SparkConf conf = new SparkConf().setAppName("Chapter
05").setMaster("local");
    JavaSparkContext ctx = new JavaSparkContext(conf);
    System.out.println("Running Spark Version : "+ctx.version());
    ctx.addFile("/Users/ksankar/fpds-vii/data/spam.data");
    JavaRDD<String> lines = ctx.textFile(SparkFiles.get("spam.data"));
    System.out.println(lines.first());
  }
}
```

```
Using Spark's default log4j profile:org/apache/spark/log4j-
defaults.properties
16/08/15 13:49:13 INFO SparkContext: Running Spark version 2.0.0
[..]
```

```
Running Spark Version : 2.0.0
[..]
16/08/15 13:49:16 INFO DAGScheduler: Job 0 finished: first at
LDSV02.java:13, took 0.576352 s
0 0.64 0.64 0 0.32 0 0 0 0 0 0.64 0 0 0 0.32 0 1.29 1.93 0 0.96 0 0 0 0 0
0 0 0 0 0 0 0 0 0 0 0 0 0 0 0 0 0 0 0 0 0 0 0 0 0 0.778 0 0 3.756 61 278 1
[..]
```

For Python, refer to the following code:

```python
from pyspark.files import SparkFiles
sc.addFile("data/spam.data")
in_file = sc.textFile(SparkFiles.get("spam.data"))
in_file.take(1)
```

Here's a screenshot of this:

```
USS-Defiant:fdps-v3 ksankar$ ~/Downloads/spark-2.0.0/bin/pyspark
Python 2.7.12 |Continuum Analytics, Inc.| (default, Jun 29 2016, 11:09:23)
[GCC 4.2.1 (Based on Apple Inc. build 5658) (LLVM build 2336.11.00)] on darwin
Type "help", "copyright", "credits" or "license" for more information.
Anaconda is brought to you by Continuum Analytics.
Please check out: http://continuum.io/thanks and https://anaconda.org
16/08/15 14:06:10 WARN NativeCodeLoader: Unable to load native-hadoop library for your platform
Welcome to
      ____              __
     / __/__  ___ _____/ /__
    _\ \/ _ \/ _ `/ __/  '_/
   /__ / .__/\_,_/_/ /_/\_\   version 2.0.0
      /_/

Using Python version 2.7.12 (default, Jun 29 2016 11:09:23)
SparkSession available as 'spark'.
>>> from pyspark.files import SparkFiles
>>> sc.addFile("data/spam.data")
>>> in_file = sc.textFile(SparkFiles.get("spam.data"))
>>> in_file.take(1)
[u'0 0.64 0.64 0 0.32 0 0 0 0 0 0.64 0 0 0 0.32 0 1.29 1.93 0 0.96 0 0 0 0 0 0 0 0 0 0
>>>
```

The resulting RDD is of the string type with each line being a unique element in the RDD. The take(1) action picks the first element from the RDD.

Frequently, your input files will be CSV or TSV files, which you will want to read and parse before you create RDDs for processing. The two ways of reading CSV files are as follows: either read and parse them using your own functions or use a CSV library, such as opencsv.

First, let's look at parsing using our own functions.

For Scala, first invoke `spark-shell`:

```
USS-Defiant:~ ksankar$ cd ~/fdps-v3/
USS-Defiant:fdps-v3 ksankar$ ~/Downloads/spark-2.0.0/bin/spark-shell
16/08/15 14:31:06 WARN NativeCodeLoader: Unable to load native-hadoop library for your platform...
16/08/15 14:31:07 WARN SparkContext: Use an existing SparkContext, some configuration may not take effect.
Spark context Web UI available at http://10.106.168.196:4040
Spark context available as 'sc' (master = local[*], app id = local-1471296667163).
Spark session available as 'spark'.
Welcome to
      ____              __
     / __/__  ___ _____/ /__
    _\ \/ _ \/ _ `/ __/  '_/
   /___/ .__/\_,_/_/ /_/\_\   version 2.0.0
      /_/

Using Scala version 2.11.8 (Java HotSpot(TM) 64-Bit Server VM, Java 1.7.0_60)
Type in expressions to have them evaluated.
Type :help for more information.

scala>
```

Here's the code for this:

```
scala> val inFile = sc.textFile("data/Line_of_numbers.csv")
scala> val numbersRDD = inFile.map(line => line.split(','))
scala> numbersRDD.take(10)
```

Note that one common error is
`org.apache.hadoop.mapred.InvalidInputException: Input`
`path does not exist.` This is because Spark looks for the file in the
`spark-2.0.0` directory if you start from there. It needs the full path.
Modify the first line to add the full path (where you have downloaded the
book files from GitHub, usually `fdps-v3`).
You also need to execute the second line to point the RDD to the right file.

Refer to the following code:

```
scala> val inFile = sc.textFile("data/Line_of_numbers.csv")
inFile: org.apache.spark.rdd.RDD[String] = MapPartitionsRDD[4] at textFile
at <console>:27

scala> val numbersRDD = inFile.map(line => line.split(','))
numbersRDD: org.apache.spark.rdd.RDD[Array[String]] = MapPartitionsRDD[5]
at map at <console>:29

scala> numbersRDD.take(10)
res2: Array[Array[String]] = Array(Array(42, 42, 55, 61,53, 49, 43, 47, 49,
60, 68, 54, 34, 35, 35, 39))
```

This is an array of strings. We need `float` or `double`:

```
Scala> val numbersRDD = inFile.map(line => line.split(',')).map(x =>
x.map(_.toDouble))
scala> val numbersRDD = inFile.map(line => line.split(',')).map(_.toDouble)
<console>:15: error: value toDouble is not a member of Array[String]
val numbersRDD = inFile.map(line => line.split(',')).map(_.toDouble)
```

This will not work as we have an array of strings. This is where `flatMap` comes in handy! It flattens the structure and returns an array:

```
scala> val numbersRDD = inFile.flatMap(line =>
line.split(',')).map(_.toDouble)
numbersRDD: org.apache.spark.rdd.RDD[Double] = MappedRDD[10] at map at
<console>:15
scala> numbersRDD.collect()
 [..]
res10: Array[Double] = Array(42.0, 42.0, 55.0, 61.0, 53.0, 49.0, 43.0,
47.0, 49.0, 60.0, 68.0, 54.0, 34.0, 35.0, 35.0, 39.0)
scala> numbersRDD.sum()
res9: Double = 766.0
scala>
```

For Python, first invoke the `pyspark` shell:

```
USS-Defiant:~ ksankar$ cd ~/Downloads/spark-2.0.0/
USS-Defiant:spark-2.0.0 ksankar$ bin/pyspark
```

```
USS-Defiant:fdps-v3 ksankar$ ~/Downloads/spark-2.0.0/bin/pyspark
Python 2.7.12 |Continuum Analytics, Inc.| (default, Jun 29 2016, 11:09:23)
[GCC 4.2.1 (Based on Apple Inc. build 5658) (LLVM build 2336.11.00)] on darwin
Type "help", "copyright", "credits" or "license" for more information.
Anaconda is brought to you by Continuum Analytics.
Please check out: http://continuum.io/thanks and https://anaconda.org
16/08/15 15:08:44 WARN NativeCodeLoader: Unable to load native-hadoop library for your platform.
Welcome to
      ____              __
     / __/__  ___ _____/ /__
    _\ \/ _ \/ _ `/ __/  '_/
   /__ / .__/\_,_/_/ /_/\_\   version 2.0.0
      /_/

Using Python version 2.7.12 (default, Jun 29 2016 11:09:23)
SparkSession available as 'spark'.
>>>
```

Refer to the following command:

```
>>> inp_file = sc.textFile("data/Line_of_numbers.csv")
>>> numbers_rdd = inp_file.map(lambda line: line.split(','))
>>> numbers_rdd.take(10)
[..]
  [[u'42', u'42', u'55', u'61', u'53', u'49', u'43', u'47', u'49',
u'60',
     u'68', u'54', u'34', u'35', u'35', u'39']]
>>>
But we want the values as integers or double
>>> numbers_rdd = inp_file.flatMap(lambda line:
    line.split(',')).map(lambda x:float(x))
>>> numbers_rdd.take(10)
    [42.0, 42.0, 55.0, 61.0, 53.0, 49.0, 43.0, 47.0, 49.0, 60.0]
>>> numbers_sum = numbers_rdd.sum()
[..]
>>> numbers_sum
766.0
>>>
```

For Java, use Eclipse or your favorite Java IDE to run the program, fdps-v3/code/LDSV03.java:

```java
import java.util.Arrays;
import java.util.List;

import org.apache.spark.SparkConf;
import org.apache.spark.api.java.*;
import org.apache.spark.api.java.function.DoubleFunction;
import org.apache.spark.api.java.function.FlatMapFunction;
import org.apache.spark.api.java.function.Function;
import org.apache.spark.api.java.function.Function2;
import org.apache.spark.SparkFiles;;

public class LDSV03 {

  public static void main(String[] args) {
    SparkConf conf = new SparkConf().setAppName("Chapter
      05").setMaster("local");
    JavaSparkContext ctx = new JavaSparkContext(conf);
    System.out.println("Running Spark Version : " +ctx.version());
    ctx.addFile("/Users/ksankar/fdps-vii/data/Line_of_numbers.csv");
    //
    JavaRDD<String> lines =
    ctx.textFile(SparkFiles.get("Line_of_numbers.csv"));
    //
    JavaRDD<String[]> numbersStrRDD = lines.map(new
```

```
      Function<String,String[]>() {
        public String[] call(String line) {return line.split(",");}
      });
      List<String[]> val = numbersStrRDD.take(1);
      for (String[] e : val) {
        for (String s : e) {
          System.out.print(s+" ");
        }
        System.out.println();
      }
      //
      JavaRDD<String> strFlatRDD = lines.flatMap(new
      FlatMapFunction<String,String>() {
        public Iterable<String> call(String line) {return
        Arrays.asList(line.split(","));}
      });
      List<String> val1 = strFlatRDD.collect();
      for (String s : val1) {
        System.out.print(s+" ");
        }
      System.out.println();
      //
      JavaRDD<Integer> numbersRDD = strFlatRDD.map(new
      Function<String,Integer>() {
        public Integer call(String s) {return Integer.parseInt(s);}
      });
      List<Integer> val2 = numbersRDD.collect();
      for (Integer s : val2) {
        System.out.print(s+" ");
        }
      System.out.println();
      //
      Integer sum = numbersRDD.reduce(new
      Function2<Integer,Integer,Integer>() {
        public Integer call(Integer a, Integer b) {return a+b;}
      });
      System.out.println("Sum = "+sum);
    }
  }
```

The results are as expected:

```
Using Spark's default log4j profile: org/apache/spark/log4j-
defaults.properties
16/01/03 09:54:19 INFO SparkContext: Running Spark version 2.0.0
[..]
Running Spark Version : 2.0.0
16/01/03 09:54:22 INFO Utils: Copying /Volumes/sdxc-01/fdps-
```

```
vii/data/Line_of_numbers.csv to
/private/var/folders/gq/70vnnyfj6913b6lms_td7gb40000gn/T/
spark-8cd10820-4a05-49a0-b01d-fc3771d78c21/userFiles-3c65ab59-0f4b-
4de5-b719-db828be61f92/Line_of_numbers.csv
16/01/03 09:54:22 INFO SparkContext: Added file /Volumes/sdxc-01/fdps-
vii/data/Line_of_numbers.csv at file:/Volumes/sdxc-01/fdps-
vii/data/Line_of_numbers.csv with timestamp 1451843662655
16/01/03 09:54:23 INFO MemoryStore: Block broadcast_0 stored as values
in memory (estimated size 225.2 KB, free 225.2 KB)
16/01/03 09:54:23 INFO MemoryStore: Block broadcast_0_piece0 stored as
bytes in memory (estimated size 19.3 KB, free 244.6 KB)
16/01/03 09:54:23 INFO BlockManagerInfo: Added broadcast_0_piece0 in
memory on localhost:50463 (size: 19.3 KB, free: 2.4 GB)
16/01/03 09:54:23 INFO SparkContext: Created broadcast 0 from textFile
at LDSV03.java:20
16/01/03 09:54:23 INFO FileInputFormat: Total input paths to process
: 1
[..]
16/01/03 09:54:23 INFO DAGScheduler: Job 0 finished: take at
LDSV03.java:25,
took 0.193101 s
42 42 55 61 53 49 43 47 49 60 68 54 34 35 35 39
16/01/03 09:54:23 INFO SparkContext: Starting job: collect at
LDSV03.java:36
[..]
16/01/03 09:54:23 INFO DAGScheduler: Job 1 finished: collect at
LDSV03.java:36, took 0.025556 s
42 42 55 61 53 49 43 47 49 60 68 54 34 35 35 39
16/01/03 09:54:23 INFO SparkContext: Starting job: collect at
LDSV03.java:45
[..]
16/01/03 09:54:23 INFO DAGScheduler: Job 2 finished: collect at
LDSV03.java:45, took 0.035017 s
42 42 55 61 53 49 43 47 49 60 68 54 34 35 35 39
16/01/03 09:54:23 INFO SparkContext: Starting job: reduce at
LDSV03.java:51
[..]
16/01/03 09:54:23 INFO DAGScheduler: Job 3 finished: reduce at
LDSV03.java:51, took 0.025595 s
Sum = 766
16/01/03 09:54:23 INFO SparkContext: Invoking stop() from shutdown hook
```

This also illustrates one of the ways of getting the data out of Spark; you can transform it to a standard Scala array using the collect() function. The collect() function is especially useful for testing, in much the same way that the parallelize() function is. The collect() function collects the job's execution results, while parallelize() partitions the input data and makes it an RDD. The collect function only works if your data fits into the memory of a single host (where the driver runs), and even in that case, it adds to a bottleneck where everything has to come back to a single machine.

The collect() function brings all of the data to the machine that runs the code so beware of accidentally using collect() on a large RDD!

The split() and toDouble() functions don't always work out so well for more complex CSV files. The opencsv library is a versatile library for Java and Scala. For Python, the CSV library does the trick. Let's use the opencsv library to parse the CSV files in Scala.

Here's the code for Scala:

```
import au.com.bytecode.opencsv.CSVReader
import java.io.StringReader

val inFile = sc.textFile("/Users/ksankar//fdps-
v3/data/Line_of_numbers.csv")
val splitLines = inFile.map(line => {
  val reader = new CSVReader(new StringReader(line))
  reader.readNext()
})
val numericData = splitLines.map(line => line.map(_.toDouble))
val summedData = numericData.map(row => row.sum)
println(summedData.collect().mkString(","))
766.0
```

While loading text files into Spark is certainly easy, having text files on local disks is often not the most convenient format to store large chunks of data. Spark supports loading from all the different Hadoop formats (sequence files, regular text files, and so on) and from all the supported Hadoop storage sources (HDFS, S3, HBase, and so on). You can also load your CSV file into HBase using some of their bulk-loading tools (such as import TSV) and get your CSV data.

Sequence files are binary flat files that consist of key-value pairs; they are one of the common ways of storing data for use with Hadoop. Loading a sequence file into Spark is similar to loading a text file, but you also need to let it know about the types of keys and values. The types must either be subclasses of Hadoop's `Writable` class or be implicitly convertible into such a type. For Scala users, some natives are convertible through implicits in `WritableConverter`. As of Version 2.0.0, the standard `WritableConverter` types are integer, long, double, float, Boolean, byte array, and string. Let's illustrate by looking at the process of loading a sequence file of string to an integer, as shown here:

For Scala, refer to the following code:

```
val data = sc.sequenceFile[String, Int](inputFile)
```

For Java, refer to the following code:

```
JavaPairRDD<Text, IntWritable> dataRDD = sc.sequenceFile(file, Text.class,
IntWritable.class);
JavaPairRDD<String, Integer> cleanData = dataRDD.map(new
PairFunction<Tuple2<Text, IntWritable>, String, Integer>() {
  @Override
  public Tuple2<String, Integer> call(Tuple2<Text, IntWritable> pair) {
    return new Tuple2<String, Integer>(pair._1().toString(),
    pair._2().get());
  }
});
```

Note that in the preceding cases, like with text input, the file need not be a traditional file; it can reside on S3, HDFS, and so on. Also note that for Java, you can't rely on implicit conversions between types.

HBase is a Hadoop-based database designed to support random read/write access to entries. Loading data from HBase is a bit different from text files and sequence in files with respect to how we tell Spark what types to use for the data.

For Scala, refer to the following code:

```
import spark._
import org.apache.hadoop.hbase.{HBaseConfiguration, HTableDescriptor}
import org.apache.hadoop.hbase.client.HBaseAdmin
import org.apache.hadoop.hbase.mapreduce.TableInputFormat
....
val conf = HBaseConfiguration.create()
conf.set(TableInputFormat.INPUT_TABLE, input_table)
  // Initialize hBase table if necessary
val admin = new HBaseAdmin(conf)
```

```
if(!admin.isTableAvailable(input_table)) {
  val tableDesc = new HTableDescriptor(input_table)
  admin.createTable(tableDesc)
}
val hBaseRDD = sc.newAPIHadoopRDD(conf, classOf[TableInputFormat],
classOf[org.apache.hadoop.hbase.io.ImmutableBytesWritable],
classOf[org.apache.hadoop.hbase.client.Result])
```

For Java, refer to the following code:

```
import spark.api.java.JavaPairRDD;
import spark.api.java.JavaSparkContext;
import spark.api.java.function.FlatMapFunction;
import org.apache.hadoop.conf.Configuration;
import org.apache.hadoop.hbase.HBaseConfiguration;
import org.apache.hadoop.hbase.HTableDescriptor;
import org.apache.hadoop.hbase.client.HBaseAdmin;
import org.apache.hadoop.hbase.mapreduce.TableInputFormat;
import org.apache.hadoop.hbase.io.ImmutableBytesWritable;
import org.apache.hadoop.hbase.client.Result;
...
JavaSparkContext sc = new JavaSparkContext(args[0], "sequence load",
System.getenv("SPARK_HOME"), System.getenv("JARS"));
Configuration conf = HBaseConfiguration.create();
conf.set(TableInputFormat.INPUT_TABLE, args[1]);
// Initialize hBase table if necessary
HBaseAdmin admin = new HBaseAdmin(conf);
if(!admin.isTableAvailable(args[1])) {
  HTableDescriptor tableDesc = new HTableDescriptor(args[1]);
  admin.createTable(tableDesc);
}
JavaPairRDD<ImmutableBytesWritable, Result> hBaseRDD = sc.newAPIHadoopRDD(
conf, TableInputFormat.class, ImmutableBytesWritable.class, Result.class);
```

The method that you used to load the HBase data can be generalized for loading all other sorts of Hadoop data. If a `helper` method in `SparkContext` does not already exist for loading the data, simply create a configuration specifying how to load the data and pass it into a `newAPIHadoopRDD` function. Different `helper` methods exist for plain text files and sequence files. A `helper` method also exists for Hadoop files similar to the sequence file API.

Saving your data

While distributed computational jobs are a lot of fun, they are much more useful when the results are stored in a useful place. While the methods for loading an RDD are largely found in the `SparkContext` class, the methods for saving an RDD are defined on the RDD classes. In Scala, implicit conversions exist so that an RDD, which can be saved as a sequence file, could be converted to the appropriate type; in Java, explicit conversions must be used.

Here are the different ways to save an RDD.

Here's the code for Scala:

```
rddOfStrings.saveAsTextFile("out.txt")
keyValueRdd.saveAsObjectFile("sequenceOut")
```

Here's the code for Java:

```
rddOfStrings.saveAsTextFile("out.txt")
keyValueRdd.saveAsObjectFile("sequenceOut")
```

Here's the code for Python:

```
rddOfStrings.saveAsTextFile("out.txt")
```

 In addition, users can save the RDD as a compressed text file using the following function:
`saveAsTextFile(path: String, codec: Class[_ <: CompressionCodec])`

References

The references are listed here:

- http://spark-project.org/docs/latest/scala-programming-guide.html#hadoop-datasets
- http://opencsv.sourceforge.net/
- http://commons.apache.org/proper/commons-csv/
- http://hadoop.apache.org/docs/current/api/org/apache/hadoop/mapred/SequenceFileInputFormat.html
- http://hadoop.apache.org/docs/current/api/org/apache/hadoop/mapred/InputFormat.html
- http://www.michael-noll.com/tutorials/running-hadoop-on-ubuntu-linux

```
    -single-node-cluster/
```

- http://spark.apache.org/docs/latest/api/python/
- http://wiki.apache.org/hadoop/SequenceFile
- http://hbase.apache.org/book/quickstart.html
- http://hbase.apache.org/apidocs/org/apache/hadoop/hbase/mapreduce/TableInputFormat.html
- https://spark.apache.org/docs/latest/api/java/org/apache/spark/api/java/JavaPairRDD.html
- https://bzhangusc.wordpress.com/214/6/18/csv-parser/

Summary

In this chapter, first you got an insight into Spark abstractions, data modalities, and how different data types can be read into a Spark environment. Then, you saw how to load data from a variety of different sources. We also looked at the basic parsing of data from text input files. Now that we can get our data loaded into a Spark RDD, it is time to explore the different operations we can perform on our data in the next chapter.

6
Manipulating Your RDD

The last few chapters have been the necessary groundwork to get Spark working. Now that you know how to load and save data in different ways, it's time for the big payoff, that is, manipulating data. The API you'll use to manipulate your RDD is similar among languages but not identical. Unlike the previous chapters, each language is covered in its own section here; should you wish, you could only read the one pertaining to the language you are interested in using.

Manipulating your RDD in Scala and Java

RDD is the primary low-level abstraction in Spark. As we discussed in the last chapter, the main programming APIs will be Datasets/DataFrames. However, underneath it all, the data will be represented as RDDs. So, understanding and working with RDDs is important. From a structural view, RDDs are just a bunch of elements-elements that can be operated in parallel.

RDD stands for Resilient Distributed Dataset, that is, it is distributed over a set of machines and the transformations are captured so that an RDD can be recreated in case there is a machine failure or memory corruption. One important aspect of the distributed parallel data representation scheme is that RDDs are immutable, which means when you do an operation, it generates a new RDD. Manipulating your RDD in Scala is quite simple, especially if you are familiar with Scala's collection library. Many of the standard functions are available directly on Spark's RDDs with the primary catch being that they are immutable.

RDDs are created either by parallelizing a collection or by reading data from external data sources. Manipulating your RDD in Java is fairly simple but a little more awkward at times than it is in Scala. There are a couple of reasons for this. The main reason has to do with **type inference** and also with the fact that Java doesn't have anonymous functions. In the following code snippets, sometimes the Java code is more unwieldy because Java lacks type inference and anonymous functions. Java 8 has `lambda`, which would make Java a lot more elegant with Spark. Secondly, as Java doesn't have implicit conversions, we have to be more explicit with our types. While the return types are Java-friendly, Spark requires the use of Scala's Tuple2 class for key-value pairs.

> In this book, we are using the Java 7 language and will not use any of the new Java 8 features.

The hallmark of a `MapReduce` system is this: `map` and `reduce`, the two primitives. We've seen the `map` function used in the earlier chapters. The `map` function works by taking in a function, which acts on each individual element in the input RDD and produces a new output element. For example, to produce a new RDD where you want to add one to every number, use `rdd.map(x => x+1)`.

Alternatively, in Java, you can use this code:

```
rdd.map(new Function<Integer, Integer>() { public Integer      call(Integer
x) { return x+1;} });
```

> There are two types of the `map` function: `map` and `flatMap`. You can easily get confused between them. The `map` function takes an element and returns another element. The element could be a single entity, a tuple, or a list; nevertheless, there is a one-to-one correspondence with the `map` function. The `flatMap` function, on the other hand, takes one element and returns zero or one or more elements. Actually, the `map` function in Hadoop, `MapReduce`, is `flatMap`. In fact, the Spark word count example is implemented using the `flatMap()`, `map()`, and `reduceByKey()` functions.

It is important to understand that the `map` function and the other Spark functions do not modify/update the existing elements; instead, they return a new RDD with new elements-RDDs are immutable. The `reduce` function takes a function that operates in pairs to combine all of the data. The `reduce` function you provide needs to be commutative and associative (that is, `f(a,b) == f(b,a)` and `f(a,f(b,c)) == f(f(a,b),c)`). For example, to sum all the elements, you need to use `rdd.reduce(x,y => x+y)` or `rdd.reduce(new Function2<Integer, Integer>(){ public Integer call(Integer x, Integer y) { return x+y;} }`.

All the functions are not commutative. For example, while multiplication is commutative (2*3 = 3*2), subtraction is not, that is, 3-2 is not the same as 2-3; this is true for division as well, that is, 4/2 is not the same as 2/4. The same applies for associativity; sum is associative, that is, 2+3+4 = (2+3)+4 or 2+(3+4), but average is not, that is, the average of (2,3,4,5,6) is not equal to *average (2,3) + average (4,5,6)*.

The `flatMap` function is a useful utility function that lets you write a function. This function returns an iterable of the type you want and then flattens the results. A simple example of this is a case where you want to parse all of the data, but some of it might fail to do so. The `flatMap` function can be used to output an empty list if it fails or a list with success if it works. Another example when the output collection has a different size than the input collection can be observed when you parse a document and split it in words; here every line may contain one or more words.

In addition to the `reduce` function, there is a corresponding `reduceByKey` function that works on the `PairRDD` classes, which are key-value pairs to produce another RDD. Unlike when you're using map on a list in Scala, your function will run on a number of different machines, and so you can't depend on the shared state with this.

Before moving on to other wonderful functions that are available for manipulating your RDD, you need to read a bit about shared states. In the example given earlier, where we added one to every integer, we didn't really share states. However, for simpler tasks, such as distributed parsing of data-which we did when loading the CSV file-it can be quite handy to share counters for things such as keeping track of the number of rejected records.

Spark supports two types of shared immutable data, which it calls **broadcast** and **accumulator** (via accumulators). To be precise, broadcast is immutable but accumulator is mutable (albeit it can only be added to):

- You can create a new broadcast by calling `sc.broadcast(value)`. You don't have to explicitly broadcast values as Spark does its magic in the background. Broadcasting ensures that the value is sent to each node only once. Broadcasts are often used for things such as side inputs (for example, a hashmap that you need to look up as part of the `map` function). This returns an object that can be used to reference the broadcast value.

- Another method for sharing states is the use of an accumulator. To create an accumulator, use `sc.accumulator(initialvalue)`. This returns an object you can add to in a distributed context and then get back the value by calling `.value()`. The `accumulableCollection` instance can be used to create a collection that is appended in a distributed fashion; however, if you find yourself using this, ask yourself whether you could use the results of a map output instead. If the predefined accumulators don't work for your use case, you can use `accumulable` to define your own accumulation type. A broadcast value can be read by all the workers, but an accumulator can be written by all the workers but read only by the driver. Consider this example: The workers add 1 to the error count whenever they encounter a bad record. Now if you want a count of the records with errors, the driver will just need to check the error value, which will be the bad records from all the workers.

> If you are writing the Scala code that interacts with a Java Spark process (say, for testing), you may find it useful to use the `int` accumulator and similar others in the Java Spark context; otherwise, your accumulator types might not quite match up.
>
> If you find that your accumulator isn't increasing in value like you expect, remember that Spark follows the principle of lazy evaluation. This means that Spark won't actually perform the maps, reductions, or other computations on RDDs until the data has to be output by an action.

Look at the previous example, where we parsed CSV files; let's make it a bit more robust. In your previous work, you had assumed that the input was well-formatted, and if any error were to occur, your entire pipeline would fail. While this can be the correct behavior for some kind of work, we may want to accept a number of malformed records while dealing with data from third parties. On the other hand, we don't want to just throw out all the records and declare it a success; we might miss an important format change and produce meaningless results. Consider the following code (`LoadCsvWithCountersExample.scala`):

```scala
import org.apache.spark.SparkConf;
import org.apache.spark.SparkContext;
import org.apache.spark.SparkFiles;
import org.apache.spark.api.java.JavaSparkContext;
import au.com.bytecode.opencsv.CSVReader;
import java.io.StringReader;

object LoadCsvWithCountersExample {
  def main(args: Array[String]) {
    val sc = new SparkContext("local","Chapter 6")
    println(s"Running Spark Version ${sc.version}")
    val invalidLineCounter = sc.accumulator(0);
    val invalidNumericLineCounter = sc.accumulator(0);
    val inFile = sc.textFile("/Volumes/sdxc-01/fdps-vii/data/
    Line_of_numbers.csv");
    val splitLines = inFile.flatMap(line => {
      try {
        val reader = new CSVReader(new StringReader(line))
        Some(reader.readNext())
      } catch {
        case _ => {
          invalidLineCounter += 1
          None
        }
      }
    })
    val numericData = splitLines.flatMap(line => {
      try {
        Some(line.map(_.toDouble))
      } catch {
        case _ => {
          invalidNumericLineCounter += 1
          None
        }
      }
    })
    val summedData = numericData.map(row => row.sum)
    println(summedData.collect().mkString(","))
```

```
        println("Errors: "+invalidLineCounter+","
        +invalidNumericLineCounter)
    }
}
```

You can run the code. It'll provide you with the following result:

```
Using Spark's default log4j profile: org/apache/spark/log4j-
defaults.properties
16/08/15 16:18:13 INFO SparkContext: Running Spark version 2.0.0
[..]
Running Spark Version 2.0.0
[..]
16/08/15 16:18:16 INFO DAGScheduler: Job 0 finished: collect at
LoadCsvWithCountersExample.scala:37, took 0.238827 s
766.0
Errors: 0,0
```

Alternatively, in Java, you can use the following code
(`LoadCsvWithCountersJavaExample.java`):

```
import org.apache.spark.SparkConf;
import org.apache.spark.api.java.JavaRDD;
import org.apache.spark.api.java.JavaSparkContext;
import org.apache.spark.api.java.function.FlatMapFunction;
import org.apache.spark.Accumulator;

import au.com.bytecode.opencsv.CSVReader;

import java.io.StringReader;
import java.util.List;
import java.util.ArrayList;

public class LoadCsvWithCountersJavaExample {
  public static void main(String[] args) throws Exception {
    SparkConf conf = new SparkConf().setAppName("Chapter
    06").setMaster("local");
    JavaSparkContext sc = new JavaSparkContext(conf);
    final Accumulator<Integer> errors = sc.accumulator(0);
    JavaRDD<String> inFile = sc.textFile("/Volumes/sdxc-01/
    fdps-vii/data/Line_of_numbers.csv");
    JavaRDD<Integer[] > splitLines = inFile.flatMap(new
    FlatMapFunction<String, Integer[]> (){
      public Iterable<Integer[]> call(String line) {
        ArrayList<Integer[]> result = new ArrayList<Integer[]>();
        try {
          CSVReader reader = new CSVReader(new StringReader
          (line));
```

```
            String[] parsedLine = reader.readNext();
            Integer[] intLine = new Integer[parsedLine.length];
            for (int i = 0; i < parsedLine.length; i++) {
              intLine[i] = Integer.parseInt(parsedLine[i]);
            }
            result.add(intLine);
          } catch (Exception e) {
            errors.add(1);
          }
          return result;
        }
      }
    );
    List <Integer[]> res = splitLines.collect();
    System.out.print("Loaded data ");
    Integer sum = 0;
    for (Integer[] e : res) {
      for (Integer val:e) {
        System.out.print(val+" ");
        sum += val;
      }
      System.out.println();
    }
    System.out.println("Sum = "+sum);
    System.out.println("Error count "+errors.value());
  }
}
```

You can run the code with parameters, and it will provide you with the following result:

```
16/01/11 20:32:43 INFO SparkContext: Running Spark version 2.0.0
[..]
16/01/11 20:32:46 INFO DAGScheduler: Job 0 finished: collect at
LoadCsvWithCountersJavaExample.java:39, took 0.240100 s
Loaded data 42 42 55 61 53 49 43 47 49 60 68 54 34 35 35 39
Sum = 766
Error count 0
```

> The preceding code example illustrates the usefulness of flatMap. In general, flatMap can be used when the required output collection is of a different size than that of the input collection. You can do this because in general, there are nested collections or types involved, which need to be flattened. Because the options in Scala can be used as sequences through an implicit conversion, you can avoid having to explicitly filter out the None result and just use flatMap.

Summary statistics can be quite useful when examining large Datasets. In the preceding example, you loaded the data as `Doubles` to use Spark's existing summary statistics capabilities on the RDD. In Java, this requires explicitly using the `JavaDoubleRDD` type. For Java, it is important to use `DoubleFunction<Integer[]>` rather than `Function<Integer[], Double>` in the example, as the second option won't result in the `JavaDoubleRDD` type. No such consideration is required for Scala as implicit conversions deal with the details. Compute the mean and the variance or compute them together with the statistics. You can extend this by adding it to the end of the preceding function to print out the summary statistics as `println(summedData.stats())`.

To do this with Java, we would do it as follows:

```
JavaDoubleRDD summedData = splitLines.map(new
DoubleFunction<Integer[]>() {
  public Double call(Integer[] in) {
    Double ret = 0.;
    for (int i = 0; i < in.length; i++) {
      ret += in[i];
    }
    return ret;
  }
}
);
System.out.println(summedData.stats());
```

While working with key-value pair data, it can be quite useful to group data with the same key together (for example, if the key represents a user or a sample). The `groupByKey` function provides an easy way to group data together by a key. This function is a special case of `combineByKey`. There are several functions in the `PairRDD` class that are all implemented very closely on top of `combineByKey`. If you find yourself using `groupByKey` or one of the other functions derived from `combineByKey` and immediately transforming the result, you should check to see whether there is a function better suited to the task. A common thing to do while starting out is to perform `groupByKey` and then sum the results with `groupByKey().map({case (x,y) => (x,y.sum)})`. Alternatively, in Java, you can use the following code:

```
pairData.groupByKey().mapValues(new Function<List<Integer>,
  Integer >(){
  public Integer call(List<Integer> x) {
    Integer sum = 0;
    for (Integer i : x) {
      sum += i;
    }
    return sum;
  }
```

```
    }
); or in python .map(lambda (x,y): (x,sum(y))).collect()
```

By using `reduceByKey`, it could be simplified to `reduceByKey((x,y) => x+y)` or in Java as follows:

```
pairData.groupByKey().mapValues(
    new Function<Iterable<Integer>, Integer >(){
        public Integer call(Iterable<Integer> x) {
            Integer sum = 0; for (Integer i : x) {
                sum += i;
            }
            return sum;
        }
    }
);
```

In fact, this is much more efficient. No big shuffle is needed, as is the case for the `groupBy` function. The only thing required is an aggregation of the values, which is important.

The `foldByKey(zeroValue)(function)` function is similar to a traditional fold operation, which works per key. In a traditional fold, a list that is provided would be called with the initial value and the first element of the list, then the resulting value and the next element of the list would be the input to the next call of the fold. Doing this requires sequentially processing the entire list, so `foldByKey` behaves slightly differently. There is a handy table of the functions of the `PairRDD` classes at the end of this section.

Sometimes, you will only want to update the values of a key-value pair data structure, such as a `PairRDD` class. You've learned about `foldByKey` and how it doesn't quite work as a traditional fold. If you're a Scala developer and you require the *traditional* fold behavior, you can perform the `groupByKey` function and then map a fold by the value over the resulting RDD. This is an example of a case where you only want to change the value and we don't care about the key of the RDD; therefore, examine the following code:

```
rdd.groupByKey().mapValues(x => {x.fold(0)((a,b) => a+b)})
```

The preceding code is interesting as it combines the Spark function, `groupByKey`, with a Scala function, `fold()`. The `groupBy()` function shuffles the data so that the values are *together*. The fold mentioned is a *local* Scala fold, run on each node. Bear in mind that performance-wise, reduce is $\log(n)$, while fold is $O(n)$.

Often your data won't come in cleanly from a single source and you will want to join the data together for processing, which can be done with coGroup. This can be done when you are joining web access logs with transaction data or just joining two different computations on the same data. Provided that the RDDs have the same key, we can join two RDDs together with rdd.coGroup(otherRdd). There are a number of different join functions for different purposes illustrated in the table at the end of this section.

The next task you will learn is distributing files among the cluster. We illustrate this by adding GeoIP support and mixing it together with the gradient descent example from the earlier chapter. Sometimes, the libraries you will use would need files distributed along with them. While it is possible to add them to the JAR file and access them as class objects, Spark provides a simple way to distribute the required files by calling addFile(), as shown here:

```scala
import scala.math

import org.apache.spark.SparkContext
import org.apache.spark.SparkContext._
import org.apache.spark.SparkFiles;
import org.apache.spark.util.Vector

import au.com.bytecode.opencsv.CSVReader

import java.util.Random
import java.io.StringReader
import java.io.File

import com.snowplowanalytics.maxmind.geoip.IpGeo

case class DataPoint(x: Vector, y: Double)

object GeoIpExample {
  def main(args: Array[String]) {
    if (args.length != 2) {
      System.err.println("Usage: GeoIpExample <master> <inputfile>")
      System.exit(1)
    }
    val master = args(0)
    val inputFile = args(1)
    val iterations = 100
    val maxMindPath = "GeoLiteCity.dat"
    val sc = new SparkContext(master, "GeoIpExample",
    System.getenv("SPARK_HOME"), Seq(System.getenv("JARS")))
    val invalidLineCounter = sc.accumulator(0)
    val inFile = sc.textFile(inputFile)
    val parsedInput = inFile.flatMap(line => {
```

```
    try {
      val row = (new CSVReader(new StringReader (line))).readNext()
      Some((row(0),row.drop(1).map(_.toDouble)))
    } catch {
      case _ => {
        invalidLineCounter += 1
        None
      }
    }
  })
  val geoFile = sc.addFile(maxMindPath)
  // getLocation gives back an option so we use flatMap to only output
    if its a some type
  val ipCountries = parsedInput.flatMapWith(_ => IpGeo(dbFile =
  SparkFiles.get(maxMindPath) ))((pair, ipGeo) => {
    ipGeo.getLocation(pair._1).map(c => (pair._1, c.countryCode)).toSeq
  })
  ipCountries.cache()
  val countries = ipCountries.values.distinct().collect()
  val countriesBc = sc.broadcast(countries)
  val countriesSignal = ipCountries.mapValues(country =>
  countriesBc.value.map(s => if (country == s) 1. else 0.))
  val dataPoints = parsedInput.join(countriesSignal).map(input => {
    input._2 match {
      case (countryData, originalData) => DataPoint(new
      Vector(countryData++originalData.slice(1,originalData.size-2)) ,
      originalData(originalData.size-1))
    }
  })
  countriesSignal.cache()
  dataPoints.cache()
  val rand = new Random(53)
  var w = Vector(dataPoints.first.x.length, _ => rand.nextDouble)
  for (i <- 1 to iterations) {
    val gradient = dataPoints.map(p =>
    (1 / (1 + math.exp(-p.y*(w dot p.x))) - 1) * p.y * p.x).reduce(_ + _)
    w -= gradient
  }
  println("Final w: "+w)
  }
}
```

In this example, you will see multiple Spark computations. The first computation is to determine all the countries where our data is so that we can map the country to a binary feature. The code then uses a public list of proxies and the reported latency to try and estimate the latency I measured. This also illustrates the use of `mapWith` (which is now `MapPartitions`). If you have a mapping job that needs to create a per-partition resource, `mapWith` (which is now `MapPartitions`) can be used.

This can be useful for connections to the backend or the creation of something similar to a PRNG. Some elements also can't be serialized over the wire (such as the `IpCountry` instance in the example), and so you will have to create them per shard. You can also see that we cache a number of our RDDs to keep them from having to be recomputed.

There are several options when working with multiple RDDs.

Scala RDD functions

These are the `PairRDD` functions based on `combineByKey`. All operate on the RDDs of the type `[K,V]`:

Function	Param options	Explanation	Return type
foldByKey	(zeroValue)(func(V,V)=>V) (zeroValue, partitioner)(func(V,V=>V) (zeroValue, partitions)(func(V,V=>V)	This function merges the values using the provided function. Unlike a traditional fold over a list, the `zeroValue` function can be added an arbitrary number of times.	RDD[K,V]
reduceByKey	(func(V,V)=>V) (func(V,V)=>V,numTasks)	This function is the parallel version of reduce that merges the values for each key using the provided function and returns an RDD.	RDD[K,V]
groupByKey	() (numPartitions)	This function groups elements together by the key.	RDD[K,Seq[V]]

Functions for joining the PairRDD classes

Often, while working with two or more key-value RDDs, it is useful to join them together. There are a few different methods to do this, depending on what your desired behavior is:

Function	Param options	Explanation	Return type
coGroup	(otherRdd[K,W]...)	Join two (or more) RDDs by the shared key. Note that if an element is found missing in one RDD but present in the other, the Seq value will simply be empty.	RDD[(K,(Seq[V],Seq[W]...))]
join	(otherRdd[K,W]) (otherRdd[K,W], partitioner) (otherRdd[K,W], numPartitions)	Join an RDD with another RDD. The result is only present for elements where the key is present in both RDDs.	RDD[(K,(V,W))]
subtractKey	(otherRdd[K,W]) (otherRdd[K,W], partitioner) (otherRdd[K,W], numPartitions)	This returns an RDD with only keys not present in the other RDD.	RDD[(K,V)]

Other PairRDD functions

Some functions only make sense when working on key-value pairs, as follows:

Function	Param options	Explanation	Return type
lookup	(key: K)	This function looks up a specific element in the RDD. It uses the RDD's partitioner to figure out which shard(s) to look at.	Seq[V]

Function	Param options	Explanation	Return type
`mapValues`	(f: V => U)	This function is a specialized version of the map for the `PairRDD` classes when you only want to change the value of the key-value pair. It takes the provided `map` function and applies it to the value. If you need to make your change based on both the key and the value, you must use one of the normal RDD `map` functions.	RDD[(K,U)]
`collectAsMap`	() (No arguments)	This function takes an RDD and returns a concrete map. Your RDD must be able to fit in the memory.	Map[K, V]
`countByKey`	()	This function counts the number of elements for each key.	Map[K, Long]
`partitionBy`	(partitioner: Partitioner, mapSideCombine: Boolean)	This function returns a new RDD with the same data but partitioned by the new partitioner. The Boolean flag, `mapSideCombine`, controls whether Spark should group values with the same key together before repartitioning. It defaults to `false` and sets to `true` if you have a large percentage of duplicate keys.	RDD[(K,V)]
`flatMapValues`	(f: V => TraversableOnce[U])	This function is similar to `MapValues`. It's a specialized version of `flatMap` for the `PairRDD` classes when you only want to change the value of the key-value pair. It takes the provided `map` function and applies it to the value. The resulting sequence is then *flattened*, that is, instead of getting `Seq[Seq[V]]`, you get `Seq[V]`. If you need to make your change based on both key and value, you must use one of the normal RDD map functions.	RDD[(K,U)]

For information on how to save the `PairRDD` classes, refer to the previous chapter.

Double RDD functions

Spark defines a number of convenience functions that work when your RDD is comprised of doubles, as follows:

Function	Arguments	Return value
Mean	()	Average
sampleStdev	()	Standard deviation for a sample rather than a population (as it divides by *N-1* rather than *N*)
Stats	()	Mean, variance, and count as `StatCounter`
Stdev	()	Standard deviation (for population)
Sum	()	The sum of elements
variance	()	Variance

General RDD functions

The remaining RDD functions are defined on all RDDs:

Function	Arguments	Returns
aggregate	(zero: U)(seqOp: (U,T) => T, combOp (U, U) => U)	This function aggregates all the elements of each partition of an RDD and then combines them using `combOp`. The zero value should be neutral (that is, for + and 1 for *).
cache	()	This function caches an RDD reused without being recomputed. It's the same as `persist(StorageLevel.MEMORY_ONLY)`.
collect	()	This function returns an array of all the elements in the RDD.
count	()	This function returns the number of elements in an RDD.
countByValue	()	This function returns a map of the value to the number of times that the value occurs.

Function	Arguments	Returns
distinct	() (partitions: Int)	This function returns an RDD that contains only distinct elements.
filter	(f: T => Boolean)	This function returns an RDD that contains only elements matching f.
filterWith	(constructA: Int => A)(f: (T, A) => Boolean)	This function is similar to filter, but f takes an additional parameter generated by constructA, which is called per-partition. The original motivation for this came when we provided the PRNG generation for each shard.
first	()	This function returns the first element of the RDD.
flatMap	(f: T => TraversableOnce[U])	This function returns an RDD of type U.
fold	(zeroValue: T)(op: (T,T) => T)	This function merges values using the provided operation, the first operation on each partition, and then merges the merged result.
foreach	(f: T => Unit)	This function applies the function f to each element.
groupBy	(f: T => K) (f: T => K, p: Partitioner) (f: T => K, numPartitions:Int)	This function takes in an RDD and produces a PairRDD class of the type (K, Seq[T]), using the result of f for the key and for each element.
keyBy	(f: T => K) (f: T => K, p: Partitioner) (f: T => K, numPartitions:Int)	This function is the same as groupBy but does not group results together with duplicate keys. It returns an RDD of (K, T).
map	(f: T => U)	This function returns an RDD of the result of applying f to every element in the input RDD.
mapPartitions	(f: Iterator[T] => Iterator[U])	This function is similar to map except that the provided function takes and returns an iterator and is applied to each partition.

Function	Arguments	Returns
mapPartitionsWithIndex	(f: (Int, Iterator[T]) => Iterator[U], preservePartitions)	This function is the same as mapPartitions but also provides the index of the original partition.
mapWith	(constructA: Int => A)(f: (T, A) => U)	This function is similar to map, but f takes an additional parameter generated by constructA, which is called per-partition. The original motivation for this came when we provided the PRNG generation for each shard.
persist	() (newLevel: StorageLevel)	This function sets the RDD storage level, which can cause the RDD to be stored after it is computed. The different StorageLevel values can be seen in StorageLevel.scala (NONE, DISK_ONLY, MEMORY_ONLY, and MEMORY_AND_DISK are the common ones).
pipe	(command: Seq[String]) (command: Seq[String], env: Map[String, String])	This function takes an RDD and calls the specified command with the optional environment. Then, it pipes each element through the command. This function results in an RDD of type string.
sample	(withReplacement: Boolean, fraction: Double, seed: Int)	This function returns an RDD of that fraction.
takeSample	(withReplacement: Boolean, num: Int, seed: Int)	This function returns an array of the requested number of elements. It works by oversampling the RDD and then grabbing a subset.
toDebugString	()	This is a handy function that outputs the recursive deps of the RDD.
union	(other: RDD[T])	This function is an RDD containing the elements of both the RDDs. Here, duplicates are not removed.
unpersist	()	This function removes all the blocks of the RDD from the memory/disk if they've persisted.

Function	Arguments	Returns
zip	(other: RDD[U])	This function is important to note as it requires that the RDDs have the same number of partitions and the same size of each partition. It returns an RDD of key-value pairs, RDD[T,U].

Java RDD functions

Many of the Java RDD functions are quite similar to the Scala RDD functions, but the type signatures are somewhat different.

Spark Java function classes

For the Java RDD API, we need to extend one of the provided function classes while implementing our function:

Name	Params	Purpose
Function<T,R>	**R call(T t)**	**This function takes something of the type T and returns something of the type R. It is commonly used for maps.**
DoubleFunction<T>	Double call(T t)	This function is the same as Function<T, Double>, but the result of the map-like call returns JavaDoubleRDD (for summary statistics).
PairFunction<T, K, V>	Tuple2<K, V> call(T t)	This function results in a JavaPairRDD class. If you're working on JavaPairRDD<A,B>, have T of the type Tuple2<A,B>.
FlatMapFunction<T, R>	Iterable<R> call(T t)	This function is used for producing an RDD through flatMap.
PairFlatMapFunction<T, K, V>	Iterable<Tuple2<K, V>> call(T t)	This function results in a JavaPairRDD class. If you're working on JavaPairRDD<A,B>, have T of the type Tuple2<A,B>.

Name	Params	Purpose
DoubleFlatMapFunction<T>	Iterable<Double> call(T t)	This function is the same as FlatMapFunction<T, Double>, but the result of the map-like call returns JavaDoubleRDD (for summary statistics).
Function2<T1, T2, R>	R call(T1 t1, T2 t2)	This function is for taking two input actions and returning an output. It is used by fold and similar.

Common Java RDD functions

These RDD functions are available regardless of the type of RDD:

Name	Params	Purpose
cache	()	**This function makes an RDD persist in memory.**
coalesce	numPartitions: Int	This function returns a new RDD with the numPartitions partitions.
collect	()	This function returns the List representation of the entire RDD.
count	()	This function returns the number of elements.
countByValue	()	This function returns a map of each unique value to the number of times that the value shows up.
distinct	() (Int numPartitions)	This function is an RDD consisting of all the distinct elements of the RDD optionally in the provided number of partitions.
filter	(Function<T, Boolean> f)	This function is an RDD, consisting only of the elements for which the provided function returns true.
first	()	This function is the first element of the RDD.

Name	Params	Purpose
flatMap	(FlatMapFunction<T, U> f) (DoubleFlatMapFunction<T> f) (PairFlatMapFunction<T, K, V> f)	This function is an RDD of the specified types (U, Double, and Pair<K, V> respectively).
fold	(T zeroValue, Function2<T, T, T> f)	This function returns the result T. Each partition is folded individually with the zero value and then the results are folded.
foreach	(VoidFunction<T> f)	This function applies the function to each element in the RDD.
groupBy	(Function<T, K> f) (Function<T, K> f, Int numPartitions)	This function returns a JavaPairRDD class of grouped elements.
map	(DoubleFunction<T> f) (PairFunction<T, K2, V2> f) (Function<T, U> f)	This function returns an RDD of an appropriate type for the input function (see the previous table) by calling the provided function on each element in the input RDD.
mapPartitions	(DoubleFunction<Iterator<T>> f) (PairFunction<Iterator<T>, K2, V2> f) (Function<Iterator<T>, U> f)	This function is similar to map, but the provided function is called per-partition. This can be useful if you have done some setup work that is necessary for each partition.
reduce	(Function2<T, T, T> f)	This function uses the provided function to reduce down all the elements.
sample	(Boolean withReplacement, Double fraction, Int seed)	This function returns a smaller RDD, consisting of only the requested fraction of the data.

Methods for combining JavaRDDs

There are a number of different functions that we can use to combine RDDs:

Name	Params	Purpose
subtract	(JavaRDD<T> other) (JavaRDD<T> other, Partitioner p) (JavaRDD<T> other, Int numPartitions)	This function returns an RDD with only the elements initially present in the first RDD and not present in the other RDD.
union	(JavaRDD<T> other)	This function is the union of the two RDDs.
zip	(JavaRDD<U> other)	This function returns an RDD of key-value pairs RDD[T,U]. It is important to note that it requires that the RDDs should have the same number of partitions and the size of each partition.

Functions on JavaPairRDDs

Some functions are only defined on the key-value `PairRDD` classes:

Name	Params	Purpose
cogroup	(JavaPairRDD<K, W> other) (JavaPairRDD<K, W> other, Int numPartitions) (JavaPairRDD<K, W> other1, JavaPairRDD<K, W> other2) (JavaPairRDD<K, W> other1, JavaPairRDD<K, W> other2, Int numPartitions)	**This function joins two (or more) RDDs by the shared key. Note that if an element is missing in one RDD but present in the other one, the list will simply be empty.**

Name	Params	Purpose
combineByKey	(Function<V, C> createCombiner Function2<C, V, C> mergeValue, Function2<C,C,C> mergeCombiners)	This function is a generic function to combine elements by key. The createCombiner function turns something of the type V into something of the type C. The mergeValue function adds V to C, and mergeCombiners is used to combine two C values into a single C value.
collectAsMap	()	This function returns a map of the key-value pairs.
countByKey	()	This function returns a map of the key to the number of elements with that key.
flatMapValues	(Function[T] f, Iterable[V] v)	This function returns an RDD of the type V.
join	(JavaPairRDD<K, W> other) (JavaPairRDD<K, W> other, Int integers)	This function joins an RDD with another RDD. The result is only present for elements where the key is present in both the RDDs.
keys	()	This function returns an RDD of only the keys.
lookup	(Key k)	This function looks up a specific element in the RDD. It uses the RDD's partitioner to figure out which shard(s) to look at.
reduceByKey	(Function2[V,V,V] f)	The reduceByKey function is the parallel version of reduce that merges the values for each key using the provided function and returns an RDD.
sortByKey	(Comparator[K] comp, Boolean ascending) (Comparator[K] comp) (Boolean ascending)	This function sorts the RDD by key; therefore, each partition contains a fixed range.
values	()	This function returns an RDD of only the values.

Manipulating your RDD in Python

Spark has a more limited Python API than Java and Scala, but it supports most of the core functionality.

The hallmark of a `MapReduce` system lies in two commands: `map` and `reduce`. You've seen the `map` function used in the earlier chapters. The `map` function works by taking in a function that works on each individual element in the input RDD and produces a new output element. For example, to produce a new RDD where you have added one to every number, you would use `rdd.map(lambda x: x+1)`. It's important to understand that the `map` function and the other Spark functions do not transform the existing elements; instead, they return a new RDD with new elements. The `reduce` function takes a function that operates in pairs to combine all of the data. This is returned to the calling program. If you were to sum all the elements, you would use `rdd.reduce(lambda x, y: x+y)`. The `flatMap` function is a useful utility function that allows you to write a function that returns an iterable of the type you want and then flattens the results. A simple example of this is a case where you want to parse all of the data, but some of it fails to parse. The `flatMap` function outputs an empty list if it fails or a list with its success if it works. In addition to `reduce`, there is a corresponding `reduceByKey` function that works on RDDs, which are key-value pairs, and produces another RDD.

Many of the mapping operations are also defined with a partition's variant. In this case, the function you need to provide takes and returns an iterator, which represents all of the data on that partition, thus performing work on a per-partition level. The `mapPartitions(func)` function can be quite useful if the operation you need to perform has to do expensive work on each shard/partition. An example of this is establishing a connection to a backend server. Another reason for using `mapPartitions(func)` is to do setup work for your `map` function that can't be serialized across the network. A good example of this is parsing some expensive side input, as shown here:

```
def f(iterator):
  // Expensive work goes here
  for i in iterator:
  yield per_element_function(i)
```

Often, your data can be expressed with key-value mappings. As such, many of the functions defined on Python's RDD class only work if your data is in a key-value mapping. The `mapValues` function is used when you only want to update the key-value pair you are working with.

In addition to performing simple operations on the data, Spark also provides support for broadcast values and accumulators. Broadcast values can be used to broadcast a read-only value to all the partitions, which can save the need to reserialize a given value multiple times. Accumulators allow all the shards to be added to the accumulator and the result can then be read on the master. You can create an accumulator by using `counter = sc.accumulator(initialValue)`. If you want the behavior to be customized, you can also provide `AccumulatorParam` to the accumulator. The return value can then be incremented as `counter += x` on any of the workers. The resulting value can then be read with `counter.value()`. The broadcast value is created with `bc = sc.broadcast(value)` and then accessed by `bc.value()` on any worker. The accumulator can only be read on the master, and the broadcast value can be read on all the shards.

Let's look at a quick Python example that shows multiple RDD operations. We have two text files, namely `2009-2014-BO.txt` and `1861-1864-AL.txt`. These are the *State Of the Union* speeches by Presidents Barack Obama and Abraham Lincoln. We want to compare the mood of the nation by comparing the salient differences in the words used.

The first step is reading the files and creating the word frequency vector, that is, each word and the number of times it is used in the speech. I am sure you would recognize this as a canonical word count `MapReduce` example, and in traditional Hadoop `MapReduce` system, it takes around 100 lines of code. In Spark, as we shall see, it takes only five lines of code:

```
from pyspark.context import SparkContext
print "Running Spark Version %s" % (sc.version)
from pyspark.conf import SparkConf
conf = SparkConf()
print conf.toDebugString()
```

The `MapReduce` code is shown here:

```
from operator import add
lines = sc.textFile("sotu/2009-2014-BO.txt")
word_count_bo = lines.flatMap(lambda x: x.split(' ')).\
  map(lambda x: (x.lower().rstrip().    lstrip().rstrip(',').rstrip('.'),
1)).\
  reduceByKey(add)
word_count_bo.count()
#6658 without lower, 6299 with lower, rstrip,lstrip 4835
lines = sc.textFile("sotu/1861-1864-AL.txt")
word_count_al = lines.flatMap(lambda x: x.split(' ')).map(lambda    x:
(x.lower().rstrip().lstrip().rstrip(',').rstrip('.'),
1)).reduceByKey(add)
word_count_al.count()
```

Sorting an RDD by any column is very easy, as shown next:

```
word_count_bo_1 = word_count_bo.sortBy(lambda x:    x[1],ascending=False)
```

We can collect the word vector. However, don't print it! It is a long list:

```
for x in word_count_bo_1.take(10):
  print x
```

Now, let's take out common words, as shown here:

```
common_words = ["us","has","all", "they", "from",
"who","what","on","by","more","as","not","their","can","new","it","but","be
","are","--
","i","have","this","will","for","with","is","that","in","our","we","a","of
","to","and","the","that's","or","make","do","you","at","it's","than","if",
"know","last","about","no","just","now","an","because","<p>we","why","we'll
","how","two","also","every","come","we've","year","over","get","take","one
","them","we're","need","want","when","like","most","-
","been","first","where","so","these","they're","good","would","there","sho
uld","-->","<!--
","up","i'm","his","their","which","may","were","such","some","those","was"
,"here","she","he","its","her","his","don't","i've","what's","didn't","shou
ldn't","(applause.)","let's","doesn't"]
```

Filtering out common words is also a single `filter` operation. Of course, as RDDs are immutable, we will create a new filtered RDD:

```
word_count_bo_clean = word_count_bo_1.filter(lambda x: x[0] not in
common_words)
word_count_al_clean = word_count_al.filter(lambda x: x[0] not in
common_words)
```

Finding the words that were spoken by Obama and not by Lincoln is a single RDD operation. You need to use `subractByKey` and then use `sortBy` on the count to see the different but most frequent words, as shown here:

```
for x in word_count_bo_clean.subtractByKey
(word_count_al_clean).sortBy(lambda x:    x[1],ascending=False).take(15):
#collect():
  print x
```

The preceding program should give you a good grip on the RDD functions and how to use them in Python.

Standard RDD functions

These functions are available on all RDDs in Python:

Name	Params	Purpose
flatMap	**f, preserves Partitioning=False**	**This function takes a function that returns an iterator of the type** U **for each input of the type** T **and returns a flattened RDD of the type** U.
mapPartitions	f, preserves Partitioning=False	This function takes a function that takes in an iterator of the type T and returns an iterator of the type U, which then results in an RDD of the type U. It's useful for map operations with expensive per-machine setup work.
filter	f	This function takes a function and returns an RDD with only the elements for which the function returns true.
distinct	()	This function returns an RDD with distinct elements (for example, 1, 1, 2 gives the output as 1, 2).
union	other	This function returns a union of two RDDs.
intersection	other	This function returns the intersection as a set (that is, no duplicates).
cartesian	other	This function returns the Cartesian product of the RDD with the other RDD.
groupBy	f, numPartitions=None	This function returns an RDD with the elements grouped together for the value that f outputs.
pipe	command, env={}	This function pipes each element of the RDD to the provided command and returns an RDD of the result.
foreach	f	This function applies the function f to each element in the RDD.

Name	Params	Purpose
reduce	f	This function reduces the elements using the provided function.
fold	zeroValue, op	With this function, each partition is folded individually with the zero value; then, the results are folded.
countByValue	()	This function returns a dictionary mapping of each distinct value to the number of times it is found in the RDD.
take	num	This function returns a list of num elements. This can be slow for the large values of num; therefore, use collect if you want to get back to the entire RDD.
Stats(),min(),max(), mean(),variance()	()	These are statistical functions.
partitionBy	numPartitions, partitionFunc=hash	This function makes a new RDD partitioned using the provided partitioning function. The partitionFunc function simply needs to map the input key to an integer number, and the partitionBy function calculates the partition by that number using numPartitions.

The PairRDD functions

These functions are only available on key-value pair functions:

Name	Params	Purpose
collectAsMap	()	**This function returns a dictionary consisting of all the key-value pairs of the RDD.**
reduceByKey	func, numPartitions=None	This function is the parallel version of reduce, which merges the values for each key using the provided function and returns an RDD.

Name	Params	Purpose
`countByKey`	`()`	This function returns a dictionary of the number of elements for each key.
`join`	other, numPartitions=None	This function joins an RDD with another RDD. The result is only present for elements where the key is present in both RDDs. The value that gets stored for each key is a tuple of the values from each RDD.
`rightOuterJoin`	other, numPartitions=None	This function joins an RDD with another RDD. It outputs a given key-value pair only if the key it's being joined to is present in the RDD. If the key is not present in the source RDD, the first value in the tuple will be `None`.
`leftOuterJoin`	other, numPartitions=None	This function joins an RDD with another RDD. It outputs a given key-value pair only if the key is present in the source RDD. If the key is not present in the other RDD, the second value in the tuple will be `None`.
`combineByKey`	createCombiner, mergeValues, mergeCombiners	This function combines elements using a key. It takes an RDD of the type `[K, V]` and returns an RDD of the type `[K, C]`. The `createCombiner` function turns something of the type `V` into something of the type `C`. The `mergeValue` function adds `V` to `C`, and `mergeCombiners` is used to combine the two `C` values into a single `C` value.
`zip`	other	This function returns key-value pairs, pairing one element from each RDD. The first key-value pair would be the first element from this RDD, and the value would be the first element from the *other* RDD; the second pair would be the respective second elements from each of the RDDs; and so on.
`groupByKey`	numPartitions=None	This function groups the values in the RDD using the key they have.

Name	Params	Purpose
cogroup	other, numPartitions=None	This function joins two (or more) RDDs using the shared key. Note that if an element is missing in one RDD but present in the other one, the list will simply be empty.

References

Some references are as follows:

- http://www.scala-lang.org/api/current/index.html#scala.collection.immutable.List
- http://spark.apache.org/docs/latest/api/scala/index.html#org.apache.spark.api.java.JavaRDD
- http://spark.apache.org/docs/latest/api/scala/index.html#org.apache.spark.api.java.JavaPairRDD
- http://spark.apache.org/docs/latest/api/scala/index.html#org.apache.spark.api.java.JavaDoubleRDD
- https://spark.apache.org/docs/latest/api/scala/index.html#org.apache.spark.SparkContext
- http://abshinn.github.io/python/apache-spark/214/1/11/using-combinebykey-in-apache-spark/
- Good examples of RDD transformations: (https://github.com/JerryLead/SparkLearning/tree/master/src)

Summary

This chapter looked at how to perform computations on data in a distributed fashion once it's loaded into an RDD. With our knowledge of how to load and save RDDs, we can now write distributed programs using Spark.

7
Spark 2.0 Concepts

Now that you have seen the fundamental underpinnings of Spark, let's take a broader look at the architecture, context, and ecosystem in which Spark operates. This is a catch-all chapter that captures a divergent set of essential topics that will help you get a broader understanding of Spark as a whole. Once you go through this, you will understand who is using Spark and how and where it is being used. This chapter will cover the following topics:

- The Datasets accompanying this book and the IDEs for data wrangling
- A quick description of a data scientist's expectation from Spark
- The Data Lake architecture and the position of Spark
- The evolution and progression of Spark Architecture to 2.0
- The Parquet data storage mechanism

So with good fundamental knowledge of the Spark framework, let's start focusing on these three topics: data scientist DevOps, data wrangling, and of course, the mechanisms in Apache Spark, including DataFrames, machine learning, and working with big data. In this chapter, we will look at the broader picture. In Chapter 8, *Spark SQL*, we will dive into DataFrames, APIs, and work on programs using DataFrame APIs. In Chapter 9, *Foundations of Datasets/DataFrames – The Proverbial Workhorse for Data Scientists*, we will visit Spark SQL. In Chapter 10, *Spark with Big Data*, we will see how Spark fits with the big data ecosystem. In Chapter 11, *Machine Learning with Spark ML Pipelines*, we'll get a chance to work with machine learning libraries. Spark R is another interesting area for data scientists to explore, and we have Chapter 12, *GraphX*, for this.

Code and Datasets for the rest of the book

The first order of business is to look at the code and Datasets that we will be using for the rest of the chapters.

Code

It is time for you to experiment with Spark APIs and wrangle with data. We have been using the Scala and Python shell in this book and you can continue to do so. You should also explore using an iPython notebook, which is an excellent way for data engineers and data scientists to experiment with data. The iPython notebooks and its Datasets are available at `https://github.com/xsankar/fdps-v3`. You'll have to download some of the data yourselves due to the restrictions in distributing them. We have provided the appropriate URL as and when the need to download data arises.

IDE

For this book, we will use `scala-shell` and `pyspark`. The Zeppelin IDE is another fine choice. Python is a better language for data scientists and has a tradition of strong scientific libraries. For those of you who prefer Scala, it is not that hard to map Python programs to Scala. If you are using Scala, my suggestion is the Zeppellin IDE.

iPython startup and test

Before attempting the notebooks, install Jupyter and iPython. We will use Python 2.7. Make sure you can create a notebook.

Assuming that you have downloaded the GitHub to the `fdps-v3/` directory, you can start iPython like this:

```
cd ~/fdps-v3/
PYSPARK_DRIVER_PYTHON=ipython PYSPARK_DRIVER_PYTHON_OPTS="notebook"
~/Downloads/spark-2.0.0/bin/pyspark
```

A couple of things to note

This attempt needs the location of `pyspark`. In the example, I have Spark in my `~/Downloads` directory.

You will see the iPython IDE in the `http://localhost:8888/` browser.

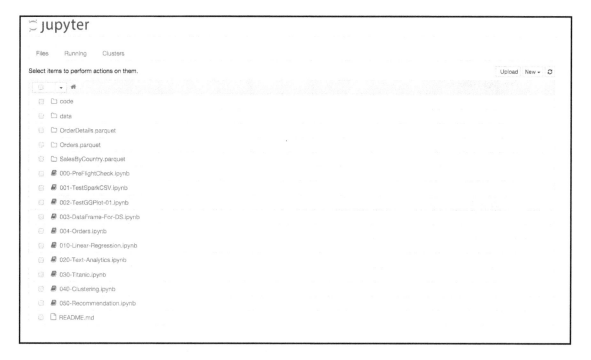

Let's make sure our installation is working fine:

1. Click on `000-PreFlightCheck.ipynb`.
2. The notebook will start in a new tab. Run the first code block and it should print the version numbers, as shown in the following screenshot:

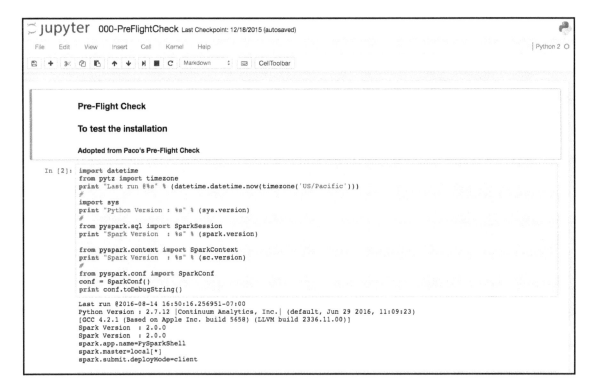

Datasets

We will use lots of Datasets in this book. Some are small, while some are relatively bigger. The following sections will provide further details on each Dataset.

Car-mileage

This is a very old Dataset, going back to 70s. It contains engine characteristics, such as mileage, hp, torque, and rear axle ratio for 32 cars. It is a tiny Dataset, which is useful for the purpose of understanding statistical operations, aggregations, na, udf, and column-type conversion operations. It is also very easy to experiment with. The `csv` file has the header that describes the data elements.

The name of the file is `data/car-data/car-mileage.csv`.

Northwind industries sales data

While writing other chapters, I was wondering what could be considered a good Dataset if I wish to bring out the various aspects of SQL. And, I hit upon an idea! Long time ago, the Northwind database was the canonical database to learn Microsoft Access, and later, the SQL server. And that would be a good Dataset for learning Spark SQL as well!

Let's use some of the tables and data to dig deeper into Spark SQL. The SQL scripts to create the Northwind database are available at `https://northwinddatabase.codeplex.com/rel eases/view/71634`. In our case, we will load data from a set of CSV files and create an appropriate Dataset in Spark. Then, we will fire off the SQL queries of increasing complexity. A good reference for this is the Spark SQL programming guide available at `htt ps://spark.apache.org/docs/latest/sql-programming-guide.html`.

The Dataset has products, orders, order details, and salespeople from the fictitious company Northwind Industries-about 800 orders, 2150 order details, and 70 products. It's a tiny Dataset but easy to experiment with and very useful in understanding SQL operations, such as `Join`, as well as temporal partition and the aggregation of data, for example, year-wise aggregation.

The files are `data/NW/NW-products.csv, data/NW/NW-orders.csv, data/NW/NW-order-details.csv`, and `data/NW/NW-employees.csv`.

Titanic passenger list

The Titanic passenger list includes data related to the passenger list of the Titanic and the survivor flag, interesting data wrangling, and classification exercise. We will use this data to understand DataFrames as well as MLib.

The name of the file is `data/titanic/titanic3.csv`.

State of the Union speeches by POTUS

This data includes the text files dating from 1760 to the present-State of the Union speeches by Washington, Lincoln, Bill Clinton, George Bush, and Barack Obama. We will use this data to understand how we can infer the mood of the nation using the ML pipelines.

The name of the file is `data/sotu/`.

Movie lens Dataset

The movie lens Dataset includes data related to movie ratings by users, curated by the group lens project. There are multiple versions available, including small, medium, large, and XL. The small version has 100 K ratings, medium has 1 million, large with 10 million, and XL with 20 million. The main use of this is to study recommendation algorithms. We will also do some interesting data wrangling with Spark DataFrames.

The name of the file is `data/medium/`.

The data scientist and Spark features

One of the interesting questions relevant to this book is, "What do data scientists want?" It is a question that is being discussed and debated in many blogs. A short answer is as follows:

- The ability to explore, model, and reason data at scale-because many of their algorithms get asymptotically better with data, and so, a small Dataset sample is not enough for exploring different algorithms
- The ability to deploy without a lot of impedance
- The facility to evolve models once they are in production and the real world is using them

In short, all we ask for is the shortest path from the lab to the factory, enabling a data scientist DevOps person! The following screenshot (combining talks from Josh Willis and Ian Buss), which displays **The Sense & Sensibility of a Data Scientist DevOps**, succinctly shows the value of Apache Spark to a data scientist by addressing three points:

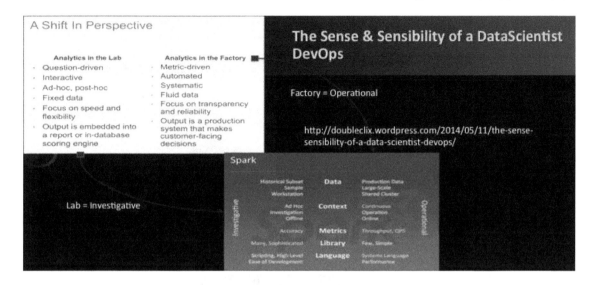

Who is this data scientist DevOps person?

Of course, we really do not want to start defining a data scientist here. There are many blogs (including mine) that explore this topic. It is enough to say that a data scientist DevOps person focuses on exploratory data analysis, visualization, lots of data wrangling, and tons of ideas. The work could span operational analytics, product analytics, decision data science, and product data science. That is, the inferences might be to answer business questions, say sales or marketing, or to embed intelligence in a product.

She (or he) would spend time equally with business/customers, algorithms, and data wrangling. The time might not be precisely one-third-for example, a person with more theoretical work might go deeper into algorithms, while a product data scientist might also dive into architecture and data modeling.

Their preferred programming language is R or Python, and they have enough statistical and programming background to work with both. The term data scientist DevOps can and will include developers who become proficient in statistics as well as statisticians who embrace programming. With this in mind, the preferred interface would be an IDE, such as iPython or Zeppelin, which can interact with a local or remote spark cluster. The focus is on agile and fast data wrangling-which is different from systems development, something that focuses on programming and the tools of choice are Java and IDEs, such as Eclipse.

Data scientists need to address reporting as well as analytics and span development-stage-production environments. Thus, they enable model development in the lab and model evolution in production.

The Data Lake architecture

The following diagram shows a canonical Spark Data Lake architecture and stack with essential elements. It consists of the **Data Hub**, **Analytics Hub**, **Reporting Hub**, **Visualization**, and **ETL** services.

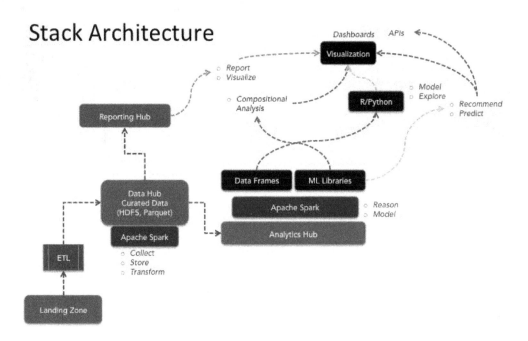

Data Hub

Data Hub is the store where all the curated data lives, fed by ETL processes, Kafka, and so on. The data is heterogeneous in terms of the topics (for example, marketing data, transactional data, web logs, social media data, and unstructured data) as well as of the temporal fidelity nature (some of the data might relate to daily workings, some by the minute, and some with much more granularity). Data curation is what keeps the data hub usable. Also remember, the schemas would change over time, and the management of schema is essential.

Reporting Hub

Reporting Hub usually contains the data in a more structured and aggregated format suitable for daily consumption by reports and visualization dashboards. Spark is deployed here mainly for ETL and transformations. There could be matching and other in-memory requirements where Spark would work very well. Visualization tools, such as Tableau, Quilk, and Pentaho, can directly access the data in Spark via SparkSQL.

Analytics Hub

Analytics Hub is where the data scientists and the readers of this book spend most of their time. Analytics Hub would have access to the vast amount of data in Data Hub, and the analytics is expected to produce intermediate Datasets, feature extractions, as well as model Datasets. DataFrames, MLlib, GraphX, and ML pipelines are all very relevant here.

Spark v2.0 and beyond

Spark v2.0 and beyond has been the catalyst for a renaissance in data science! Datasets, DataFrames, ML pipelines, and new and improved algorithms in MLlib have paved the way for data wrangling at scale. I think Version 2.0 marks the spot where Spark turned into a mature framework. It could handle huge workloads in terms of the number of machines as well as the volume of data. The community update at the Spark Summit 2015 in San Francisco included a slide that showed the power of Spark:

- The largest cluster-8,000 nodes (Tencent)
- The largest single job-1 petabyte and more (Alibaba and Tencent)
- The longest running job-1 petabyte and more for a week (Alibaba)
- The top streaming intake-1 terabyte/hour (Janelia farm)
- The largest shuffle-1 petabyte during sort benchmark (databricks)
- Netflix uses Spark for ad-hoc query and experimentation; they have 1,500 and more Spark nodes with 100 terabyte memory, chugging through 15 petabyte and more of S3 data and 7 petabyte of Parquet
- Tencent, probably the biggest known Spark installation, has 400 terabyte and more of memory in 8,000 and more machines and 150 petabyte data, running ETL and SQL

Apache Spark – evolution

It is interesting to trace the evolution of Apache Spark from an abstract perspective. Spark started out as a fast engine for big data processing-fast to run the code and write code as well. The original value proposition for Spark was that it offered faster in-memory computation graphs with compatibility with the Hadoop ecosystem, plus interesting and very usable APIs in Scala, Java, and Python. RDDs ruled the world. The focus was on iterative and interactive apps that operated on data multiple times, which was not a good use case for Hadoop.

The evolution didn't stop there. As Matei pointed out in his talk at MIT, users wanted more, and the Spark programming model evolved to include the following functionalities:

- More complex, multi-pass analytics (for example, ML pipelines and graph)
- More interactive ad-hoc queries
- More real-time stream processing
- More parallel machine learning algorithms beyond the basic RDDs
- More types of data sources as input and output
- More integration with R to span statistical computing beyond single-node tools
- More integration with apps such as visualization dashboards
- More performance with even larger Datasets and complex applications

Spark Versions 1.3,1.4, 1.5, and 1.6 rose to the occasion and answered these requests as follows:

Functionality	Spark feature
More complex multi-pass analytics	ML pipelines and GraphX
More interactive ad-hoc queries	Datasets and DataFrames
More real-time stream processing	Spark streaming
More parallel machine learning algorithms beyond the basic RDDs	MLlib
More types of data sources as input and output	`DataFrameReader` and `DataFrameWriter`
More integration with R to span statistical computing beyond single-node tools	SparkR
More integration with apps such as visualization dashboards	`SparkSQL` and `jdbc` drivers

More performance with even larger Datasets and complex applications	Tungsten for optimized execution and unified execution across all languages

Of course, Spark has added a lot more features than in the preceding table, for example, the interface with kafka, flume, and kinesis, which we will not get into in this book.

The various talks at the Spark Summit 2015 in San Francisco paint a clear picture of the trajectory and locus of Apache Spark:

- A very clear focus on Spark as a unified engine across diverse data sources, workloads, and environments
- Another important direction is Project Tungsten for optimizing execution, making Spark faster, and preparing for the next five years
- The third focus is the DAG visualization and debugging tools

The following diagram shows how Spark's projection for the future maps across the actual features in the Spark platform:

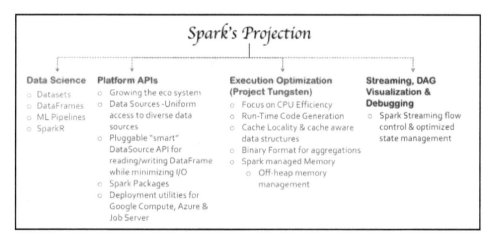

The interface to data sources is guided by the vision of high-level interfaces similar to the single-node tools. DataFrames are inspired by popular data transformation frameworks, such as Pandas in Python and the R DataFrames; the ML pipeline is inspired by Scikit-learn and Spark R interfaces with R.

The data source interface is far advanced than just having the ability to read MongoDB or Cassandra databases, or even the `jdbc` drivers. The algorithms, pushdown predicates, and the ability to leverage various smart optimizations in the storage native to the data sources are all part of the data source interface layers. The data would be returned as Datasets/DataFrames, which in turn can be consumed by the apps or the layers (refer to the diagram in the next section).

The engine improvements are taking priority at databricks because Spark is now handling more complex jobs, and CPUs are not getting any faster. Another main reason for the engine improvements is the JVM and the GC overhead-one of the goals of Project Tungsten is the off-heap memory management, which can optimize how memory is handled by the execution graphs and RDDs. Another interesting feature is the caching, leveraging data locality and cache-aware data structures. Caching improves performance because it avoids recomputation as well as data reads from the disk, as the data is available in the caches.

In addition to visible API improvements, each version of Spark achieves performance improvements as well. In fact, Spark 2.0, under the cover improvements, include shared optimization pipelines, efficient joins, and space efficiency. The Datasets do column-wise compression with four times less memory space and faster serialization performance.

Apache Spark – the full stack

With all of this background information behind us, let's take a quick look at the full Spark stack (shown in the following diagram), which used to be a lot simpler, showing how the Spark ecosystem is continually evolving:

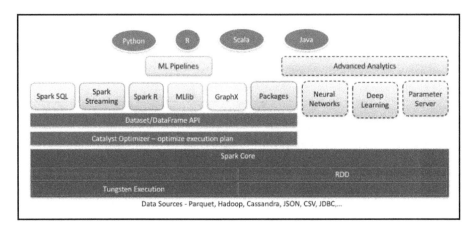

The Spark stack currently includes the following features:

- It provides the Spark SQL feature. This feature uses SQL for data manipulation while maintaining the underlying Spark computations. It also provides the vital interface via exposing the Datasets to external systems through JDBC/ODBC, arguably the best value of Spark SQL.
- Advanced analytics, which is still evolving; look out for features such as parameter server and neural networks in the later versions of Spark.
- It provides the Dataset/DataFrame API, of course. It is one of parts we are focusing on in this book and we will see more of it in the following chapters.
- The catalyst optimizer is an interesting beast. It is the proverbial software layer that separates a declarative API/interface from efficient computation pragmatics. We will look at this layer a little closely in the next chapter when we talk about DataFrames.
- The data sources layer makes it possible to integrate Spark with other external systems. Of course, it is not a layer, but has the capabilities embedded in other layers. As we know, data exists in multiple heterogeneous systems, namely text files, relational databases, NOSQL systems, and so forth. Spark's focus is on abstracting the data sources and the focus on integration with as many data sources as possible as a conceptual layer (rather than specific point drivers).
- The Spark streaming and the GraphX are important parts of the system, but we will not focus on them in this book.

The art of a big data store – Parquet

For an efficient and performant computing stack, we also need an equally optimal storage mechanism. Parquet fits the bill and can be considered as a best practice. The pattern uses the HDFS file system, curates the Datasets, and stores them in the Parquet format.

Parquet is a very efficient columnar format for data storage, initially developed by contributors from Twitter, Cloudera, Criteo, Berkely AMP Lab, LinkedIn, and Stripe. The Google Dremel paper (Dremel, 2010) inspired the basic algorithms and design of Parquet. It is now a top-level Apache project, `parquet-apache`, and is the default format for reading and writing operations in Spark DataFrames. Almost all the big data products, from MPP databases to query engines to visualization tools, interface natively with Parquet. Let's take a quick look at the science of data storage in the big data domain, what we need from a store, and the capabilities of Parquet.

Column projection and data partition

Column projection and data partition are used to enable you to read less data and only the data you need. Reading less data and optimizing it is a big part of the DataFrame story, especially distributed DataFrame at scale spanning 10s of machines, even 100s or 1000s. Parquet implements the concept of shredding columns and storing them in partitions. As a result, one only needs to read the columns needed, as opposed to row storage where the entire row is read and the columns not needed are ignored, but encounter the read penalty. Row read is expensive if we need only a few columns. Also, because of the partitions, one can surgically read subsets of columnar data without exhaustive seeks, thus adding another level of efficiency. Of course, column-oriented schemes would be slower for reading all columns.

Compression

Compression is very important for performance, saving bandwidth as well as increasing storage efficiency. I/O is expensive, so is compression-column store compression is efficient because of multiple reasons. First, usually columns are more homogeneous, resulting in better compression; second, columns can be compressed with encoding schemes without heavyweight compression. In fact, Parquet achieves good compression ratio with schemes, such as bit packing, run length encoding, delta encoding, prefix coding, and dictionary encoding. An interesting side effect of the encoding is that many times, the scheme turns string comparison to integer comparison, thus increasing performance.

Smart data storage and predicate pushdown

Predicate pushdown allows the store to skip data that don't match the selection predicates. Parquet stores the statistics about the data chunks that can be used by query planners and for predicate pushdown semantics. Thus, column pruning, skipping data blocks, happens at the Parquet drivel layer.

Support for evolving schema

By nature, big data evolves, and we really cannot go back and rewrite older schemas as data structures change, especially when new columns are added. Of course, no system can create newer columns in old data and populate for us, but it can be flexible when we add more attributes. Parquet stores the schema and the design allows evolvability.

The Parquet schema merging capability makes it possible to evolve schema by having multiple Parquet files with different but compatible schemas. Naturally, one has to be careful to keep the schema compatibility in mind.

In short, the Parquet format provides a good balance with query optimization and storage efficiency. However, it has limitations as well:

- It doesn't perform well for single record additions; one gets the best performance when data is stored in chunks
- Like we discussed earlier, it would be relatively slower for reading all the columns

Performance

Spark Version 2.0 improved Parquet throughput, from 11 M rows/second to 90 M rows/second, an eight-fold increase. One benchmark shows multiple operators throughput has increased from 14 M rows/second in Spark 1.6 to 125 M rows/second in Spark 2.0. We can definitely say that Spark and Parquet will achieve more performance and features in the future.

References

The references are stated as follows:

- http://cdn.oreillystatic.com/en/assets/1/event/126/Apache%2Spark_%2 What_s%2new_%2what_s%2coming%2Presentation.pdf
- https://spark-summit.org/215-east/wp-content/uploads/215/3/SSE15-1- Matei-Zaharia.pdf
- http://www.slideshare.net/databricks/spark-community-update-spark-su mmit-san-francisco-215
- https://doubleclix.wordpress.com/214/5/11/the-sense-sensibility-of- a-data-scientist-devops/
- http://www.slideshare.net/databricks/spark-sql-deep-dive-melbroune
- http://www.slideshare.net/databricks/introducing-dataframes-in-spark -for-large-scale-data-science
- http://www.slideshare.net/databricks/bdtc2

- http://www.slideshare.net/SparkSummit/deep-dive-into-project-tungsten-josh-rosen
- https://databricks.com/blog/215/6/22/understanding-your-spark-application-through-visualization.html
- http://www.slideshare.net/databricks/dynamic-allocation-in-spark
- http://cdn.oreillystatic.com/en/assets/1/event/1/Parquet_%2An%20Open%2Columnar%2Storage%2for%2Hadoop%2Presentation%21.pdf
- http://www.slideshare.net/julienledem/how-to-use-parquet-hadoopsummitsanjose215
- http://www.slideshare.net/alexlevenson/hadoop-summit-215-performance-optimization-at-scale
- https://parquet.apache.org/
- http://www.slideshare.net/SparkSummit/data-storage-tips-for-optimal-spark-performancevida-ha-databricks
- https://blogs.apache.org/foundation/entry/the_apache_software_foundation_announces75
- http://yunus.hacettepe.edu.tr/~tonta/courses/spring23/dok322/
- https://code.google.com/p/northwindextended/
- http://www.slideshare.net/databricks/215-616-spark-summit
- http://research.google.com/pubs/pub36632.html

Summary

This is an interesting chapter where we discussed the broader and wider picture of where Spark fits in the big data and analytics ecosystem. First, we looked at the Datasets that accompany this book as well as some interesting IDEs. We then discussed the role of data scientists and what they expect from a Spark stack, which led to our discussion to the Spark-based Data Lake architecture and then the Spark stack. We also looked at Parquest as an efficient storage format.

8
Spark SQL

Spark SQL provides an important feature in the Spark ecosystem, that is, integration with different data sources as well as the capability to interact with other subsystems, such as visualization. As we know, in modern data stacks, no stack is an island by itself, and in many ways, the versatility of integration with other components is an important capability. Obviously, the role of Spark SQL is not to replace SQL databases. We see it more as a versatile query interface for Spark data that complements the data wrangling and input capabilities of Spark. The ability to scale complex data operations makes sense only when one can utilize the results in flexible ways, and Spark SQL achieves that. We'll cover the following topics in this chapter:

- The Spark SQL architecture
- Datasets/DataFrames
- SQL programming

The Spark SQL architecture

Interestingly, as I was writing this chapter, Michael Armbrust from Databricks wrote a blog about the data sources API and presented an architecture diagram; this is what inspired me to create the following diagram:

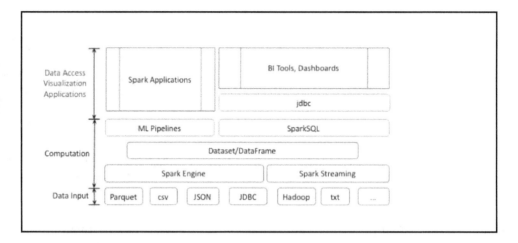

The bottom layer is a flexible data access layer (and store) that works via multiple formats, usually a distributed filesystem such as HDFS. The computation layer is the place where we leverage the distributed-at-scale processing of the Spark engine, including the streaming data. The computation layer usually acts on RDDs. The **Dataset/DataFrame** layer provides the API layer. The Spark SQL then overlays the Dataset/DataFrame layer and provides data access for applications, dashboards, BI tools, and so forth. There is a huge amount of SQL knowledge among various people, with roles ranging from data analysts and programmers to data engineers, who have developed interesting SQL queries over their data. Spark needs to leverage this knowledge of SQL queries, and it does this via Spark SQL.

Spark SQL how-to in a nutshell

Prior to Spark 2.0.0, the heart of Spark SQL was SchemaRDD, which, as you can guess, associates a schema with an RDD. Of course, internally it does a lot of magic by leveraging the ability to scale and distribute processing and providing flexible storage.

In many ways, data access via Spark SQL is deceptively simple; we mean the process of creating one or more appropriate RDDs by paying attention to the layout, data types, and so on, and then accessing them via SchemaRDDs. We get to use all the interesting features of Spark to create the RDDs: structured data from Hive or Parquet, unstructured data from any source, and the ability to apply RDD operations at scale. Then, you need to overlay the respective schemas to the RDDs by creating SchemaRDDs. Voilà! You now have the ability to run SQL over RDDs. You can see the SchemaRDDs being created in the log entries.

Spark SQL with Spark 2.0

The preceding section was true until Spark 2.0 (actually Datasets have been available since Spark 1.6.0)! The transition had been in progress since Spark 1.3.0, when DataFrames were introduced. Finally in Spark 2.0, all the elegant designs came together and Datasets became the way to wrangle with data. The basic workflow and semantics still exist; we have a Dataset in the disk in some form, say comma-separated values (`csv`), `tab`, or `pipe` delimited. We need to read the data and tell Spark the organization and the types; we also need a way to represent the data in memory at scale in a distributed fashion and find interesting ways to do operations on the data. While pre-Spark 2.0 had RDDs and schemaRDD to express data semantics and tables, Spark 2.0 unified the interface to Datasets/DataFrames.

Even how we print data elements has become very easy now. Earlier, we had to use either `result.take(10).foreach(println)` or `result.take(30).foreach(e=>println("%15s | %9.2f |".format(e(0),e(1))))` to get a reasonably formatted output. These are still good patterns for printing RDDs, but DataFrames/Datasets can be printed using the `result.show()` method. As you will see, it does an excellent job. Sometimes, we will use the `head()` call to see more details, such as the underlying object; most of the time it is `sql.row`, but still it gives us the layout, which comes in handy when we want to filter or use map operations.

In the next few sections, we will see how all of these come together. In this chapter, we will look at SQL statements, and in later chapters, we will explore the rich data wrangling capabilities of Datasets/DataFrames.

Because of the transition to 2.0 and the changes, we now have both versions of the code. For example, `sparkSQL.scala` is the pre-2.0 way of doing things; it will still work with 2.0 but will display deprecated messages. You should always start the Spark shell to show the deprecated messages like this:

spark-shell -deprecation

This command will display a message when it encounters a deprecated method, and you can then change the call. This is how I created the `sparkSQL2.scala` file, which uses the 2.0 code.

Spark SQL programming

Let's now get our hands dirty and work through various examples. We will start with a simple Dataset and then progressively perform more sophisticated SQL statements. We will use the NorthWind Dataset.

Datasets/DataFrames

In short, Datasets are semantic domain-specific objects, which means they are very rich in terms of typing and they possess all the functions of RDDs. In short, the best of both worlds! A DataFrame is an untyped view into a Dataset, basically a collection of rows. This is useful for doing abstract generic operations on a Dataset, that is, operations that depend only on the positions of elements in a row and other factors. We will learn more in later sections.

 As languages, such as Python and R, do not have compile-time type checking, Datasets and DataFrames are collapsed and called DataFrames.

Another change in 2.0 is `sparksession`, which replaces `sqlcontext`, `hivecontext`, and others. The `sparksession` instance has a very rich and flexible `read` method that can handle different data formats, such as `.csv`, `.parquet`, `.json`, and `.jdbc`. The `read()` method has options that reflect format-related characteristics, such as header, delimiter, and others.

Combining all the new interfaces and capabilities, we will create Datasets from the `read` operations available from `sparksession` and see how we can apply the `sql` statements.

SQL access to a simple data table

Let's load a small CSV file into the employee Dataset, as shown here:

```
//
// sparkSQL2.scala
//
// Code for Spark 2.0 way of doing things
//
// register case class external to main
//
[..]
val filePath = "/Users/ksankar/fdps-v3/"
```

```
println(s"Running Spark Version ${sc.version}")
//
val employees = spark.read.option("header","true").
csv(filePath + "data/NW-Employees.csv").as[Employee]
println("Employees has "+employees.count()+" rows")
employees.show(5)
employees.head()
```

The code is straightforward. We create a `case` class that represents the employee table. We then parse the CSV file and create a Dataset that has the `Employee` class as its elements.

The data files are available at `https://github.com/xsankar/fdps-v3`. After you download the data, change `filePath` (the preceding code) to the directory where you have `fdps-v3`.

The screenshot of the process and the output from running the code from the Spark shell are shown here.

We start the Spark shell with the following command:

`/Volumes/sdxc-01/spark-2.0.0-preview/bin/spark-shell –deprecation`

Refer to the following screenshot:

```
USS-Defiant:fdps-v3 ksankar$ /Volumes/sdxc-01/spark-2.0.0-preview/bin/spark-shell -deprecation
Using Spark's default log4j profile: org/apache/spark/log4j-defaults.properties
Setting default log level to "WARN".
To adjust logging level use sc.setLogLevel(newLevel).
16/06/18 21:56:21 WARN NativeCodeLoader: Unable to load native-hadoop library for your platform... using builtin-java classes where applicable
16/06/18 21:56:22 WARN AbstractHandler: No Server set for org.spark_project.jetty.server.handler.ErrorHandler@23ce68fc
Spark context Web UI available at http://10.0.1.3:4040
Spark context available as 'sc' (master = local[*], app id = local-1466312182773).
Spark session available as 'spark'.
Welcome to
      ____              __
     / __/__  ___ _____/ /__
    _\ \/ _ \/ _ `/ __/  '_/
   /___/ .__/\_,_/_/ /_/\_\   version 2.0.0-preview
      /_/

Using Scala version 2.11.8 (Java HotSpot(TM) 64-Bit Server VM, Java 1.7.0_60)
Type in expressions to have them evaluated.
Type :help for more information.

scala>
```

Note a couple of things. As in older versions, the Spark context is available as `sc`; however, the new `sparkSession` instance is also available as Spark and that is what we will use.

Let's load the file `sparkSql2.scala`. It will run all the commands; we will parse the output and the code to understand the various operations.

```
scala> :load /Users/ksankar/fdps-v3/code/sparkSql2.scala
Loading /Users/ksankar/fdps-v3/code/sparkSql2.scala...
defined class Employee
defined class Order
defined class OrderDetails
filePath: String = /Users/ksankar/fdps-v3/
Running Spark Version 2.0.0-preview
employees: org.apache.spark.sql.Dataset[Employee] = [EmployeeID: string, LastName: string ... 9 more fields]
Employees has 9 rows
+----------+---------+---------+--------------------+---------+--------+--------+-----+--------+-------+--------+
|EmployeeID| LastName|FirstName|               Title|BirthDate|HireDate|    City|State|     Zip|Country|ReportsTo|
+----------+---------+---------+--------------------+---------+--------+--------+-----+--------+-------+--------+
|         1|   Fuller|   Andrew|Sales Representative| 12/6/48| 4/29/92| Seattle|   WA|  98122|    USA|       2|
|         2|  Davolio|    Nancy|Vice President, S...| 2/17/52| 8/12/92|  Tacoma|   WA|  98401|    USA|       0|
|         3|Leverling|    Janet|Sales Representative| 8/28/63| 3/30/92|Kirkland|   WA|  98033|    USA|       2|
|         4|  Peacock| Margaret|Sales Representative| 9/17/37|  5/1/93| Redmond|   WA|  98052|    USA|       2|
|         5|Dodsworth|     Anne|       Sales Manager|  3/2/55|10/15/93|  London| SW1 8JR|     UK|       2|
+----------+---------+---------+--------------------+---------+--------+--------+-----+--------+-------+--------+
only showing top 5 rows
```

We declare a `case` class and `Employee` and then parse the file to the Dataset of the employees, as shown here:

```scala
case class Employee(EmployeeID : String,
  LastName : String, FirstName : String, Title : String,
  BirthDate : String, HireDate : String,
  City : String, State : String, Zip : String, Country : String,
  ReportsTo : String)
//
case class Order(OrderID : String, CustomerID : String, EmployeeID :
String,
  OrderDate : String, ShipCountry : String)
//
case class OrderDetails(OrderID : String, ProductID : String, UnitPrice :
Double, Qty : Int, Discount : Double)
```

All the magic is done in the `read` method of the `sparkSession` variable, `spark`. We use the `csv` method, giving it a filename as well as an option to say we have the headers. The file looks like the following screenshot:

EmployeeID	LastName	FirstName	Title	BirthDate	HireDate	City	State	Zip	Country	ReportsTo
1	Fuller	Andrew	Sales Repres	12/6/48	4/29/92	Seattle	WA		98122	USA	2
2	Davolio	Nancy	Vice Presider	2/17/52	8/12/92	Tacoma	WA		98401	USA	0
3	Leverling	Janet	Sales Repres	8/28/63	3/30/92	Kirkland	WA		98033	USA	2
4	Peacock	Margaret	Sales Repres	9/17/37	5/1/93	Redmond	WA		98052	USA	2

The column titles in the header row correspond to the names in our `case` class and `Employee`, and the file is a `.csv` file. Spark is intelligent enough to match the data and our `case` class, and it subsequently creates the Dataset. We can see that the Dataset has nine rows and the `show(5)` command displays the first five rows in a tabular format.

The next step is to create a view in the Dataset that can be used for queries using SQL.

The code is as follows:

```
employees.createOrReplaceTempView("EmployeesTable")
var result = spark.sql("SELECT * from EmployeesTable")
result.show(5)
result.head(3)
//
employees.explain(true)
```

We create a view, `EmployeesTable`, over which an SQL statement is applied. The result is a DataFrame, which we verify using the `show()` command. Also, `explain` shows us the query plan as expected.

```
res3: Employee = Employee(1,Fuller,Andrew,Sales Representative,12/6/48,4/29/92,Seattle,WA,98122,USA,2)
result: org.apache.spark.sql.DataFrame = [EmployeeID: string, LastName: string ... 9 more fields]
+----------+--------+---------+--------------------+---------+--------+--------+-----+------+-------+--------+
|EmployeeID|LastName|FirstName|               Title|BirthDate|HireDate|    City|State|   Zip|Country|ReportsTo|
+----------+--------+---------+--------------------+---------+--------+--------+-----+------+-------+--------+
|         1|  Fuller|   Andrew|Sales Representative| 12/6/48| 4/29/92| Seattle|   WA| 98122|   USA|      2|
|         2| Davolio|    Nancy|Vice President, S...| 2/17/52| 8/12/92| Tacoma|    WA| 98401|   USA|      0|
|         3|Leverling|   Janet|Sales Representative| 8/28/63| 3/30/92|Kirkland|   WA| 98033|   USA|      2|
|         4| Peacock| Margaret|Sales Representative| 9/17/37| 5/1/93| Redmond|    WA| 98052|   USA|      2|
|         5|Dodsworth|    Anne|       Sales Manager| 3/2/55|10/15/93| London|     |SW1 8JR|    UK|      2|
+----------+--------+---------+--------------------+---------+--------+--------+-----+------+-------+--------+
only showing top 5 rows

res6: Array[org.apache.spark.sql.Row] = Array([1,Fuller,Andrew,Sales Representative,12/6/48,4/29/92,Seattle,WA,98122,USA,2], [2,Davolio,Nancy,Vice Preside
nt, Sales,2/17/52,8/12/92,Tacoma,WA,98401,USA,0], [3,Leverling,Janet,Sales Representative,8/28/63,3/30/92,Kirkland,WA,98033,USA,2])
== Parsed Logical Plan ==
Relation[EmployeeID#0,LastName#1,FirstName#2,Title#3,BirthDate#4,HireDate#5,City#6,State#7,Zip#8,Country#9,ReportsTo#10] csv

== Analyzed Logical Plan ==
EmployeeID: string, LastName: string, FirstName: string, Title: string, BirthDate: string, HireDate: string, City: string, State: string, Zip: string, Cou
ntry: string, ReportsTo: string
Relation[EmployeeID#0,LastName#1,FirstName#2,Title#3,BirthDate#4,HireDate#5,City#6,State#7,Zip#8,Country#9,ReportsTo#10] csv

== Optimized Logical Plan ==
Relation[EmployeeID#0,LastName#1,FirstName#2,Title#3,BirthDate#4,HireDate#5,City#6,State#7,Zip#8,Country#9,ReportsTo#10] csv

== Physical Plan ==
WholeStageCodegen
:  +- Scan csv [EmployeeID#0,LastName#1,FirstName#2,Title#3,BirthDate#4,HireDate#5,City#6,State#7,Zip#8,Country#9,ReportsTo#10] Format: CSV, InputPaths: f
ile:/Users/ksankar/fdps-v3/data/NW-Employees.csv, PushedFilters: [], ReadSchema: struct<EmployeeID:string,LastName:string,FirstName:string,Title:string,Bi
rthDate:string,HireDate:...
```

Let's try a filter query, namely `SELECT * from Employees WHERE State = 'WA'`, and see how it works. Here is the code for this query:

```
result = spark.sql("SELECT * from EmployeesTable WHERE State = 'WA'")
result.show(5)
result.head(3)
//
result.explain(true)
```

Here's the screenshot for this query:

```
result: org.apache.spark.sql.DataFrame = [EmployeeID: string, LastName: string ... 9 more fields]
+----------+--------+--------+--------------------+---------+--------+--------+-----+-----+-------+---------+
|EmployeeID|LastName|FirstName|               Title|BirthDate|HireDate|    City|State|  Zip|Country|ReportsTo|
+----------+--------+--------+--------------------+---------+--------+--------+-----+-----+-------+---------+
|         1|  Fuller|  Andrew| Sales Representative|  12/6/48| 4/29/92| Seattle|   WA|98122|    USA|        2|
|         2| Davolio|   Nancy|Vice President, S...|  2/17/52| 8/12/92|  Tacoma|   WA|98401|    USA|        0|
|         3|Leverling|  Janet| Sales Representative|  8/28/63| 3/30/92|Kirkland|   WA|98033|    USA|        2|
|         4| Peacock|Margaret| Sales Representative|  9/17/37|  5/1/93| Redmond|   WA|98052|    USA|        2|
|         8|Callahan|   Laura|Inside Sales Coor...|   1/7/58|  3/3/94| Seattle|   WA|98105|    USA|        2|
+----------+--------+--------+--------------------+---------+--------+--------+-----+-----+-------+---------+

res9: Array[org.apache.spark.sql.Row] = Array([1,Fuller,Andrew,Sales Representative,12/6/48,4/29/92,Seattle,WA,98122,USA,2], [2,Davolio,Nancy,Vice Preside
nt, Sales,2/17/52,8/12/92,Tacoma,WA,98401,USA,0], [3,Leverling,Janet,Sales Representative,8/28/63,3/30/92,Kirkland,WA,98033,USA,2])
```

The query plan is slightly more detailed:

```
== Parsed Logical Plan ==
'Project [*]
+- 'Filter ('State = WA)
   +- 'UnresolvedRelation `EmployeesTable`, None

== Analyzed Logical Plan ==
EmployeeID: string, LastName: string, FirstName: string, Title: string, BirthDate: string, HireDate: string, City: string, State: string, Zip: string, Cou
ntry: string, ReportsTo: string
Project [EmployeeID#0,LastName#1,FirstName#2,Title#3,BirthDate#4,HireDate#5,City#6,State#7,Zip#8,Country#9,ReportsTo#10]
+- Filter (State#7 = WA)
   +- SubqueryAlias employeestable
      +- Relation[EmployeeID#0,LastName#1,FirstName#2,Title#3,BirthDate#4,HireDate#5,City#6,State#7,Zip#8,Country#9,ReportsTo#10] csv

== Optimized Logical Plan ==
Filter (isnotnull(State#7) && (State#7 = WA))
+- Relation[EmployeeID#0,LastName#1,FirstName#2,Title#3,BirthDate#4,HireDate#5,City#6,State#7,Zip#8,Country#9,ReportsTo#10] csv

== Physical Plan ==
WholeStageCodegen
:  +- Project [EmployeeID#0,LastName#1,FirstName#2,Title#3,BirthDate#4,HireDate#5,City#6,State#7,Zip#8,Country#9,ReportsTo#10]
:     +- Filter (isnotnull(State#7) && (State#7 = WA))
:        +- Scan csv [EmployeeID#0,LastName#1,FirstName#2,Title#3,BirthDate#4,HireDate#5,City#6,State#7,Zip#8,Country#9,ReportsTo#10] Format: CSV, InputPa
ths: file:/Users/ksankar/fdps-v3/data/NW-Employees.csv, PushedFilters: [IsNotNull(State), EqualTo(State,WA)], ReadSchema: struct<EmployeeID:string,LastNam
e:string,FirstName:string,Title:string,BirthDate:string,HireDate:...
```

Great! It worked as expected. You can see that the filter did get into the query plan.

Handling multiple tables with Spark SQL

Now that we have mastered the art of Spark SQL, let's try multiple Datasets and slightly larger Datasets. The `Orders` table's Dataset has 830 records and the `Order Details` table has approximately 2,000 records. These tables will give us a good representation of a few queries with joins that span the two tables.

Let's start by loading the `Orders` table, as shown here:

```
case class Order(OrderID : String, CustomerID : String, EmployeeID :
String, OrderDate : String, ShipCountry : String)
//
...
...
val orders = spark.read.option("header","true").
csv(filePath + "data/NW-Orders.csv").as[Order]
println("Orders has "+orders.count()+" rows")
```

```
orders.show(5)
orders.head()
orders.dtypes
```

Here, I ran into a few interesting miscues, which were very revealing but at the same time showed the work Spark is doing for us beneath the hood.

The first error was a little puzzling:

```
scala> :load /Users/ksankar/fdps-v3/code/sparkSql2.scala
Loading /Users/ksankar/fdps-v3/code/sparkSql2.scala...
defined class Order
defined class OrderDetails
filePath: String = /Users/ksankar/fdps-v3/
Running Spark Version 2.0.0-preview
org.apache.spark.sql.AnalysisException: cannot resolve '`EmployeeID`' given input columns: [ShipCuntry, OrderDate, OrderID, EmpliyeeID, CustomerID];
    at org.apache.spark.sql.catalyst.analysis.package$AnalysisErrorAt.failAnalysis(package.scala:42)
    at org.apache.spark.sql.catalyst.analysis.CheckAnalysis$$anonfun$checkAnalysis$1$$anonfun$apply$2.applyOrElse(CheckAnalysis.scala:61)
    at org.apache.spark.sql.catalyst.analysis.CheckAnalysis$$anonfun$checkAnalysis$1$$anonfun$apply$2.applyOrElse(CheckAnalysis.scala:58)
    at org.apache.spark.sql.catalyst.trees.TreeNode$$anonfun$transformUp$1.apply(TreeNode.scala:287)
```

I realized that the header of the fourth column in the `data` file had a spelling mistake: `EmpliyeeId` instead of `EmployeeID`! Once I corrected the error in the `data` file, I ran into the second error:

```
scala> :load /Users/ksankar/fdps-v3/code/sparkSql2.scala
Loading /Users/ksankar/fdps-v3/code/sparkSql2.scala...
defined class Order
defined class OrderDetails
filePath: String = /Users/ksankar/fdps-v3/
Running Spark Version 2.0.0-preview
org.apache.spark.sql.AnalysisException: cannot resolve '`ShipCountry`' given input columns: [EmployeeID, OrderID, CustomerID, OrderDate, ShipCuntry];
    at org.apache.spark.sql.catalyst.analysis.package$AnalysisErrorAt.failAnalysis(package.scala:42)
    at org.apache.spark.sql.catalyst.analysis.CheckAnalysis$$anonfun$checkAnalysis$1$$anonfun$apply$2.applyOrElse(CheckAnalysis.scala:61)
    at org.apache.spark.sql.catalyst.analysis.CheckAnalysis$$anonfun$checkAnalysis$1$$anonfun$apply$2.applyOrElse(CheckAnalysis.scala:58)
    at org.apache.spark.sql.catalyst.trees.TreeNode$$anonfun$transformUp$1.apply(TreeNode.scala:287)
    at org.apache.spark.sql.catalyst.trees.TreeNode$$anonfun$transformUp$1.apply(TreeNode.scala:287)
    at org.apache.spark.sql.catalyst.trees.CurrentOrigin$.withOrigin(TreeNode.scala:68)
```

This was easy to fix. There was another spelling mistake related to `ShipCountry`, the last column. After correcting the column title in the data file, I ran the code again; then the next error popped up:

```
res115: Order = Order(10248,VINET,5,7/2/96,France)
res116: Array[(String, String)] = Array((OrderID,IntegerType), (CustomerID,StringType), (EmployeeID,IntegerType), (OrderDate,StringType), (ShipCountry,StringType))
org.apache.spark.sql.AnalysisException: Cannot up cast `UnitPrice` from double to float as it may truncate
The type path of the target object is:
- field (class: "scala.Float", name: "UnitPrice")
- root class: "OrderDetails"
You can either add an explicit cast to the input data or choose a higher precision type of the field in the target object;
    at org.apache.spark.sql.catalyst.analysis.Analyzer$ResolveUpCast$.org$apache$spark$sql$catalyst$analysis$Analyzer$ResolveUpCast$$fail(Analyzer.scala:1917)
    at org.apache.spark.sql.catalyst.analysis.Analyzer$ResolveUpCast$$anonfun$apply$33$$anonfun$applyOrElse$13.applyOrElse(Analyzer.scala:1943)
    at org.apache.spark.sql.catalyst.analysis.Analyzer$ResolveUpCast$$anonfun$apply$33$$anonfun$applyOrElse$13.applyOrElse(Analyzer.scala:1934)
    at org.apache.spark.sql.catalyst.trees.TreeNode$$anonfun$3.apply(TreeNode.scala:265)
    at org.apache.spark.sql.catalyst.trees.TreeNode$$anonfun$3.apply(TreeNode.scala:265)
    at org.apache.spark.sql.catalyst.trees.CurrentOrigin$.withOrigin(TreeNode.scala:68)
    at org.apache.spark.sql.catalyst.trees.TreeNode.transformDown(TreeNode.scala:264)
```

I had declared the `case` class as follows:

```
case class OrderDetails(OrderID : String, ProductID : String, UnitPrice :
Float, Qty : Int, Discount : Float)
```

The `UnitPrice` instance needs to be changed to `Double`. The error message was detailed enough. So I changed the `case` class definition and ran the code again:

```
case class OrderDetails(OrderID : String, ProductID : String, UnitPrice :
Double, Qty : Int, Discount : Float)
```

Here's a screenshot with the changes introduced:

```
res132: Order = Order(10248,VINET,5,7/2/96,France)
res133: Array[(String, String)] = Array((OrderID,IntegerType), (CustomerID,StringType), (EmployeeID,IntegerType), (OrderDate,StringType), (ShipCountry,Str
ingType))
org.apache.spark.sql.AnalysisException: Cannot up cast `Discount` from double to float as it may truncate
The type path of the target object is:
- field (class: "scala.Float", name: "Discount")
- root class: "OrderDetails"
You can either add an explicit cast to the input data or choose a higher precision type of the field in the target object;
    at org.apache.spark.sql.catalyst.analysis.Analyzer$ResolveUpCast$.org$apache$spark$sql$catalyst$analysis$Analyzer$ResolveUpCast$$fail(Analyzer.scala:191
7)
    at org.apache.spark.sql.catalyst.analysis.Analyzer$ResolveUpCast$$anonfun$apply$33$$anonfun$apply$OrElse$13.applyOrElse(Analyzer.scala:1943)
```

Then the next error popped up; this time the type of discount was changed to `Double`:

```
res149: Order = Order(10248,VINET,5,7/2/96,France)
res150: Array[(String, String)] = Array((OrderID,IntegerType), (CustomerID,StringType), (EmployeeID,IntegerType), (OrderDate,StringType), (ShipCountry,Str
ingType))
org.apache.spark.sql.AnalysisException: cannot resolve '`ProductID`' given input columns: [ProductId, OrderID, UnitPrice, Qty, Discount];
    at org.apache.spark.sql.catalyst.analysis.package$AnalysisErrorAt.failAnalysis(package.scala:42)
    at org.apache.spark.sql.catalyst.analysis.CheckAnalysis$$anonfun$checkAnalysis$1$$anonfun$apply$2.applyOrElse(CheckAnalysis.scala:61)
    at org.apache.spark.sql.catalyst.analysis.CheckAnalysis$$anonfun$checkAnalysis$1$$anonfun$apply$2.applyOrElse(CheckAnalysis.scala:58)
    at org.apache.spark.sql.catalyst.trees.TreeNode$$anonfun$transformUp$1.apply(TreeNode.scala:287)
```

Once the errors were fixed, the code ran fine and the orders Dataset and the view were created fine:

```
orders: org.apache.spark.sql.Dataset[Order] = [OrderID: string, CustomerID: string ... 3 more fields]
Orders has 830 rows
+-------+----------+----------+---------+-----------+
|OrderID|CustomerID|EmployeeID|OrderDate|ShipCountry|
+-------+----------+----------+---------+-----------+
|  10248|     VINET|         5|  7/2/96|     France|
|  10249|     TOMSP|         6|  7/3/96|    Germany|
|  10250|     HANAR|         4|  7/6/96|     Brazil|
|  10251|     VICTE|         3|  7/6/96|     France|
|  10252|     SUPRD|         4|  7/7/96|    Belgium|
+-------+----------+----------+---------+-----------+
only showing top 5 rows

res13: Order = Order(10248,VINET,5,7/2/96,France)
res14: Array[(String, String)] = Array((OrderID,StringType), (CustomerID,StringType), (EmployeeID,StringType), (OrderDate,StringType), (ShipCountry,String
Type))
```

The `read` method has an option to infer a schema automatically. I think this is a very good idea. I have been doing this in R for a long time. So let's try this option.

```
val orders = spark.read.option("header","true").
option("inferSchema","true").
csv(filePath + "data/NW-Orders.csv").as[Order]
println("Orders has "+orders.count()+" rows")
orders.show(5)
orders.head()
orders.dtypes // verify column types
```

This code worked out fine. Notice the slight change in the types for `OrderID` and `EmployeeID`. They changed from `String` to `Integer`. Here's a screenshot of this:

```
orders: org.apache.spark.sql.Dataset[Order] = [OrderID: int, CustomerID: string ... 3 more fields]
Orders has 830 rows
+-------+----------+----------+---------+-----------+
|OrderID|CustomerID|EmployeeID|OrderDate|ShipCountry|
+-------+----------+----------+---------+-----------+
|  10248|     VINET|         5|  7/2/96 |    France |
|  10249|     TOMSP|         6|  7/3/96 |   Germany |
|  10250|     HANAR|         4|  7/6/96 |    Brazil |
|  10251|     VICTE|         3|  7/6/96 |    France |
|  10252|     SUPRD|         4|  7/7/96 |   Belgium |
+-------+----------+----------+---------+-----------+
only showing top 5 rows

res17: Order = Order(10248,VINET,5,7/2/96,France)
res18: Array[(String, String)] = Array((OrderID,IntegerType), (CustomerID,StringType), (EmployeeID,IntegerType), (OrderDate,StringType), (ShipCountry,Stri
ngType))
```

We apply a similar pattern for order details. By now, we are an old hand at doing this. The following code is for the loading process of the table:

```
val orderDetails = spark.read.option("header","true").
option("inferSchema","true").
csv(filePath + "data/NW-Order-Details.csv").as[OrderDetails]
println("Order Details has "+orderDetails.count()+" rows")
orderDetails.show(5)
orderDetails.head()
orderDetails.dtypes // verify column types
//
//orders.createTempView("OrdersTable")
orders.createOrReplaceTempView("OrdersTable")
result = spark.sql("SELECT * from OrdersTable")
result.show(10)
result.head(3)
//
orderDetails.createOrReplaceTempView("OrderDetailsTable")
var result = spark.sql("SELECT * from OrderDetailsTable")
result.show(10)
result.head(3)
```

When we create the view, if the view already exists you will get the
`TempTableAlreadyExists` exception:

```
res170: OrderDetails = OrderDetails(10248,11,14.0,12,0.0)
res171: Array[(String, String)] = Array((OrderID,IntegerType), (ProductID,IntegerType), (UnitPrice,DoubleType), (Qty,IntegerType), (Discount,DoubleType))
org.apache.spark.sql.catalyst.analysis.TempTableAlreadyExistsException: Temporary table 'OrderTable' already exists;
  at org.apache.spark.sql.catalyst.catalog.SessionCatalog.createTempView(SessionCatalog.scala:324)
  at org.apache.spark.sql.SparkSession.createTempView(SparkSession.scala:524)
  at org.apache.spark.sql.Dataset.createTempView(Dataset.scala:2328)
  ... 71 elided
```

The solution is to use `createOrReplaceView` instead of `cretaeTempView`. Once I had
changed `orders.createTempView("OrderTable")` to
`orders.createOrReplaceTempView("OrderTable")`, the error disappeared.

The output of this is shown in the following screenshot. This is no different from our earlier
work. We have 830 orders in our orders table and 2,155 order details.

```
orderDetails: org.apache.spark.sql.Dataset[OrderDetails] = [OrderID: int, ProductID: int ... 3 more fields]
Order Details has 2155 rows
+-------+---------+---------+---+--------+
|OrderID|ProductID|UnitPrice|Qty|Discount|
+-------+---------+---------+---+--------+
|  10248|       11|     14.0| 12|     0.0|
|  10248|       42|      9.8| 10|     0.0|
|  10248|       72|     34.8|  5|     0.0|
|  10249|       14|     18.6|  9|     0.0|
|  10249|       51|     42.4| 40|     0.0|
+-------+---------+---------+---+--------+
only showing top 5 rows
```

In this chapter, we are trying to create a few queries. So, we really do not need hundreds of
records. However, the Dataset has enough records for you to try out various queries on
your own. The Dataset is big enough to do meaningful queries but too small to work on a
laptop with limited resources. This would be a good exercise for you to experiment with
Spark SQL.

Now comes the interesting part. Let's join the two tables and see how that query works:

```
//
// Now the interesting part
//
result = spark.sql("SELECT OrderDetailsTable.OrderID, ShipCountry,
UnitPrice, Qty, Discount FROM OrdersTable INNER JOIN OrderDetailsTable ON
OrdersTable.OrderID = OrderDetailsTable.OrderID")
result.show(10)
result.head(3)
//
// Sales By Country
//
```

```
result = spark.sql("SELECT ShipCountry, SUM(OrderDetailsTable.UnitPrice *
Qty * Discount) AS ProductSales FROM OrdersTable INNER JOIN
OrderDetailsTable ON OrdersTable.OrderID = OrderDetailsTable.OrderID GROUP
BY ShipCountry")
result.count()
result.show(10)
result.head(3)
result.orderBy($"ProductSales".desc).show(10) // Top 10 by Sales
```

Refer to the following screenshot:

```
res28: Array[org.apache.spark.sql.Row] = Array([10248,11,14.0,12,0.0], [10248,42,9.8,10,0.0], [10248,72,34.8,5,0.0])
result: org.apache.spark.sql.DataFrame = [OrderID: int, ShipCountry: string ... 3 more fields]
+-------+-----------+---------+---+--------+
|OrderID|ShipCountry|UnitPrice|Qty|Discount|
+-------+-----------+---------+---+--------+
|  10248|     France|     34.8|  5|     0.0|
|  10248|     France|      9.8| 10|     0.0|
|  10248|     France|     14.0| 12|     0.0|
|  10249|    Germany|     42.4| 40|     0.0|
|  10249|    Germany|     18.6|  9|     0.0|
|  10250|     Brazil|     16.8| 15|    0.15|
|  10250|     Brazil|     42.4| 35|    0.15|
|  10250|     Brazil|      7.7| 10|     0.0|
|  10251|     France|     16.8| 20|     0.0|
|  10251|     France|     15.6| 15|    0.05|
+-------+-----------+---------+---+--------+
only showing top 10 rows
```

It works fine! Good stuff! The second query, `Sales by Country`, is more interesting.

The output looks as expected. We can also use `orderBy` and see the top 10 countries by sales:

```
result: org.apache.spark.sql.DataFrame = [ShipCountry: string, ProductSales: double]
res31: Long = 22
+-----------+------------------+
|ShipCountry|      ProductSales|
+-----------+------------------+
|     Sweden|5028.5599999999995|
|    Germany|         14355.9965|
|     France|  4140.437499999999|
|  Argentina|               0.0|
|    Belgium|1310.1250000000002|
|    Finland|          968.3975|
|      Italy|           934.995|
|     Norway|               0.0|
|      Spain|           1448.69|
|    Denmark|          2121.2275|
+-----------+------------------+
only showing top 10 rows

res33: Array[org.apache.spark.sql.Row] = Array([Sweden,5028.5599999999995], [Germany,14355.9965], [France,4140.437499999999])
+-----------+------------------+
|ShipCountry|      ProductSales|
+-----------+------------------+
|        USA|17982.369499999997|
|    Germany|         14355.9965|
|    Austria|11492.791500000001|
|     Brazil|          8029.7585|
|    Ireland|           7337.485|
|     Canada|5137.8099999999995|
|     Sweden|5028.5599999999995|
|     France|  4140.437499999999|
|  Venezuela|          4004.261|
|    Denmark|          2121.2275|
+-----------+------------------+
only showing top 10 rows
```

Interestingly, this worked on the first try, the credit for which goes to the Spark developers. We could also format the printout with currency as well. I leave that as an exercise to be done by you! Try and run different queries and verify that the results are as expected.

Aftermath

As seen in the preceding screenshot, this was a good exercise. Also, Spark 2.0 has made the interfaces simpler and powerful. We are thoroughly impressed! We just created the last query and it ran fine. The Spark developers have done a good job. Good work, guys!

The Dataset also includes the `product` table, which I leave to you as an exercise. For example, you can work on a query that returns sales by product or one that shows the products that are selling more. The Dataset also has date fields, such as `order dates`, which you can use to query sales by quarters, and reports, such as `Product sales for 1997`. The dates are now read in as strings. They need to be converted to the `TIMESTAMP` data type.

References

The references are listed here:

- `https://northwinddatabase.codeplex.com/releases/view/71634`
- `https://databricks.com/blog/215/1/9/spark-sql-data-sources-api-unified-data-access-for-the-spark-platform.html`
- `https://spark.apache.org/docs/latest/sql-programming-guide.html`

Summary

This was an important chapter that discussed the integration aspects of Spark and SQL. We have covered the main parts, namely Datasets and programmatic access. However, there are more capabilities, such as the JDBC/ODBC server for direct SQL queries. On the integration side, you will see more integration capabilities in `Chapter 10`, *Spark with Big Data*. Spark SQL will be getting more features in the future versions, and I think this will be one of the areas that will grow at a much faster pace.

9
Foundations of Datasets/DataFrames – The Proverbial Workhorse for DataScientists

From a data wrangling perspective, Datasets are the most important feature of Spark 2.0.0. In this chapter, we will first look at Datasets from a stack perspective, including layering, optimizations, and so forth. Then we will delve more deeply into the actual Dataset APIs and cover the various operations, starting from reading various formats to creating Datasets and finally covering the rich capabilities for queries, aggregations, and scientific operations. We will use the car and orders Datasets for our examples.

Datasets – a quick introduction

A Spark Dataset is a group of specified heterogeneous columns, akin to a spreadsheet or a relational database table. RDDs have always been the basic building blocks of Spark and they still are. But RDDs deal with objects; we might know what the objects are but the framework doesn't. So things such as type checking and semantic queries are not possible with RDDs. Then came DataFrames, which added schemas; we can associate schemas with an RDD. DataFrames also added SQL and SQL-like capabilities.

Spark 2.0.0 added Datasets, which have all the original DataFrame APIs as well as compile-time type checking, thus making our interfaces richer and more robust. So now we have three mechanisms:

- Our preferred mechanism is the semantic-rich Datasets
- Our second option is the use of DataFrames as untyped views in a Dataset
- For low-level operations, we'll use RDDs as the underlying basic distributed objects

In short, we should always use the Dataset APIs and abstractions. RDDs are akin to low-level APIs, which we do go to, occasionally. In fact, in this book, I had a few such occasions/places where I couldn't find appropriate Dataset APIs. Maybe there are Dataset options that I don't know about. So familiar RDD operations do come to the rescue. The advantage is that you can move from Datasets to RDDs and vice versa. So when needed, the pattern to follow is this: convert to RDD, do the low-level operation, and then convert back to a Dataset.

A few points to remember:

- For Python and R, the class is still DataFrame, but with all the Dataset APIs. So you can think as of it as this: Datasets in Python and R are called DataFrames. The APIs map exactly, so it is easy to keep the mental model straight.
- In Scala and Java, Datasets are the main interface and there is no DataFrame class.
- You will still see the name DataFrame, as in DataFrame Reader, DataFrame Writer, and so on. For all practical purposes, the words DataFrame and Dataset are interchangeable. And you will know when the difference matters.

Dataset APIs – an overview

Before we delve into Datasets and data wrangling, let's take a broader view of the APIs; we will focus on the relevant functions we need. This will give us a firm foundation when we wrangle with data later in this chapter. Refer to the following diagram:

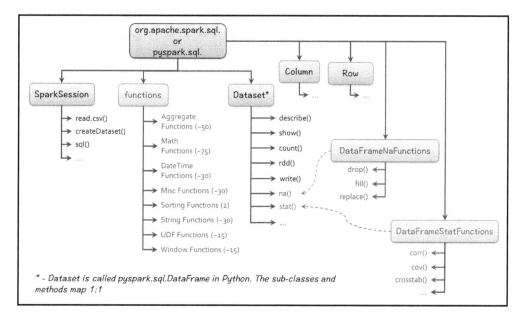

The preceding diagram shows the broader hierarchy of the `org.apache.spark.sql` classes. Interestingly, `pyspark.sql` mirrors this hierarchy, except for DataFrame, which is basically the Scala Dataset. What I like about the PySpark interface is that it is very succinct and crisp, offering the same power, performance, and functionality as Scala or Java. But Scala has more elaborate hierarchies and more abstractions. One of the tricks to learn more about its functions is to refer to the Scala documentation, which I found to be a lot more detailed.

Each of these classes is rich with a lot of functions. The diagram shows only the most common ones we need in this chapter. You should refer to either `https://spark.apache.o rg/docs/latest/api/scala/index.html#org.apache.spark.sql.package` or `https://s park.apache.org/docs/latest/api/python/pyspark.sql.html` to get full coverage.

In this book, and more so in this chapter, we encourage polyglot programming, moving between a compiled language, such as Scala/Java, and an interpreted one, such as Python/R. For data wrangling, the interpreted languages Python/R are more suitable. And the Scala Dataset/Python DataFrame makes it very easy to be in both languages, without any performance penalty.

org.apache.spark.sql.SparkSession/pyspark.sql.SparkSession

SparkSession is the single entry point, and it has the create, read, and SQL functions that are relevant to us:

- The `createDataset()` is a good way to create a Dataset from an RDD.
- The `SparkSession.read` library is very rich in semantics. You can read CSV files (`SparkSession.read.csv()`), text files (`SparkSession.read.text()`), Parquet (`SparkSession.read.parquet()`), JDBC(`SparkSession.read.jdbc()`), JSON (`SparkSession.read.json()`), and other formats. Each format has its own options appropriate to the respective format so that you can have good control over how the files are read and Datasets created.
- The `write()` method is also equally capable, and it is available as a function in the Dataset, for example, `df.write.csv()`.
- The `SparkSession.sql()` method takes a SQL query. We have covered this in `Chapter 8`, *Spark SQL*.
- If for any reason, you need SparkContext, it is encapsulated. So the `SparkSession.sparkContext` method returns the underlying SparkContext, which you can use to create RDDs as well as manage cluster resources.

org.apache.spark.sql.Dataset/pyspark.sql.DataFrame

The `sql.Dataset/sql.DataFrame` class is the primary choice for data wrangling in Scala/Python. It has more than 100 functions. Some of the functions, such as `na.*` and `stat.*`, are mapped from the `sql.DataFrameNaFunctions` and `sql.DataFrameStatFunctions` packages. This is for convenience, as the `na` and `stat` functions are used extensively for data exploration.

org.apache.spark.sql.{Column,Row}/pyspark.sql.(Column,Row)

While there is no need to use the `Column` and `Row` objects, operations, such as `map()`, are done at the row level and aggregation functions, such as sum, mean, and variance, are done at the column level. These are done transparently, but it is good to be aware that the underlying objects are `Row` and `Column`. Sometimes, low-level operations require us to recognize that we are dealing with a `Row/Column` object, and so we must index the values appropriately.

org.apache.spark.sql.Column

The `sql.Column` class is very simple and elegant in what it does.

First of all, it enables you to select a column by either the `df("<columnName>")` or `df.<columnName>` notation.

As we saw, there are two ways of accessing a column, either the dotted way (`df.<columnName>`, for example, `orders.date`) or the quoted way (`df["columnName"]`, for example, `orders["date"]`). You're recommended to use `df("<columnName>")` because a column name can collide with a DataFrame method if we use `df.<columnName>`. Also, the dotted method won't work when we want to create a new column or if the column name has embedded spaces.

Second, we are able to perform column-wise operations such as `+,-, *,/,%` (modulo),`&&`,`||`, `<`,`<=`,`>`, and `>=`. This way, we can perform an operation of this nature: `df("total") = df("price") * df("qty")`. We will see the total price example at the end of this subsection. The `sql.Column` class has some interesting operations: the inequality operator is `!==`, the usual equal to operator is `===`, and an equality test that is safe for null values is `<=>`. We will check out a snippet of the inequality test to calculate the accuracy of a classification algorithm.

Third, we are able to perform meta operations, such as type conversion, alias, not null, and so forth. Column types can be converted using a cast operator like this: `df_cars.mpg.cast("double")`. Column names can be changed using the alias operator. Scala has the `as()` operator, and Python has the alias method, `df_cars.mpg.cast("double").alias('mpg')`.

It is a good practice to not change column names in the middle of a program, unless it is essential. Comment on what is being done and why. You will thank yourself later!

Finally, it provides you with operations that affect the Dataset/DataFrame organization. You can drop a column with `df.drop(<columnName>);` of course, as Datasets/DataFrames are immutable, you will get a new Dataset/DataFrame minus the column.

org.apache.spark.sql.Row

The `sql.Row` class is a lot simpler than `sql.Column`. The `Row` object by itself is usually transparent and implicit; one example is, operations such as Map, which operates over a DataFrame row by row. Thus, the parameter type for a lambda is `Row`. The elements of `Row` can be accessed by an ordinal, that is, `row(0)`, or by a name (`row("<name of field>");` the length/size gives the number of elements.

org.apache.spark.sql.functions/pyspark.sql.functions

Of all the classes, I think `sql.functions` class is the richest and provides the power that a Dataset has. In a nutshell, `sql.functions` have methods such as `split()` and `dateDiff()`, which work at the column level. The normal versions of these functions, whether they are in Scala or Python, act on single variables. The `sql.functions` class enables us to apply these functions to the Dataset columns in a distributed and optimized fashion.

Dataset interfaces and functions

Now let's work out a few interesting examples, starting out with a simple one and then moving on to progressively complex operations.

The code files are in `fdps-v3/code`, and the data files are in `fdps-v3/data`. You can run the code either from a Scala IDE or just from the Spark Shell.

Start Spark Shell from the bin directory where you have installed the spark:

```
/Volumes/sdxc-01/spark-2.0.0/bin/spark-shell
```

Inside the shell, the following command will load the source:

```
:load /Users/ksankar/fdps-v3/code/DS01.scala
```

Read/write operations

As we saw earlier, `SparkSession.read.*` gives us a rich set of features to read different types of data with flexible control over the options. `Dataset.write.*` does the same for writing data:

```scala
val spark = SparkSession.builder
      .master("local")
      .appName("Chapter 9")
      .config("spark.logConf","true")
      .config("spark.logLevel","ERROR")
      .getOrCreate()
println("Running Spark Version ${spark.version}")
//
val startTime = System.nanoTime()
//
// Read Data
//
val filePath = "/Users/ksankar/fdps-v3/"
val cars = spark.read.option("header","true").
option("inferSchema","true").
csv(filePath + "data/spark-csv/cars.csv")
println("Cars has "+cars.count()+" rows")
cars.show(5)
cars.printSchema()
//
// Write data
// csv format with headers
cars.write.mode("overwrite").option("header","true").csv(filePath +
"data/cars-out-csv.csv")
    // Parquet format
cars.write.mode("overwrite").partitionBy("year").parquet(filePath +
"data/cars-out-pqt")
```

We start the Spark Shell, load the `DS01.scala` file, and run the `DS01.main()` function.

The data read completes successfully and we can see the data and the schema as follows:

```
scala> DS01.main(Array("Hello","World"))
/Users/ksankar
16/07/27 14:55:14 WARN SparkSession$Builder: Use an existing SparkSession,
Running Spark Version 2.0.0
Cars has 4 rows
+----+-----+-----+--------------------+-----+
|year| make|model|             comment|blank|
+----+-----+-----+--------------------+-----+
|2012|Tesla|    S|          No comment|     |
|1997| Ford| E350|Go get one now th...|     |
|2015|Chevy| Volt|                    |     |
|2016|Volvo| XC90|         Good Car !|     |
+----+-----+-----+--------------------+-----+

root
 |-- year: integer (nullable = true)
 |-- make: string (nullable = true)
 |-- model: string (nullable = true)
 |-- comment: string (nullable = true)
 |-- blank: string (nullable = true)
```

The write also completes successfully. We can see the files and the directories as follows:

```
▼ 📁 data
     .DS_Store
  ▼ 📁 cars-out-pqt
       .DS_Store
       _SUCCESS
    ▼ 📁 year=1997
         .part-r-00000-e29cce70-59b0-417f-8645-30d4a5a92ccd.snappy.parquet.crc
         part-r-00000-e29cce70-59b0-417f-8645-30d4a5a92ccd.snappy.parquet
    ▼ 📁 year=2012
         .part-r-00000-e29cce70-59b0-417f-8645-30d4a5a92ccd.snappy.parquet.crc
         part-r-00000-e29cce70-59b0-417f-8645-30d4a5a92ccd.snappy.parquet
    ▶ 📁 year=2015
    ▶ 📁 year=2016
  ▼ 📁 cars-out-csv.csv
       _SUCCESS
       .part-r-00000-4f49a365-52b8-450e-a7f3-76a71dd2b3e6.csv.crc
       part-r-00000-4f49a365-52b8-450e-a7f3-76a71dd2b3e6.csv
```

Because we used `partitionBy("year")`, Spark created four subdirectories. The partitioning is useful for push-down queries; for example, if a query has **year=1997**, then the data for only that year will need to be selected while ignoring all of the other data. Remember that our data comprises only four records, but it might very well be a million records and part of a big data lake. In that case, the partitioning will save us a lot of reading.

We can also see that the compression is snappy, by default.

> To read the file back, we could use the
> `SparkSession.read.parquet(filePath + "data/cars-out-pqt")`
> call to create a new Dataset.

The CSV write also succeeds and we can inspect the file to check whether it has the headers. It does! The mode parameter in write controls what happens when the file, exists as follows:

Mode Parameter	Description
`SaveMode.Overwrite` or overwrite	This is used to overwrite existing files
`SaveMode.Append` or append	This is used to append to an existing file
`SaveMode.Ignore` or ignore	This is used to ignore the `Data Exists` error silently and not save. Use this parameter with caution
`SaveMode.Errorif` exists or error	This is used to raise an exception if the file exists (default). How do we reset this?

> A little bit of history: prior to 1.4, SQLContext had lots of data source functions, including JSON. In 1.4, these functions were moved to the `pyspark.sql.DataFrameReader` class and specifically the `read()` function. In 2.0, the `read()` functions are consolidated under the `SparkSession` class. The read/write framework is also very extensible in 2.0, and we can add support for new data storage formats with the driver classes.

Aggregate functions

One of the first things a data scientist would do to explore new data is calculate general functions such as min, max, mean, and standard deviation. The next step is to find the numbers by groups, which gives one an idea about how the groups are laid out in the sample data. In this section, we will explore the car mileage data:

```
val filePath = "/Users/ksankar/fdps-v3/"
val cars = spark.read.option("header","true").
  option("inferSchema","true").
csv(filePath + "data/car-data/car-mileage.csv")
println("Cars has "+cars.count()+" rows")
cars.show(5)
cars.printSchema()
```

```
//
cars.describe("mpg","hp","weight","automatic").show()
//
cars.groupBy("automatic").avg("mpg","torque").show()
//
cars.groupBy().avg("mpg","torque").show()
cars.agg(avg(cars("mpg")), mean(cars("torque")) ).show()
```

Here, the `describe` method shows the min, max, mean, and standard deviation. We can also find the numbers by groups, say what is the mpg for automatic versus manual transmissions? Interestingly, if we want to get the numbers outside describe, we can use the `agg` function and give it with the function and the column. Remember the function comes from the hundreds of functions available in `sql.functions`. We import the required function like this:

```
import org.apache.spark.sql.functions.{avg,mean}
```

The code file is `DS02.scala`. We load the code and run the `DS02` object. The output is as expected:

```
+-------+-----------------+-----------------+----------------+------------------+
|summary|              mpg|               hp|          weight|         automatic|
+-------+-----------------+-----------------+----------------+------------------+
|  count|               32|               32|              32|                32|
|   mean|         20.223125|          136.875|       3586.6875|           0.71875|
| stddev|6.318289089312789|44.98082028541039|947.943187269323|0.4568034093991743|
|    min|             11.2|               70|            1905|                 0|
|    max|             36.5|              223|            5430|                 1|
+-------+-----------------+-----------------+----------------+------------------+


+---------+-----------------+----------------+
|automatic|         avg(mpg)|     avg(torque)|
+---------+-----------------+----------------+
|        1|17.32478260869565|257.363636363636|
|        0|27.63000000000006|         109.375|
+---------+-----------------+----------------+


+---------+-----------+
| avg(mpg)|avg(torque)|
+---------+-----------+
|20.223125|      217.9|
+---------+-----------+


+---------+-----------+
| avg(mpg)|avg(torque)|
+---------+-----------+
|20.223125|      217.9|
+---------+-----------+
```

We get the summary of the whole Dataset. Also, the aggregation functions work well. So long as you understand `groupBy()` and use `sql.functions` with `agg()`, you have enough power to explore the data.

For example, the preceding mpg cross-table might lead us to the conclusion that manual automobiles have better mileage. Let's take a closer look:

```
cars.groupBy("automatic").avg("mpg","torque","hp","weight").show()
```

The code gives following output in response:

```
+---------+------------------+-----------------+-----------------+------------------+
|automatic|          avg(mpg)|     avg(torque)|          avg(hp)|       avg(weight)|
+---------+------------------+-----------------+-----------------+------------------+
|        1|17.324782608695646|257.3636363636364|            157.0| 4037.391304347826|
|        0|27.630000000000006|          109.375|85.44444444444444|2434.8888888888887|
+---------+------------------+-----------------+-----------------+------------------+
```

Looking at the mean of **torque** and **hp**, we realize that, for this Dataset, the cars with automatic transmission also have larger torque and higher hp. And, they also weigh more. So we cannot make a generalization that manual transmission provides better mileage.

Interestingly, `groupBy()` has an alias: `groupby()`. I prefer the camel case, but lowercase is not a mistake!

There are two types of aggregations: one on column values and the other on subsets of column values, that is, grouped values of some other columns. Full column aggregation functions act on all the values on a column (actually shorthand for the null group by, that is, `df.groupBy().agg...`); for example, if you want the average sales for the last three years combined, you can use `sql.functions.avg("sales")`. But if you want the average sales by year, you will need to use `sql.functions.groupby("year").agg("sales":"avg")`.

Statistical functions

Next, let's explore statistical functions. As we saw in the API diagram in the *Dataset APIs – an overview* section, the functions are available under `sql.stat.*`:

```
val cor = cars.stat.corr("hp","weight")
    println("hp to weight : Correlation = %.4f".format(cor))
val cov = cars.stat.cov("hp","weight")
    println("hp to weight : Covariance = %.4f".format(cov))
```

```
//
cars.stat.crosstab("automatic","NoOfSpeed").show()
//
```

The code is in `DS03.scala`. We load and run the `DS03` object. The output is is as follows:

```
scala> :load /Users/ksankar/fdps-v3/code/DS03.scala
Loading /Users/ksankar/fdps-v3/code/DS03.scala...
import org.apache.spark.sql.SparkSession
defined object DS03

scala> DS03.main(Array("Hello","World"))
/Users/ksankar
16/07/27 17:13:05 WARN SparkSession$Builder: Use an existing SparkSession
Running Spark Version 2.0.0
Cars has 32 rows
hp to weight : Correlation = 0.8834
hp to weight : Covariance = 37667.5403
+------------------+---+---+---+
|automatic_NoOfSpeed|  3|  4|  5|
+------------------+---+---+---+
|                 1| 23|  0|  0|
|                 0|  1|  5|  3|
+------------------+---+---+---+

Elapsed time: 6.20 seconds
*** That's All Folks ! ***
```

The output looks good. The correlation provides an understandable number rather than covariance. The cross tab is an interesting and very useful function. The `CrossTabulation` function provides a table of the frequency distribution for a set of variables. We can see that the automatic transmission engines have only three speed values, while the manual have 3, 4, and 5 speed values.

Let's use the `crosstab` function to explore the Titanic Dataset. This Dataset is a list of passengers with their attributes, such as name and age, and information related to whether they are traveling with spouse/siblings and so forth. And most importantly, it provides information on whether they have survived. A good Dataset to explore and ask questions is as follows:

- How many of each gender survived?
- Did age make any difference?
- Did passengers traveling with spouses/siblings have a better chance of survival?

In `Chapter 11`, *Machine Learning with Spark ML Pipelines*, we will use machine learning libraries to predict the survival. Here, we want to get a feel for the data and see whether there are any trends. And this would be a good measure of the data science capabilities of Spark. Refer to the following code:

```
val filePath = "/Users/ksankar/fdps-v3/"
  val passengers = spark.read.option("header","true").
  option("inferSchema","true").
  csv(filePath + "data/titanic3_02.csv")
  println("Passengers has "+passengers.count()+" rows")
    //passengers.show(5)
    //passengers.printSchema()
    //
  val passengers1 =
passengers.select(passengers("Pclass"),passengers("Survived"),passengers("G
ender"),passengers("Age"),passengers("SibSp"),passengers("Parch"),passenger
s("Fare"))
  passengers1.show(5)
  passengers1.printSchema()
    //
  passengers1.groupBy("Gender").count().show()
  passengers1.stat.crosstab("Survived","Gender").show()
    //
  passengers1.stat.crosstab("Survived","SibSp").show()
    //
    // passengers1.stat.crosstab("Survived","Age").show()
  val ageDist =  passengers1.select(passengers1("Survived"),
(passengers1("age") - passengers1("age") %
10).cast("int").as("AgeBracket"))
  ageDist.show(3)
  ageDist.stat.crosstab("Survived","AgeBracket").show()
```

The `read.csv` file loads the data. We select a few columns that are of interest to us and apply aggregate functions such as count and crosstab to get our answers.

The code is in `DS04.scala`. We load and run the `DS04` object. The output is interesting:

```
scala> DS04.main(Array("Hello","World"))
/Users/ksankar
16/07/27 18:08:56 WARN SparkSession$Builder: Use an existing SparkSession,
Running Spark Version 2.0.0
Passengers has 1309 rows
+------+--------+------+------+-----+-----+--------+
|Pclass|Survived|Gender|   Age|SibSp|Parch|    Fare|
+------+--------+------+------+-----+-----+--------+
|     1|       1|female|  29.0|    0|    0|211.3375|
|     1|       1|  male|0.9167|    1|    2|  151.55|
|     1|       0|female|   2.0|    1|    2|  151.55|
|     1|       0|  male|  30.0|    1|    2|  151.55|
|     1|       0|female|  25.0|    1|    2|  151.55|
+------+--------+------+------+-----+-----+--------+
only showing top 5 rows

root
 |-- Pclass: integer (nullable = true)
 |-- Survived: integer (nullable = true)
 |-- Gender: string (nullable = true)
 |-- Age: double (nullable = true)
 |-- SibSp: integer (nullable = true)
 |-- Parch: integer (nullable = true)
 |-- Fare: double (nullable = true)
```

The data load and the schema look good as shown in the preceding screenshot. Now check this out:

```
+------+-----+
|Gender|count|
+------+-----+
|female|  466|
|  male|  843|
+------+-----+


+---------------+------+----+
|Survived_Gender|female|male|
+---------------+------+----+
|              1|   339| 161|
|              0|   127| 682|
+---------------+------+----+
```

In the preceding screenshot, we see that most of the males perished and the females survived:

```
+--------------+---+---+---+---+---+---+---+
|Survived_SibSp|  0|  1|  2|  3|  4|  5|  8|
+--------------+---+---+---+---+---+---+---+
|             1|309|163| 19|  6|  3|  0|  0|
|             0|582|156| 23| 14| 19|  6|  9|
+--------------+---+---+---+---+---+---+---+
```

The SibSp flag (sibling/spouse) is an indication, but not fully conclusive. Maybe we could try SibSp and gender. I leave that as an exercise for you to pursue.

If we do a crosstab on the age, we'll get a long table for each number, as shown here:

```
16/07/27 17:44:01 WARN Utils: Truncated the string representation of a plan since it was too large. This behavior can be adjusted by setting 'spark.debug.ma
xToStringFields' in SparkEnv.conf.
+---------+----+----+----+----+----+----+----+----+----+----+----+----+----+----+----+----+----+----+----+----+----+----+----+----+----+----+----+----+----+---
-+----+----+----+----+----+----+----+----+----+----+----+----+----+----+----+----+----+----+----+----+----+----+----+----+----+----+----+----+----+----+----+---
---+----+----+----+----+----+----+----+----+----+----+----+----+----+----+---+----+
|Survived_Age|0.1667|0.3333|0.4167|0.6667|0.75|0.8333|0.9167|1.0|10.0|11.0|11.5|12.0|13.0|14.0|14.5|15.0|16.0|17.0|18.0|18.5|19.0|20.0|20.5|21.0|22.0|22
.5|23.0|23.5|24.0|24.5|25.0|26.0|26.5|27.0|28.0|28.5|29.0|3.0|30.0|30.5|31.0|32.0|32.5|33.0|34.0|34.5|35.0|36.0|36.5|37.0|38.0|38.5|39.0|4.0|40.0|40.5|41.0|
42.0|43.0|44.0|45.0|45.5|46.0|47.0|48.0|49.0|5.0|50.0|51.0|52.0|53.0|54.0|55.0|55.5|56.0|57.0|58.0|59.0|6.0|60.0|60.5|61.0|62.0|63.0|64.0|65.0|66.0|67.0|7.0
|70.0|70.5|71.0|74.0|76.0|8.0|80.0|9.0|null|
+---------+----+----+----+----+----+----+----+----+----+----+----+----+----+----+----+----+----+----+----+----+----+----+----+----+----+----+----+----+----+---
-+----+----+----+----+----+----+----+----+----+----+----+----+----+----+----+----+----+----+----+----+----+----+----+----+----+----+----+----+----+----+----+---
---+----+----+----+----+----+----+----+----+----+----+----+----+----+----+---+----+
|         |  1|  1|  0|  1|  1|  2|  3|  2|  7|  0|  1|  0|  3|  3|  4|  0|  5|  8|  7| 14|  0| 11|  4|  8|  0| 11| 20|
  0| 10|  0| 22|  0| 11| 11|  0| 13|  8|  0| 13|  5| 15|  0| 12| 11|  1|  9|  6|  0| 13| 14|  1|  2|  6|  0|  8|  7|  6|  0|  2|
  6|  3|  3| 14|  0|  0|  3| 10|  5|  4|  6|  3|  3|  4|  5|  4|  0|  2|  0|  4|  1|  3|  4|  0|  0|  2|  2|  2|  0|  0|  0|  2
|  0|  0|  0|  0|  1|  4|  1|  4| 73|
|         |  0|  0|  1|  0|  0|  1|  0|  0|  3|  4|  1|  0|  2|  4|  2|  1| 11| 13| 25|  3| 18|  8| 15|  1| 30| 23|
  1| 16|  1| 25|  1| 23| 19|  1| 17| 24|  3| 17|  2| 25|  2| 11| 13|  3| 12| 10|  2| 10| 17|  1|  7|  8|  1| 12|  3| 12|  3|  9|
 12|  6|  7|  7|  2|  6| 11|  4|  4|  1|  9|  5|  3|  0|  5|  4|  1|  2|  5|  2|  2|  3|  3|  1|  5|  3|  2|  3|  3|  1|  1|  2
|  2|  1|  2|  1|  0|  2|  0|  6|190|
+---------+----+----+----+----+----+----+----+----+----+----+----+----+----+----+----+----+----+----+----+----+----+----+----+----+----+----+----+----+----+---
-+----+----+----+----+----+----+----+----+----+----+----+----+----+----+----+----+----+----+----+----+----+----+----+----+----+----+----+----+----+----+----+---
---+----+----+----+----+----+----+----+----+----+----+----+----+----+----+---+----+
```

So we need to find a better scheme. And of course, this is easy with the following code:

```scala
val ageDist =  passengers1.select(passengers1("Survived"),
(passengers1("age") - passengers1("age") %
10).cast("int").as("AgeBracket"))
ageDist.show(3)
ageDist.stat.crosstab("Survived","AgeBracket").show()
```

If you look at the code closely, you will see that operations such as % and – are not normal Scala operations, but rather those from `sql.Column`. This is where the `Column` object and the operations defined there come in handy.

So let's create a new `ColumnAgeBracket` and a new Dataset with `AgeBracket` and the `Survived` columns, then crosstab `AgeBracket` with `Survived`. The output looks much better:

```
+--------+----------+
|Survived|AgeBracket|
+--------+----------+
|      1|        20|
|      1|         0|
|      0|         0|
+--------+----------+
only showing top 3 rows


+----------------+---+---+---+---+---+---+---+---+---+----+
|Survived_AgeBracket|  0| 10| 20| 30| 40| 50| 60| 70| 80|null|
+----------------+---+---+---+---+---+---+---+---+---+----+
|                   1| 50| 56|127| 98| 52| 32| 10|  1|  1|  73|
|                   0| 32| 87|217|134| 83| 38| 22|  6|  0| 190|
+----------------+---+---+---+---+---+---+---+---+---+----+
```

Lots of people in the 20s and 30s, which means about 50 percent of the people survived. There are lots of people whose age is null.

Anyway, in short, the Spark 2.0.0 Dataset did pass the data wrangling test with flying colors! With a few lines of code, we were able to get some answers. In `Chapter 11`, *Machine Learning with Spark ML Pipelines,* we will explore whether we can predict survival using the decision tree machine learning algorithm.

Scientific functions

Unlike the `na` and `stat` functions, scientific functions are not mapped. So we have to import them from `sql.functions` and then invoke them. Scientific functions include `log()`, `log10()`, `sqrt()`, `cbrt()`,`exp()`, `pow()`, `sin()`, `cos()`, `tan()`, `acos()`, `asin()`, `atan()`, `toDegrees()`, and `toRadians()`. Some interesting functions include `expm1(<columnName>)`, which computes the exponent of value-1, `log10p()` , the log of value plus 1 (presumably to accommodate when the value is 0), and `hypot()`, the hypotenuse. All these functions take column names or a column object, which is very versatile in that sense. Let's see some quick examples.

We will use the `log`, `log10`, `sqrt`, and `hypo` functions. We need to import them:

```
importorg.apache.spark.sql.functions.{log,log10,sqrt,hypot}
```

Next, create an RDD and then a Dataset out of it:

```
val aList : List[Int] = List(10,100,1000)
varaRDD = spark.sparkContext.parallelize(aList)
val sqlContext = spark.sqlContext
importsqlContext.implicits._
val ds = spark.createDataset(aRDD)
ds.show()
```

Then, run the functions on the Dataset:

```
ds.select( ds("value"), log(ds("value")).as("ln")).show()
ds.select( ds("value"), log10(ds("value")).as("log10")).show()
ds.select( ds("value"), sqrt(ds("value")).as("sqrt")).show()
```

Of course, these are functions from the SQL package, not from normal Scala functions.

The code is DS05.scala. We load the file and run the object DS05. The result looks like this:

```
scala> :load /Users/ksankar/fdps-v3/code/DS05.scala
Loading /Users/ksankar/fdps-v3/code/DS05.scala...
import org.apache.spark.sql.SparkSession
import org.apache.spark.sql.functions.{log, log10, sqrt, hypot}
defined object DS05

scala> DS05.main(Array("Hello","World"))
/Users/ksankar
16/07/27 19:39:34 WARN SparkSession$Builder: Use an existing SparkSession,
Running Spark Version 2.0.0
+-----+
|value|
+-----+
|   10|
|  100|
| 1000|
+-----+

+-----+-----------------+
|value|               ln|
+-----+-----------------+
|   10|2.302585092994046|
|  100|4.605170185988092|
| 1000|6.907755278982137|
+-----+-----------------+

+-----+-----+
|value|log10|
+-----+-----+
|   10|  1.0|
|  100|  2.0|
| 1000|  3.0|
+-----+-----+
```

The log will indicate null if the value of a row is :

```
+-----+----------------+
|value|              ln|
+-----+----------------+
|    0|            null|
|   10|2.302585092994046|
|  100|4.605170185988092|
| 1000|6.907755278982137|
+-----+----------------+
```

In such cases, `log1p()` comes in handy. This is good for machine learning formulas. Many formulas add the value 1 before the log, that is, `log(x+1)`, to take care of when `x = 0`:

```
+-----+----------------+
|value|            ln1p|
+-----+----------------+
|    0|             0.0|
|   10|2.3978952727983707|
|  100| 4.61512051684126|
| 1000| 6.90875477931522|
+-----+----------------+
```

For example, the NFL ELO Algorithm's [NFL-ELO, 2015] Margin Of Victory Multiplier is calculated as *ln(abs(PointDifference)+1)*, which becomes when Pd=0. This is fine because when score the difference between the two teams is 0, a draw, their respective ELOs don't change (maybe the weaker team should get a small bump up of their ELO).

Next, we read a file that has two sides of triangles and then run the `hypot` function:

```
val filePath = "/Users/ksankar/fdps-v3/"
val data = spark.read.option("header","true").
option("inferSchema","true").
csv(filePath + "data/hypot.csv")
println("Data has "+data.count()+" rows")
data.show(5)
data.printSchema()
    //
data.select( data("X"),data("Y"),hypot(data("X"),data("Y")).as("hypot")
).show()
```

The result is as expected. We have six perfect Pythagorean triples:

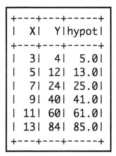

```
+---+---+-----+
|  X|  Y|hypot|
+---+---+-----+
|  3|  4|  5.0|
|  5| 12| 13.0|
|  7| 24| 25.0|
|  9| 40| 41.0|
| 11| 60| 61.0|
| 13| 84| 85.0|
+---+---+-----+
```

Data wrangling with Datasets

Now that we have covered Dataset API and how to use them in the abstract, let's take a small Dataset, apply our new skills, and extend the techniques we have learned. The **Northwind Sales** data has orders, order details, and products. Let's ask some questions and see how succinctly the Spark Dataset can answer them. The questions we need answers for are as follows:

- How many orders were placed by each customer?
- How many orders were placed in each country?
- How many orders were placed for each month/year?
- What is the total number of sales for each customer, year-wise?
- What is the average order by customer, year-wise?

Reading data into the respective Datasets

Our first mission, if we have to choose one, will be to read data into the respective Datasets. This is probably the easiest part; we have the versatile `read.csv()` file to do this.

The code is in `DS06.scala`. It has the code for all the steps, but we will work through the details step by step.

The read is easy, so we will just inspect the results. We have 830 orders and 2,155 order details. The schema looks fine for both the Datasets:

```
DS05.ma:load /Users/ksankar/fdps-v3/code/DS06.scala
Loading /Users/ksankar/fdps-v3/code/DS06.scala...
import org.apache.spark.sql.SparkSession
defined object DS06

scala> DS06.main(Array("Hello","World"))
/Users/ksankar
16/07/27 22:09:07 WARN SparkSession$Builder: Use an existing SparkSession,
Running Spark Version 2.0.0
Orders has 830 rows
+-------+----------+----------+---------+----------+
|OrderID|CustomerID|EmployeeID|OrderDate|ShipCountry|
+-------+----------+----------+---------+----------+
|  10248|     VINET|         5|   7/2/96|    France|
|  10249|     TOMSP|         6|   7/3/96|   Germany|
|  10250|     HANAR|         4|   7/6/96|    Brazil|
|  10251|     VICTE|         3|   7/6/96|    France|
|  10252|     SUPRD|         4|   7/7/96|   Belgium|
+-------+----------+----------+---------+----------+
only showing top 5 rows

root
 |-- OrderID: integer (nullable = true)
 |-- CustomerID: string (nullable = true)
 |-- EmployeeID: integer (nullable = true)
 |-- OrderDate: string (nullable = true)
 |-- ShipCountry: string (nullable = true)

Order Details has 2155 rows
+-------+---------+---------+---+--------+
|OrderID|ProductId|UnitPrice|Qty|Discount|
+-------+---------+---------+---+--------+
|  10248|       11|     14.0| 12|     0.0|
|  10248|       42|      9.8| 10|     0.0|
|  10248|       72|     34.8|  5|     0.0|
|  10249|       14|     18.6|  9|     0.0|
|  10249|       51|     42.4| 40|     0.0|
+-------+---------+---------+---+--------+
```

Aggregate and sort

If we go back to the questions we saw earlier, the first two are not that hard. The `groupBy()`, `count()`, and `sort()` method will do the trick. So let's get the easy part over and done with:

```
val orderByCustomer= orders.groupBy("CustomerID").count()
orderByCustomer.sort(orderByCustomer("count").desc).show(5) // We have out
ans#1
//
val orderByCountry= orders.groupBy("ShipCountry").count()
orderByCountry.sort(orderByCountry("count").desc).show(5) // ans#2
```

As you can see, we use the column object's `desc` property to sort by descending order. The results are as expected.

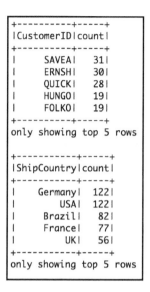

```
+----------+-----+
|CustomerID|count|
+----------+-----+
|     SAVEA|   31|
|     ERNSH|   30|
|     QUICK|   28|
|     HUNGO|   19|
|     FOLKO|   19|
+----------+-----+
only showing top 5 rows

+-----------+-----+
|ShipCountry|count|
+-----------+-----+
|    Germany|  122|
|        USA|  122|
|     Brazil|   82|
|     France|   77|
|         UK|   56|
+-----------+-----+
only showing top 5 rows
```

Date columns, totals, and aggregations

Now for the rest of the questions, we need to do a few aggregations and also create a couple of new columns. The steps are as follows:

1. Add the `OrderTotal` column to the Orders Dataset. Here are the steps to do this:
   1. Add the line total to the order details.
   2. Aggregate the total using the `orderID`.
   3. Join the order details and orders to add the order total.
   4. Check whether there are any null columns.
2. Add a date column.
3. Add the month and year.

The OrderTotal column

We have orders and order lines with the amount, quantity, and discount. We need to add an order total column to the orders table.

First, calculate the total for each line:

```
val orderDetails1 = orderDetails.select(orderDetails("OrderID"),
((orderDetails("UnitPrice") * orderDetails("Qty")) -
((orderDetails("UnitPrice") * orderDetails("Qty")) *
orderDetails("Discount")
)).as("OrderPrice"))
orderDetails1.show(5)
```

There are a lot of parentheses, but other than this the code is straightforward. Remember that the operations are actually performed on the columns. The output is as expected:

```
+-------+----------+
|OrderID|OrderPrice|
+-------+----------+
|  10248|     168.0|
|  10248|      98.0|
|  10248|     174.0|
|  10249|     167.4|
|  10249|    1696.0|
+-------+----------+
only showing top 5 rows
```

Now we can aggregate by the `orderID`, resulting in a Dataset that has the total for each order:

```
val orderTot =
orderDetails1.groupBy("OrderID").sum("OrderPrice").alias("OrderTotal")
orderTot.sort("OrderID").show(5)
```

The output is fine:

```
+-------+------------------+
|OrderID|   sum(OrderPrice)|
+-------+------------------+
|  10248|             440.0|
|  10249|            1863.4|
|  10250|1552.6000000000001|
|  10251|            654.06|
|  10252|            3597.9|
+-------+------------------+
```

It is easy to add the order total to the orders Dataset by joining the aggregated Dataset:

```
val orders1 = orders.join(orderTot,
orders("OrderID").equalTo(orderTot("OrderID")), "inner")
      .select(orders("OrderID"),
orders("CustomerID"),
orders("OrderDate"),
orders("ShipCountry").alias("ShipCountry"),
orderTot("sum(OrderPrice)").alias("Total"))
    //
orders1.sort("CustomerID").show()
    //
    // # 1.4. Check if there are any null columns
orders1.filter(orders1("Total").isNull).show()
    //
```

The join does the magic, and there are no nulls:

```
+-------+----------+-------------------+-----------+------------------+
|OrderID|CustomerID|          OrderDate|ShipCountry|             Total|
+-------+----------+-------------------+-----------+------------------+
|  11011|     ALFKI|1998-04-07 00:00:...|    Germany|             933.5|
|  10692|     ALFKI|1997-10-01 00:00:...|    Germany|             878.0|
|  10702|     ALFKI|1997-10-11 00:00:...|    Germany|             330.0|
|  10835|     ALFKI|1998-01-13 00:00:...|    Germany|             845.8|
|  10643|     ALFKI|1997-08-23 00:00:...|    Germany|             814.5|
|  10952|     ALFKI|1998-03-14 00:00:...|    Germany|             471.2|
|  10308|     ANATR|1996-09-16 00:00:...|     Mexico|              88.8|
|  10926|     ANATR|1998-03-02 00:00:...|     Mexico|             514.4|
|  10759|     ANATR|1997-11-26 00:00:...|     Mexico|             320.0|
|  10625|     ANATR|1997-08-06 00:00:...|     Mexico|            479.75|
|  10507|     ANTON|1997-04-13 00:00:...|     Mexico|          749.0625|
|  10365|     ANTON|1996-11-25 00:00:...|     Mexico|403.20000000000005|
|  10535|     ANTON|1997-05-11 00:00:...|     Mexico|            1940.85|
|  10573|     ANTON|1997-06-17 00:00:...|     Mexico|            2082.0|
|  10682|     ANTON|1997-09-23 00:00:...|     Mexico|             375.5|
|  10677|     ANTON|1997-09-20 00:00:...|     Mexico|           813.365|
|  10856|     ANTON|1998-01-26 00:00:...|     Mexico|             660.0|
|  10383|     AROUT|1996-12-14 00:00:...|         UK|             899.0|
|  10355|     AROUT|1996-11-13 00:00:...|         UK|             480.0|
|  10453|     AROUT|1997-02-19 00:00:...|         UK|             407.7|
+-------+----------+-------------------+-----------+------------------+
only showing top 20 rows


+-------+----------+---------+-----------+-----+
|OrderID|CustomerID|OrderDate|ShipCountry|Total|
+-------+----------+---------+-----------+-----+
+-------+----------+---------+-----------+-----+
```

Date operations

Date manipulation is much easier with 2.0.0 Datasets; they have very versatile conversion functions, which act on a column. We convert the order date to the date type and then extract the `Year` and `Month` columns:

```
val orders2 =      orders1.withColumn("Date",to_date(orders1("OrderDate")))
   orders2.show(2)
   orders2.printSchema()
   //
   // # 3. Add month and year
val orders3 =
orders2.withColumn("Month",month(orders2("OrderDate"))).withColumn("Year",y
ear(orders2("OrderDate")))
   orders3.show(2)
```

The `withColumn` function is very useful. You get a new Dataset with all the original columns plus the new column(s).

Be careful with the `to_date()` function. It takes the date in the yy-mm-dd format. Anything else doesn't work. Hopefully they will add a from-to format to specify the format of the string that we want to convert from.

The output is as expected:

```
+-------+----------+-------------------+-----------+------+----------+
|OrderID|CustomerID|          OrderDate|ShipCountry| Total|      Date|
+-------+----------+-------------------+-----------+------+----------+
|  10248|     VINET|1996-07-02 00:00:...|     France| 440.0|1996-07-02|
|  10249|     TOMSP|1996-07-03 00:00:...|    Germany|1863.4|1996-07-03|
+-------+----------+-------------------+-----------+------+----------+
only showing top 2 rows

root
 |-- OrderID: integer (nullable = true)
 |-- CustomerID: string (nullable = true)
 |-- OrderDate: timestamp (nullable = true)
 |-- ShipCountry: string (nullable = true)
 |-- Total: double (nullable = true)
 |-- Date: date (nullable = true)


+-------+----------+-------------------+-----------+------+----------+-----+----+
|OrderID|CustomerID|          OrderDate|ShipCountry| Total|      Date|Month|Year|
+-------+----------+-------------------+-----------+------+----------+-----+----+
|  10248|     VINET|1996-07-02 00:00:...|     France| 440.0|1996-07-02|    7|1996|
|  10249|     TOMSP|1996-07-03 00:00:...|    Germany|1863.4|1996-07-03|    7|1996|
+-------+----------+-------------------+-----------+------+----------+-----+----+
```

Final aggregations for the answers we want

Now that we have the Dataset with all the required columns, it is a question of applying the right aggregations:

```
// Q 3. How many orders by month/year ?
val ordersByYM = orders3.groupBy("Year","Month").sum("Total").as("Total")
   ordersByYM.sort(ordersByYM("Year"),ordersByYM("Month")).show()
```

Because we want year-wise and month-wise data, we group the data using two columns and sum the order total. To display the information, we can sort the data using two columns:

```
+----+-----+------------------+
|Year|Month|        sum(Total)|
+----+-----+------------------+
|1996|    7|30741.89499999997|
|1996|    8|         22726.875|
|1996|    9|           27691.4|
|1996|   10|         38380.125|
|1996|   11| 45694.44499999999|
|1996|   12|          52494.33|
|1997|    1| 51612.96999999994|
|1997|    2|38483.63499999995|
|1997|    3|40918.81999999985|
|1997|    4|         57116.7125|
|1997|    5|50270.330000000016|
|1997|    6|         34392.0825|
|1997|    7|         52744.6775|
|1997|    8|          46991.785|
|1997|    9| 57723.22749999999|
|1997|   10| 62253.62600000001|
|1997|   11|51294.80899999994|
|1997|   12| 67920.22850000001|
|1998|    1|107049.96049999999|
|1998|    2|         85240.8275|
+----+-----+------------------+
```

The yearly total sales for each customer are a simple aggregation:

```
// Q 4. Total Sales for each customer by year
var ordersByCY =
orders3.groupBy("CustomerID","Year").sum("Total").as("Total")
ordersByCY.sort(ordersByCY("CustomerID"),ordersByCY("Year")).show()
```

Once we know the trick, aggregation by another set of columns is just routine:

```
+----------+----+------------------+
|CustomerID|Year|       sum(Total)|
+----------+----+------------------+
|     ALFKI|1997|           2022.5|
|     ALFKI|1998|           2250.5|
|     ANATR|1996|             88.8|
|     ANATR|1997|           799.75|
|     ANATR|1998|            514.4|
|     ANTON|1996|403.20000000000005|
|     ANTON|1997|         5960.7775|
|     ANTON|1998|            660.0|
|     AROUT|1996|           1379.0|
|     AROUT|1997| 6406.900000000001|
|     AROUT|1998|          5604.75|
|     BERGS|1996|           4324.4|
|     BERGS|1997|         13849.015|
|     BERGS|1998|         6754.1625|
|     BLAUS|1997|           1079.8|
|     BLAUS|1998|           2160.0|
|     BLONP|1996|           9986.2|
|     BLONP|1997|          7817.88|
|     BLONP|1998|            730.0|
|     BOLID|1996|            982.0|
+----------+----+------------------+
```

The average total sales for each customer is another simple symmetric aggregation operation:

```
// Q 5. Average order by customer by year
ordersByCY = orders3.groupBy("CustomerID","Year").avg("Total").as("Total")
ordersByCY.sort(ordersByCY("CustomerID"),ordersByCY("Year")).show()
```

The fifth question is very similar to the fourth question, but we want the average, not the total. Again, this can be done using an easy column operation:

```
+---------+----+-----------------+
|CustomerID|Year|       avg(Total)|
+---------+----+-----------------+
|    ALFKI|1997| 674.1666666666666|
|    ALFKI|1998| 750.1666666666666|
|    ANATR|1996|              88.8|
|    ANATR|1997|           399.875|
|    ANATR|1998|             514.4|
|    ANTON|1996|403.20000000000005|
|    ANTON|1997|         1192.1555|
|    ANTON|1998|             660.0|
|    AROUT|1996|             689.5|
|    AROUT|1997| 915.2714285714286|
|    AROUT|1998|         1401.1875|
|    BERGS|1996|1441.4666666666665|
|    BERGS|1997|         1384.9015|
|    BERGS|1998|         1350.8325|
|    BLAUS|1997|            269.95|
|    BLAUS|1998|             720.0|
|    BLONP|1996|3328.7333333333336|
|    BLONP|1997|           1116.84|
|    BLONP|1998|             730.0|
|    BOLID|1996|             982.0|
+---------+----+-----------------+
```

Finally, the sixth question can be solved by just dropping the year and calculating the average for each customer:

```
// Q 6. Average order by customer
val ordersCA = orders3.groupBy("CustomerID").avg("Total").as("Total")
ordersCA.sort(ordersCA("avg(Total)").desc).show()
```

The output is as expected:

```
+---------+------------------+
|CustomerID|       avg(Total)|
+---------+------------------+
|    QUICK| 3938.475178571429|
|    ERNSH|3495.8326166666666|
|    SAVEA| 3366.514516129032|
|    RATTC|2838.7666944444445|
|    HUNGO|2630.5213157894736|
|    SIMOB|         2402.4425|
|    HANAR|2345.8121428571426|
|    FOLIG|           2333.38|
|    PICCO|          2312.886|
|    MEREP|2220.9376923076925|
|    KOENE|2207.7417142857144|
|    SUPRD|2007.3983333333333|
|    QUEEN| 1978.269038461539|
|    WHITC|1954.5432142857146|
|    RICSU|         1934.3779|
|    EASTC|        1845.129375|
|    SEVES|1801.7027777777776|
|    FRANK|1777.1039666666668|
|    BLONP|1684.9163636363637|
|    GREAL|1682.4954545454545|
+---------+------------------+
```

References

Here are some links you can refer to for more information:

- `https://databricks.com/blog/216/7/14/a-tale-of-three-apache-spark-a pis-rdds-dataframes-and-datasets.html`, which provides information on three Apache Spark APIs, RDDs, DataFrames, and Datasets; when to use them; and why to use them.
- `http://www.slideshare.net/databricks/spark-summit-san-francisco-216-matei-zaharia-keynote-apache-spark-2`
- `https://databricks.com/blog/216/5/11/spark-2--technical-preview-eas ier-faster-and-smarter.html`
- `https://doubleclix.wordpress.com/215/1/2/the-art-of-nfl-ranking-the -elo-algorithm-and-fivethirtyeight/`

Summary

This was an interesting chapter. Finally, we got to work with Dataset APIs, using real data. We also got a glimpse of API organization. Datasets and their associated classes have a lot of interesting functions for you to explore. Python APIs are very much similar to Scala APIs and sometimes a little easier. The IPython notebook is available at `https://github.com/xs ankar/fdps-v3/blob/master/extras/3-DataFrame-For-DS.ipynb`. Data wrangling with Python, and especially with Python notebooks, is the preferred way for data scientists.

10
Spark with Big Data

As we mentioned in Chapter 8, *Spark SQL*, the big data compute stack doesn't work in isolation. Integration points across multiple stacks and technologies are essential. In this chapter, we will look at how Spark works with some of the big data technologies that are part of the Hadoop ecosystem. We will cover the following topics in this chapter:

- **Parquet**: This is an efficient storage format
- **HBase**: This is the database in the Hadoop ecosystem

Parquet – an efficient and interoperable big data format

We explored the Parquet format in Chapter 7, *Spark 2.0 Concepts*. To recap, Parquet is essentially an interoperable storage format. Its main goals are space efficiency and query efficiency. Parquet's origin is based on Google's Dremel and was developed by Twitter and Cloudera. It is now an Apache incubator project. The nested storage format from Google Dremel is implemented in Parquet. It stores data in a columnar format and has an evolvable schema. This enables you to optimize queries (it can restrict the columns that you need to access and so you need not bring all the columns into the memory and discard the ones not needed), and it allows storage optimization (by decoding at the column level, which gives a much higher compression ratio). Another interesting feature is that Parquet can store nested Datasets. This feature can be leveraged in curated data lakes to store subject-based data. In addition to the ability to restrict column fetches during queries, Parquet 2.0 could implement push-down predicates. At the time of writing, the current Parquet version is 1.6.

Saving files in the Parquet format

In Chapter 9, *Spark SQL*, we loaded the Orders tables from the .csv format. Let's save the data in the Parquet format. Usually, one would take a .csv file, do transformations, and then store it in the Parquet format (for example, the Sales By Country Dataset that we created). The relevant part of the code is shown as follows. The full source is available at fdps-v3/code/BigData01v2-sshell.scala:

```
//
// Parquet Operations
//
orders.write.parquet(filePath + "Orders_Parquet")
```

It is that simple! With Spark 2.0.0, all of the write is consolidated and so we use the write.parquet() method for writing Parquet files. The methods, such as write.csv(), write.json(), and write.jdbc() help us save data in other formats.

```
USS-Defiant:~ ksankar$ cd ~/fdps-v3
USS-Defiant:fdps-v3 ksankar$ ~/Downloads/spark-2.0.0/bin/spark-shell
16/08/16 14:28:26 WARN NativeCodeLoader: Unable to load native-hadoop library for your platform.
  applicable
16/08/16 14:28:27 WARN SparkContext: Use an existing SparkContext, some configuration may not t
Spark context Web UI available at http://10.106.168.10:4040
Spark context available as 'sc' (master = local[*], app id = local-1471382907528).
Spark session available as 'spark'.
Welcome to
      ____              __
     / __/__  ___ _____/ /__
    _\ \/ _ \/ _ `/ __/  '_/
   /___/ .__/\_,_/_/ /_/\_\   version 2.0.0
      /_/

Using Scala version 2.11.8 (Java HotSpot(TM) 64-Bit Server VM, Java 1.7.0_60)
Type in expressions to have them evaluated.
Type :help for more information.

scala> :load "code/BigData01v2-sshell.scala"
Loading code/BigData01v2-sshell.scala...
defined class Order
defined class OrderDetails
Running Spark Version 2.0.0
```

`INFO` messages show us some of the inner details:

```
Saving in Parquet Format ....
[..]
16/08/16 13:49:53 INFO DefaultWriterContainer: Using user defined output
    committer class org.apache.parquet.hadoop.ParquetOutputCommitter
16/08/16 13:49:53 INFO FileOutputCommitter: File Output Committer Algorithm version is 1
16/08/16 13:49:53 INFO ParquetWriteSupport: Initialized Parquet WriteSupport with Catalyst schema:
{
  "type" : "struct",
  "fields" : [ {
    "name" : "OrderID",
    "type" : "string",
    "nullable" : true,
    "metadata" : { }
  }, {
    "name" : "CustomerID",
    "type" : "string",
    "nullable" : true,
    "metadata" : { }
  }, {
    "name" : "EmployeeID",
    "type" : "string",
    "nullable" : true,
    "metadata" : { }
  }, {
    "name" : "OrderDate",
    "type" : "string",
    "nullable" : true,
    "metadata" : { }
  }, {
    "name" : "ShipCountry",
    "type" : "string",
    "nullable" : true,
    "metadata" : { }
  } ]
}
and corresponding Parquet message type:
message spark_schema {
  optional binary OrderID (UTF8);
  optional binary CustomerID (UTF8);
  optional binary EmployeeID (UTF8);
  optional binary OrderDate (UTF8);
  optional binary ShipCountry (UTF8);
}
[..]
16/08/16 13:49:54 INFO DAGScheduler: Job 9 finished: parquet at BigData01v2.scala:32, took 0.652350 s
16/08/16 13:49:54 INFO DefaultWriterContainer: Job job_201608161349_0000 committed.
```

Even though we store the Parquet file in the local filesystem in this example, in an actual production system we would need to use HDFS to store the files. We can inspect the log entries and see that it has started a job with the `ParquetTableOperations` class. The scheme used to save this is **Run Length Encoding** (**RLE**). As you can see, we only need a couple of lines of code, and Spark does all of the hard work under the covers. It creates a directory, data, and metadata files underneath the main directory. It has created one (compressed) file, corresponding to one job for one partition, as shown next:

```
▼  Orders_Parquet
     _SUCCESS
     .part-r-00000-58647b09-2997-4c74-b136-47a3e372fe12.snappy.parquet.crc
     part-r-00000-58647b09-2997-4c74-b136-47a3e372fe12.snappy.parquet
```

Loading Parquet files

Now let's load the `Orders` Parquet files and see whether the data got saved correctly. The code, again, is deceptively simple, as shown here:

```
val parquetOrders = spark.read.parquet(filePath + "Orders_Parquet")
```

We use the `read.parquet()` method in the `SparkSession` object:

```
Reading back the Parquet Format ....
16/08/16 13:49:54 INFO SparkContext: Starting job: parquet at BigData01v2.scala:37
[..]
16/08/16 13:49:54 INFO FileSourceStrategy: Pruning directories with:
16/08/16 13:49:54 INFO FileSourceStrategy: Post-Scan Filters:
16/08/16 13:49:54 INFO FileSourceStrategy: Pruned Data Schema: struct<>
16/08/16 13:49:54 INFO FileSourceStrategy: Pushed Filters:
[..]
16/08/16 13:49:54 INFO DAGScheduler: Job 11 finished: count at BigData01v2.scala:38, took 0.064199 s
Orders_Parquet has 830 rows
[..]
16/08/16 13:49:54 INFO DAGScheduler: Job 12 finished: show at BigData01v2.scala:39, took 0.044264 s
+-------+----------+----------+---------+-----------+
|OrderID|CustomerID|EmployeeID|OrderDate|ShipCountry|
+-------+----------+----------+---------+-----------+
|  10248|     VINET|         5|   7/2/96|     France|
|  10249|     TOMSP|         6|   7/3/96|    Germany|
|  10250|     HANAR|         4|   7/6/96|     Brazil|
+-------+----------+----------+---------+-----------+
only showing top 3 rows
```

As you can see, the first few lines create all of the scaffolding and required definitions. The lazy evaluation does not do anything unless we ask for some action, such as `show(3)`. Spark does all the work reading the data. You can see that Spark figured out that there is a single file to process along with the field names and their types.

Note that you cannot overwrite a Parquet file, as shown here:

```
Exception in thread "main" org.apache.spark.sql.AnalysisException: path file:/Users/ksankar/fdps-v3/Orders.parquet already exists.;
        at org.apache.spark.sql.execution.datasources.InsertIntoHadoopFsRelation.run(InsertIntoHadoopFsRelation.scala:76)
        at org.apache.spark.sql.execution.ExecutedCommand.sideEffectResult$lzycompute(commands.scala:58)
        at org.apache.spark.sql.execution.ExecutedCommand.sideEffectResult(commands.scala:56)
        at org.apache.spark.sql.execution.ExecutedCommand.doExecute(commands.scala:70)
        at org.apache.spark.sql.execution.SparkPlan$$anonfun$execute$5.apply(SparkPlan.scala:132)
        at org.apache.spark.sql.execution.SparkPlan$$anonfun$execute$5.apply(SparkPlan.scala:130)
        at org.apache.spark.rdd.RDDOperationScope$.withScope(RDDOperationScope.scala:150)
```

Saving processed RDDs in the Parquet format

Now let's save our `SalesByCountry` report in the Parquet format. As we saw earlier, it is very simple and streamlined. We create views to the orders and order detail Datasets, run a SQL query, and write the resulting Dataset:

```
//
// Create views for tables
//
orders.createOrReplaceTempView("OrdersTable")
orderDetails.createOrReplaceTempView("OrderDetailsTable")
val result = spark.sql("SELECT ShipCountry, SUM(OrderDetailsTable.UnitPrice
* Qty * Discount) AS ProductSales FROM OrdersTable INNER JOIN
OrderDetailsTable ON OrdersTable.OrderID = OrderDetailsTable.OrderID GROUP
BY ShipCountry")
result.show(3)
result.write.parquet(filePath + "SalesByCountry_Parquet")
```

By now, we know the drill; as expected, the files are created, as shown next:

```
16/01/21 21:23:37 INFO SparkContext: Starting job: parquet at BigData01.scala:63
16/01/21 21:23:37 INFO DAGScheduler: Got job 10 (parquet at BigData01.scala:63) with 1 output partitions
[..]
16/01/21 21:24:23 INFO CodecConfig: Compression: GZIP
[..]
16/01/21 21:24:23 INFO ParquetOutputFormat: Writer version is: PARQUET_1_0
16/01/21 21:24:23 INFO CatalystWriteSupport: Initialized Parquet WriteSupport with Catalyst schema:
{
  "type" : "struct",
  "fields" : [ {
    "name" : "ShipCountry",
    "type" : "string",
    "nullable" : true,
    "metadata" : { }
  }, {
    "name" : "ProductSales",
    "type" : "double",
    "nullable" : true,
    "metadata" : { }
  } ]
}
and corresponding Parquet message type:
message spark_schema {
  optional binary ShipCountry (UTF8);
  optional double ProductSales;
}
[..]
16/01/21 21:24:28 INFO ParquetRelation: Listing file:/Users/ksankar/fdps-v3/SalesByCountry.parquet on driver
** Done **
```

HBase

HBase is the NoSQL datastore in the Hadoop ecosystem. Integration with a database is essential for Spark. It can read data from an HBase table or write to one. In fact, Spark supports HBase very well via the `HadoopdataSet` calls.

> If you want to experiment with HBase, you can install a standalone local version of HBase, as described in `http://hbase.apache.org/book.html# quickstart`.

Before working through the examples, let's create a table and three records in HBase. For testing, you can install a local standalone version of HBase that works from the local filesystem. So there's no need for Hadoop or HDFS. However, this won't be suitable for production.

I created a `test` table with three records via the HBase shell, as shown in the following screenshot:

```
USS-Defiant:hbase-1.1.2 ksankar$ bin/hbase shell
2016-01-21 19:06:52,189 WARN  [main] util.NativeCodeLoader: Unable to load native-hadoop library for your p
latform... using builtin-java classes where applicable
HBase Shell; enter 'help<RETURN>' for list of supported commands.
Type "exit<RETURN>" to leave the HBase Shell
Version 1.1.2, rcc2b70cf03e3378800661ec5cab11eb43fafe0fc, Wed Aug 26 20:11:27 PDT 2015

hbase(main):001:0> create 'test', 'cf'
0 row(s) in 1.4520 seconds

=> Hbase::Table - test
hbase(main):002:0> put 'test', 'row1', 'cf:a', 'value1'
0 row(s) in 0.1180 seconds

hbase(main):003:0> put 'test', 'row2', 'cf:b', 'value2'
0 row(s) in 0.0110 seconds

hbase(main):004:0> put 'test', 'row3', 'cf:c', 'value3'
0 row(s) in 0.0130 seconds

hbase(main):005:0> █
```

Loading from HBase

The HBase test code in the Apache Spark examples is a good start to testing our HBase connectivity and loading data. The code is not that difficult, but we do need to keep track of the data types, that is, keys as bytes, values as strings, and so on. The relevant part of the test code is given here (the full source file is `fdps-v3/code/BigData02.scala`):

```
val sc = new SparkContext("local","Chapter 10")
println(s"Running Spark Version ${sc.version}")
//
val conf = HBaseConfiguration.create()
conf.set(TableInputFormat.INPUT_TABLE, "test")

val admin = new HBaseAdmin(conf)
println(admin.isTableAvailable("test"))

val hBaseRDD = sc.newAPIHadoopRDD(conf, classOf[TableInputFormat],
classOf[org.apache.hadoop.hbase.io.ImmutableBytesWritable],
classOf[org.apache.hadoop.hbase.client.Result])
  println(hBaseRDD.count())
  //
  hBaseRDD.foreach(println) // will print bytes
  hBaseRDD.foreach(e=> ( println("%s | %s |".format(
Bytes.toString(e._1.get()),e._2) ) ) )
  //
println("** Read Done **")
```

The output of this code is shown in the following screenshot:

```
[..]
16/01/21 19:58:43 INFO SparkContext: Running Spark version 1.6.0
[..]
16/01/21 19:58:45 INFO BlockManagerMaster: Registered BlockManager
Running Spark Version 1.6.0
16/01/21 19:58:46 INFO RecoverableZooKeeper: Process identifier=hconnection-0x2385c98f connecting to ZooKeeper ensemble=localhost:2181
16/01/21 19:58:46 INFO ZooKeeper: Client environment:zookeeper.version=3.4.6-1569965, built on 02/20/2014 09:09 GMT
16/01/21 19:58:46 INFO ZooKeeper: Client environment:host.name=172.17.155.111
16/01/21 19:58:46 INFO ZooKeeper: Client environment:java.version=1.7.0_60
[..]
16/01/21 19:58:47 INFO SparkContext: Starting job: count at BigData02.scala:30
[..]
16/01/21 19:58:47 INFO DAGScheduler: Job 0 finished: count at BigData02.scala:30, took 0.332159 s
3
[..]
16/01/21 19:58:47 INFO TableInputFormatBase: Input split length: 0 bytes.
(72 6f 77 31,keyvalues={row1/cf:a/1453432063539/Put/vlen=6/seqid=0})
(72 6f 77 32,keyvalues={row2/cf:b/1453432077161/Put/vlen=6/seqid=0})
(72 6f 77 33,keyvalues={row3/cf:c/1453432088857/Put/vlen=6/seqid=0})
[..]
row1 | keyvalues={row1/cf:a/1453432063539/Put/vlen=6/seqid=0} |
row2 | keyvalues={row2/cf:b/1453432077161/Put/vlen=6/seqid=0} |
row3 | keyvalues={row3/cf:c/1453432088857/Put/vlen=6/seqid=0} |
[..]
16/01/21 19:58:48 INFO DAGScheduler: Job 2 finished: foreach at BigData02.scala:33, took 0.148513 s
** Read Done **
```

This is just the starting point. You need to convert the bytes from HBase to the actual data types of your data structures. You need to experiment a bit to get it right.

Saving to HBase

Now let's store a new record in our test table: key as `row4` and value as `value4`. It does require a few more classes and manipulations but nothing fancy, as shown here:

```
//
// create a pair RDD "row4":"value4"
// save it in column family "d"
//
val testMap = Map("row4" -> "value4")
val pairs = sc.parallelize(List(("row4","value4")))
pairs.foreach(println)
//
//Function to convert our RDD to the required format for HBase
//
def convert(triple: (String, String)) = {
  val p = new Put(Bytes.toBytes(triple._1))
  p.add(Bytes.toBytes("cf"), Bytes.toBytes("d"), Bytes.toBytes(triple._2))
  (new org.apache.hadoop.hbase.io.ImmutableBytesWritable, p)
}
//
val jobConfig: JobConf = new JobConf(conf, this.getClass)
jobConfig.setOutputFormat(classOf[TableOutputFormat])
jobConfig.set(TableOutputFormat.OUTPUT_TABLE, "test")
//
new PairRDDFunctions(pairs.map(convert)).saveAsHadoopDataset (jobConfig)
//
println("** Write Done **")
```

The program runs and prints the output, as shown in the following screenshot:

```
16/01/21 19:58:48 INFO SparkContext: Starting job: foreach at BigData02.scala:42
[..]
(row4,value4)
[..]
16/01/21 19:58:48 INFO SparkContext: Starting job: saveAsHadoopDataset at BigData02.scala:56
[..]
** Write Done **
```

Now let's go back to the HBase shell and verify that the fourth record is added, as shown in the following screenshot:

```
hbase(main):005:0> scan 'test'
ROW                     COLUMN+CELL
 row1                   column=cf:a, timestamp=1453432063539, value=value1
 row2                   column=cf:b, timestamp=1453432077161, value=value2
 row3                   column=cf:c, timestamp=1453432088857, value=value3
 row4                   column=cf:d, timestamp=1453435128457, value=value4
4 row(s) in 0.0350 seconds
```

Good! We can see the fourth record and a later timestamp.

Other HBase operations

We can also get metadata about the HBase server and the environment, as shown here:

```
val status = admin.getClusterStatus();
println("HBase Version : " +status.getHBaseVersion())
println("Average Load : "+status.getAverageLoad())
println("Backup Master Size : " + status.getBackupMastersSize())
println("Balancer On : " + status.getBalancerOn())
println("Cluster ID : "+ status.getClusterId())
println("Server Info : " + status.getServerInfo())
```

The output prints out the details, as you can see in the following screenshot:

```
HBase Version : 1.1.2
Average Load : 3.0
Backup Master Size : 0
Balancer On : true
Cluster ID : b581d584-3054-4383-8734-6185eab2ec78
Server Info : [172.17.155.111,55460,1453431893881]
```

Reference

The references are listed here:

- https://github.com/apache/spark/tree/master/examples/src/main/scala/org/apache/spark/examples
- http://parquet.incubator.apache.org/documentation/latest/
- http://www.slideshare.net/cloudera/hadoop-summit-36479635?ref=http://parquet.incubator.apache.org/presentations/
- Google Dremel paper at http://research.google.com/pubs/pub36632.html

- https://blog.twitter.com/213/dremel-made-simple-with-parquet
- http://planetcassandra.org/getting-started-with-apache-spark-and-cassandra/
- http://blog.cloudera.com/blog/214/12/new-in-cloudera-labs-sparkonhbase/
- http://www.vidyasource.com/blog/Programming/Scala/Java/Data/Hadoop/Analytics/214/1/25/lighting-a-spark-with-hbase
- https://github.com/apache/spark/blob/master/examples/src/main/scala/org/apache/spark/examples/HBaseTest.scala
- https://federicodayan.wordpress.com/21/9/28/hbase-textgetbytes-and-immutablebyteswritabletostring/
- https://github.com/apache/parquet-format

Summary

This chapter focused on the integration of Spark with other big data technologies. The Parquet format is an excellent way to expose the data processed by Spark to external systems, and Impala makes this very easy. The advantage of the Parquet format is that it is very efficient in terms of storage and expressive enough to capture the schema. We also looked at the process of interfacing with HBase. Thus, we can have our cake and eat it too! This means that we can leverage Spark for distributed scalable data processing, without losing the capability to integrate with other big data technologies. The next chapter, probably my favorite, is about machine learning. We will explore ML pipelines.

11
Machine Learning with Spark ML Pipelines

One of the major attractions of Spark is its ability to scale computations massively, and this is exactly what you need for machine learning algorithms. But the caveat is that all machine learning algorithms cannot be effectively parallelized. Each algorithm has its own challenges for parallelization, whether it is task parallelism or data parallelism. Having said that, Spark is becoming the de-facto platform for building machine learning algorithms and applications. Spark 2.0.0 has come a long way since version 1.1.0, with more algorithms and interesting APIs. For the latest information on this, you can refer to the Spark site at `https://spark.apache.org/docs/latest/ml-guide.html`, which is the authoritative source.

In this chapter, we will first cover machine learning interfaces and organization, including the new ml pipeline, which has become mainstream in 2.0.0. Then, we will delve into the following machine learning algorithms:

- Basic statistics
- Linear regression
- Classification
- Clustering
- Recommendation

Spark's machine learning algorithm table

Apache Spark covers a wide spectrum of machine learning algorithms. The algorithms implemented in Spark 2.0.0 consist of packages: `org.apache.spark.ml` for Scala and Java and `pyspark.ml` for Python.

Prior to 1.6.0, the libraries were in the `org.apache.spark.mllib` and `pyspark.mllib` packages, but from 2.0, the MLlib APIs are in maintenance mode. So you should use the ML APIs. In this chapter, we will do so, with clarifying notes wherever needed.

The following table summarizes the machine learning algorithms and data transformation features available in Spark 2.0.0:

Algorithm	Feature	Notes
Basic statistics	Summary statistics	Here mean, stdev, count, max, min, and numNonZeros are all part of `dataframe.count()`, `dataframe.describe()`, and sql.functions
	Correlations and covariance	Here, sql.functions are invoked as `dataframe.stat.corr(0 and cov)`
	Stratified sampling	This provides two methods, `sampleBykey` and `sampleByKeyExact`, with and without replacement
	Hypothesis testing	This is to test the statistical significance, Pearson's *chi-squared* test for goodness of fit and independence tests
	Tests of data streams for A/B testing	Since 1.6.0, these are used to check the capability of both Welch's and Student's respective two-sample t-test over streams
	Random data generation	Generate data using functions such as Normal, Poisson, Exponential, gamma, and lognormal
Regression	Linear models	This includes linear regression: Least Square, Lasso, and the Ridge regression
Classification	Binary classification	This includes logistic regression, SVM, decision trees, random forests, gradient boosted trees, and naïve Bayes
	Multiclass classification	This includes logistic, decision trees, naïve Bayes, and random forests
Recommendation	Collaborative filtering	This includes alternating between least squares

Clustering	K-means	This includes K-means, Gaussian Mixture, and Streaming K-means
Dimensionality Reduction	SVD and PCA	
Feature Extraction and Transformation	TF-IDF, Word2Vec StandardScaler, andNormalizer	
Optimization	Gradient Descent, SGD, and L-BFGS	
Frequent pattern mining	The FP-growth Algorithm	
Model import/export		

Spark machine learning APIs – ML pipelines and MLlib

Until around 1.6.0, the north-facing data abstraction method was RDD, and the MLlib APIs implemented machine learning on RDDs. MLlib was introduced in Spark 0.8 and, for the most part, were straightforward library calls to ML algorithms; however, this didn't reflect the data pipelines inherent in machine learning. With the advent of DataFrames and Datasets, MLlib transformed as well with more capabilities, and the resulting framework is the ML pipeline.

MLlib APIs are in maintenance mode from 2.0.0 and will be deprecated in 3.0.0. But be aware that there are still some APIs that are not migrated to the ML world; for example, the random generator still outputs an RDD. So you will have to use MLlib to generate a random normal, poisson, or other distributions, then convert the RDD into a DataFrame, and finally use ML for transformation and machine learning algorithms.

ML pipelines

ML pipelines were developed to address the fact that machine learning is not just a bunch of algorithms, such as classification and regression, but a pipeline of actions performed over a Dataset. Let's take a quick look at the tasks involved in a typical machine learning process. The following figure shows the top-level activities:

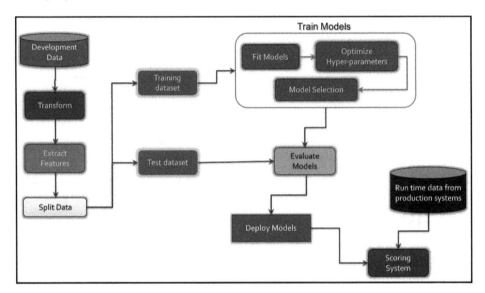

The first step is to get some data for the data science work. If you are using internal data, the data should be made anonymous and all PII information purged.

Once we have the data, we'll transform it: for example, we can convert a comma-separated CSV format into a DataFrame consisting of strings and numbers.

Then we extract the features that can be used to train our machine learning models. The feature extraction can be as simple as separating lines into words or normalizing words, such as deleting special characters and converting words to lowercase. This might also involve turning columns into categories, for example, Yes/No to 1/0 or Survived/Dead to 1/0.

Once we have the features, the next step is to split them into training and testing sets. Usually, it is a 80-20 random split; that is, we train the model using 80 percent of the data and evaluate the model with the remaining 20 percent of the data. But it might not be so easy. If our data is related to time series, a random split will, not work. If the data has a high-class imbalance (that is, 99% of the data belongs to one class-as in the case of data about rare diseases), a different strategy will be required, something that takes the class distribution into consideration.

The training itself has multiple steps:

1. First we try different models and fit the training data into the algorithms to develop the models.
2. Different algorithms have parameters: batch size, number of runs, tolerances, and so forth. So even while developing the models, we need to tune the hyper parameters.
3. Finally, we might try different algorithms and choose the best one that fits the problem.

The tuning and model selection are done via validation.

Once the model is selected with the optimized parameters, the test data is run with the model, which gives the performance of the model.

The model is then deployed into production where it uses the actual runtime data for predictions.

Bear in mind that the preceding paragraph is a generalization of a vast body of work with underlying mathematics, statistics, and heuristics from practical experience.

MLlib mainly focuses on the fit-models box, and the new ML pipelines address all parts of the workflow. Let's take a quick table view of the ML pipeline capabilities with respect to the machine learning workflow.

Workflow Stage	ML Feature	Notes
Transfom	org.apache.spark.ml.feature	Uses SQL functions such **assplit**
Extract Features	org.apache.spark.ml.feature	Uses Binarizer, Bucketizer, Normalizer, PAC, oneHotEncoder, Tokenizer, StandardScaler, StopWordsRemover, and Word2Vec
Split Data	org.apache.spark.ml.tuning org.apache.spark.sql.functions.split	Uses TrainValidationSplit
Fit Model	org.apache.spark.ml.regression, org.apache.spark.ml.recommendation	The machine learning algorithms live here
Model Optimization	org.apache.spark.ml.tuning	This is done through CrossValidator, and ParamGridBuilder
Model Evaluation	org.apache.spark.ml.evaluation.RegressionEvaluator	This calculates RMSE and MSE
Model Deployment	org.apache.spark.ml.util	Uses MLReader and MLWriter

As you can see, ML pipelines have extensive capabilities that address the machine learning workflow.

> As the goal of this chapter is to provide a basic introduction, we won't go deeper into pipeline construction and other aspects. But we will use the ML patterns, transformer, feature extraction, model evaluation, and others, as we work through the various algorithms. We will point out the patterns as we encounter them in our examples.

Spark ML examples

Now, let's look at how to develop machine learning applications. Naturally, we need interesting Datasets to implement the algorithms; we will use appropriate Datasets for the algorithms shown in the next section. In this book, we will use Scala, but I have included **iPython** notebooks for the algorithm examples in Python.

> The code and data files are available in the GitHub repository at `https://github.com/xsankar/fdps-v3`. Well keep it updated with the corrections.

The API organization

As an introduction, the following figure gives you a bird's eye view of the classes and methods that are relevant. Sometimes, one gets lost in the numerous classes and deep hierarchies.

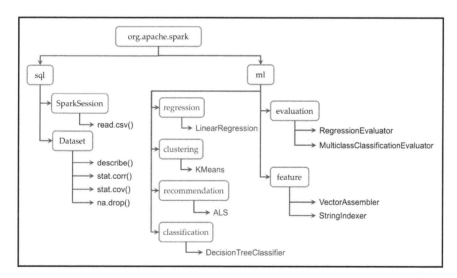

This organization is definitely something you should get used to. The MLlib library was more straightforward, but with far fewer capabilities. ML is definitely better, once you get the hang of it. It took me a few days to convert the examples; I had to visit/revisit the documentation multiple times. That is why I created the preceding diagram; this should make it easier for you to get a quick roadmap of the process while learning. Once done, it becomes easier to navigate the API documentation and find what one needs. Mastering the pipeline correctly will take a little while.

Basic statistics

Let's read the car mileage data and then compute some basic statistics. In Spark 2.0.0, DataFrameReader has the capability to read CSV files and create Datasets. And the Dataset has the `describe()` function, which calculates the count, mean, standard deviation, min, and max values. For correlation and covariance, we use the `stat.corr()` and `stat.cov()` methods. Spark 2.0.0 Datasets have made our statistics work a lot easier.

Now let's run the program, parse the code, and compare the results.

The code files are in `fdps-v3/code` and the data files in `fdps-v3/data`. You can run the code either from a Scala IDE or just from the Spark shell startup.

Start the Spark shell from the `bin` directory where you have installed Spark:

```
/Volumes/sdxc-01/spark-2.0.0/bin/spark-shell
```

Inside the shell, you'll find this command:

```
load /Users/ksankar/fdps-v3/code/ML01v2.scala
```

This command loads the source as follows:

```
USS-Defiant:~ ksankar$ /Volumes/sdxc-01/spark-2.0.0/bin/spark-shell
16/07/25 17:31:52 WARN NativeCodeLoader: Unable to load native-hadoop library for your platform... using builtin-java classes where applicable
16/07/25 17:31:53 WARN SparkContext: Use an existing SparkContext, some configuration may not take effect.
Spark context Web UI available at http://10.106.169.39:4040
Spark context available as 'sc' (master = local[*], app id = local-1469493113252).
Spark session available as 'spark'.
Welcome to
      ____              __
     / __/__  ___ _____/ /__
    _\ \/ _ \/ _ `/ __/  '_/
   /___/ .__/\_,_/_/ /_/\_\   version 2.0.0
      /_/

Using Scala version 2.11.8 (Java HotSpot(TM) 64-Bit Server VM, Java 1.7.0_60)
Type in expressions to have them evaluated.
Type :help for more information.

scala> :load /Users/ksankar/fdps-v3/code/ML01v2.scala
Loading /Users/ksankar/fdps-v3/code/ML01v2.scala...
import org.apache.spark.sql.SparkSession
import org.apache.spark.sql.functions.corr
import org.apache.spark.ml.regression.LinearRegression
import org.apache.spark.ml.feature.VectorAssembler
import org.apache.spark.ml.linalg.Vectors
import org.apache.spark.ml.evaluation.RegressionEvaluator
defined object ML01v2

scala>
```

It creates the `ML01v2` object. To run the object, use the following command:

ML01v2.main(Array("Hello","World"))

The result will be like this:

```
scala> ML01v2.main(Array("Hello","World"))
/Users/ksankar
16/07/25 17:37:22 WARN SparkSession$Builder: Use an existing SparkSession, some configuration may not take effect.
Running Spark Version 2.0.0
Cars has 32 rows
+-----+------------+---+------+------+-------+-----------+---------+------+-----+------+---------+
| mpg|displacement| hp|torque|CRatio|RARatio|CarbBarrells|NoOfSpeed|length|width|weight|automatic|
+-----+------------+---+------+------+-------+-----------+---------+------+-----+------+---------+
| 18.9|       350.0|165|  260|   8.0|   2.56|          4|        3| 200.3| 69.9|  3910|        1|
| 17.0|       350.0|170|  275|   8.5|   2.56|          4|        3| 199.6| 72.9|  3860|        1|
| 20.0|       250.0|105|  185|  8.25|   2.73|          1|        3| 196.7| 72.2|  3510|        1|
|18.25|       351.0|143|  255|   8.0|    3.0|          2|        3| 199.9| 74.0|  3890|        1|
|20.07|       225.0| 95|  170|   8.4|   2.76|          1|        3| 194.1| 71.8|  3365|        0|
+-----+------------+---+------+------+-------+-----------+---------+------+-----+------+---------+
only showing top 5 rows

root
 |-- mpg: double (nullable = true)
 |-- displacement: double (nullable = true)
 |-- hp: integer (nullable = true)
 |-- torque: integer (nullable = true)
 |-- CRatio: double (nullable = true)
 |-- RARatio: double (nullable = true)
 |-- CarbBarrells: integer (nullable = true)
 |-- NoOfSpeed: integer (nullable = true)
 |-- length: double (nullable = true)
 |-- width: double (nullable = true)
 |-- weight: integer (nullable = true)
 |-- automatic: integer (nullable = true)
```

Loading data

Loading data is a lot easier with the `read.csv` file and Datasets:

```
val spark = SparkSession.builder
    .master("local")
    .appName("Chapter 11")
    .config("spark.logConf","true")
    .config("spark.logLevel","ERROR")
    .getOrCreate()
println(s"Running Spark Version ${spark.version}")
//
valfilePath = "/Users/ksankar/fdps-v3/"
val cars = spark.read.option("header","true").
option("inferSchema","true").
csv(filePath + "data/car-data/car-milage.csv")
println("Cars has "+cars.count()+" rows")
cars.show(5)
cars.printSchema()
```

We use the options `header = true` and `inferschema = true`. The first line in the Dataset (`car-milage.csv`) has the column name. The `show()` method prints out the first few rows nicely. The `printSchema()` method shows the data and the types, as inferred from the data file. Looks fine for us!

Computing statistics

This work is also a lot easier with Spark 2.0.0 and Datasets. The reason the statistics are encapsulated in an easy function is because data scientists look at the basic statistics as the first step in data exploration.

The code is simple and the results as follows:

```
//
// Let us find summary statistics
//
cars.describe("mpg","hp","weight","automatic").show()
//
// correlations
//
varcor = cars.stat.corr("hp","weight")
println("hp to weight : Correlation = %2.4f".format(cor))
varcov = cars.stat.cov("hp","weight")
println("hp to weight : Covariance = %2.4f".format(cov))
//
```

```
cor = cars.stat.corr("RARatio","width")
println("Rear Axle Ratio to width : Correlation = %2.4f".format(cor))
cov = cars.stat.cov("RARatio","width")
println("Rear Axle Ratio to width : Covariance = %2.4f".format(cov))
```

The output of the preceding code is as follows, and it looks OK:

```
+-------+-----------------+-----------------+-----------------+-------------------+
|summary|              mpg|               hp|           weight|          automatic|
+-------+-----------------+-----------------+-----------------+-------------------+
|  count|               32|               32|               32|                 32|
|   mean|         20.223125|          136.875|         3586.6875|            0.71875|
| stddev|6.318289089312789|44.98082028541039|947.9431872693230|0.45680340939917435|
|    min|             11.2|               70|             1905|                  0|
|    max|             36.5|              223|             5430|                  1|
+-------+-----------------+-----------------+-----------------+-------------------+

hp to weight : Correlation = 0.8834
hp to weight : Covariance = 37667.5403
Rear Axle Ratio to width : Correlation = -0.4344
Rear Axle Ratio to width : Covariance = -1.2469
```

While it might seem too much work to calculate the correlation of a tiny Dataset, remember that this will scale to Datasets consisting of 1,000,000 rows or even a billion rows!

Linear regression

Linear regression involves a little more work than statistics. We need the data in a vector form along with a few more parameters; such as the learning rate, that is, the step size. We will also split the Dataset into `training` and `test`, as shown in the later part of this chapter.

Data transformation and feature extraction

The `ml.feature` library has a class vector assembler that transforms the data into a vector of features:

```
//
// Linear Regression
//
// Transformation to a labeled data that Linear Regression Can use
val cars1 = cars.na.drop()
val assembler = new VectorAssembler()
assembler.setInputCols(Array("displacement","hp","torque","CRatio","RARatio
","CarbBarrells","NoOfSpeed","length","width","weight","automatic"))
assembler.setOutputCol("features")
val cars2 = assembler.transform(cars1)
```

```
cars2.show(40)
```

The result is a Dataset with a new column `features`, which contains vectorized features:

```
+-----+------------+---+------+------+-------+-----------+----------+------+-----+------+---------+--------------------+
| mpg|displacement| hp|torque|CRatio|RARatio|CarbBarrells|NoOfSpeed|length|width|weight|automatic|            features|
+-----+------------+---+------+------+-------+-----------+----------+------+-----+------+---------+--------------------+
| 18.9|       350.0|165|   260|   8.0|   2.56|          4|         3| 200.3| 69.9|  3910|        1|[350.0,165.0,260....|
| 17.0|       350.0|170|   275|   8.5|   2.56|          4|         3| 199.6| 72.9|  3860|        1|[350.0,170.0,275....|
| 20.0|       250.0|105|   185|  8.25|   2.73|          1|         3| 196.7| 72.2|  3510|        1|[250.0,105.0,185....|
|18.25|       351.0|143|   255|   8.0|    3.0|          2|         3| 199.9| 74.0|  3890|        1|[351.0,143.0,255....|
|20.07|       225.0| 95|   170|   8.4|   2.76|          1|         3| 194.1| 71.8|  3365|        0|[225.0,95.0,170.0...|
| 11.2|       440.0|215|   330|   8.2|   2.88|          4|         3| 184.5| 69.0|  4215|        1|[440.0,215.0,330....|
|22.12|       231.0|110|   175|   8.0|   2.56|          2|         3| 179.3| 65.4|  3020|        1|[231.0,110.0,175....|
|21.47|       262.0|110|   200|   8.5|   2.56|          2|         3| 179.3| 65.4|  3180|        1|[262.0,110.0,200....|
| 34.7|        89.7| 70|    81|   8.2|   3.91|          2|         4| 155.7| 64.0|  1905|        0|[89.7,70.0,81.0,8...|
| 30.4|        96.9| 75|    83|   9.0|   4.3 |          2|         5| 165.2| 65.0|  2320|        0|[96.9,75.0,83.0,9...|
| 16.5|       350.0|155|   250|   8.5|   3.08|          4|         3| 195.4| 74.4|  3885|        1|[350.0,155.0,250....|
+-----+------------+---+------+------+-------+-----------+----------+------+-----+------+---------+--------------------+
```

Data split

Here, we split the data based on weight. In the next section, we will use the `randomSplit()` function for the classification:

```
    //
    // Split into training & test
    //
val train = cars2.filter(cars1("weight") <= 4000)
val test = cars2.filter(cars1("weight") > 4000)
test.show()
println("Train = "+train.count()+" Test = "+test.count())
```

The results are as expected:

```
+-----+------------+---+------+------+-------+-----------+----------+------+-----+------+---------+--------------------+
| mpg|displacement| hp|torque|CRatio|RARatio|CarbBarrells|NoOfSpeed|length|width|weight|automatic|            features|
+-----+------------+---+------+------+-------+-----------+----------+------+-----+------+---------+--------------------+
| 11.2|       440.0|215|   330|   8.2|   2.88|          4|         3| 184.5| 69.0|  4215|        1|[440.0,215.0,330....|
|14.39|       500.0|190|   360|   8.5|   2.73|          4|         3| 224.1| 79.8|  5290|        1|[500.0,190.0,360....|
|14.89|       440.0|215|   330|   8.2|   2.71|          4|         3| 231.0| 79.7|  5185|        1|[440.0,215.0,330....|
|21.47|       360.0|290|   290|   8.4|   2.45|          2|         3| 214.2| 76.3|  4250|        1|[360.0,180.0,290....|
|13.27|       460.0|223|   366|   8.0|    3.0|          4|         3| 228.0| 79.8|  5430|        1|[460.0,223.0,366....|
|19.73|       318.0|140|   255|   8.5|   2.71|          2|         3| 215.3| 76.3|  4370|        1|[318.0,140.0,255....|
| 13.9|       351.0|148|   243|   8.0|   3.25|          2|         3| 215.5| 78.5|  4540|        1|[351.0,148.0,243....|
|13.27|       351.0|148|   243|   8.0|   3.26|          2|         3| 216.1| 78.5|  4715|        1|[351.0,148.0,243....|
|13.77|       360.0|195|   295|  8.25|   3.15|          4|         3| 209.3| 77.4|  4215|        1|[360.0,195.0,295....|
+-----+------------+---+------+------+-------+-----------+----------+------+-----+------+---------+--------------------+

Train = 21 Test = 9
```

In the regression model, we create an algorithm object, set the appropriate parameters, and fit the training data to the algorithm to get the model. We will now inspect the various attributes of the model:

```
    val algLR = new LinearRegression()
    algLR.setMaxIter(100)
    algLR.setRegParam(0.3)
    algLR.setElasticNetParam(0.8)
    algLR.setLabelCol("mpg")
    //
    val mdlLR = algLR.fit(train)
    //
    println(s"Coefficients: ${mdlLR.coefficients} Intercept:
${mdlLR.intercept}")
    val trSummary = mdlLR.summary
println(s"numIterations: ${trSummary.totalIterations}")
println(s"Iteration Summary History: ${trSummary.objectiveHistory.toList}")
trSummary.residuals.show()
println(s"RMSE: ${trSummary.rootMeanSquaredError}")
println(s"r2: ${trSummary.r2}")
```

The output is interesting in the sense that the model has APIs to expose the attributes. Our R2 is .86, not that bad:

```
Coefficients: (11,[1,4,6,8,9],[-0.006861678246669865,2.8043197801610513,-0.7300904297334968,-0.2567322317253541,-0
5247338
numIterations: 72
Iteration Summary History: List(0.47619047619047616, 0.3797292659056507, 0.14205853716292927, 0.13425116878339244,
0.12082130252886975, 0.12016157238991124, 0.11895269501579105, 0.11706046702110359, 0.11642707184360138, 0.1158570
+--------------------+
|           residuals|
+--------------------+
|   2.0790900659615232|
|   0.7461850761798416|
|   0.9818585319734794|
RMSE: 2.2095233421225062
r2: 0.8610318374217147
```

Predictions using the model

We use the `transform()` method and the `test` Dataset to predict. The call adds a new column to our Dataset (actually a new Dataset with the new column added):

```
//
// Now let us use the model to predict our test set
//
val predictions = mdlLR.transform(test)
predictions.show()
```

You can see the new column named predictions:

```
+-----+------------+---+------+------+------+----------+--------+------+-----+------+---------+--------------------+------------------+
| mpg|displacement| hp|torque|CRatio|RARatio|CarbBarrels|NoOfSpeed|length|width|weight|automatic|            features|        prediction|
+-----+------------+---+------+------+------+----------+--------+------+-----+------+---------+--------------------+------------------+
| 11.2|       440.0|215| 330|  8.2| 2.88|         4|       3| 184.5| 69.0|  4215|        1|[440.0,215.0,330....|16.158065895143636|
|14.39|       500.0|190| 360|  8.5| 2.73|         4|       3| 224.1| 79.8|  5290|        1|[500.0,190.0,360....| 8.031935143543777|
|14.89|       440.0|215| 330|  8.2| 2.71|         4|       3| 231.0| 79.7|  5185|        1|[440.0,215.0,330....| 8.328541174947645|
|21.47|       360.0|180| 290|  8.4| 2.45|         2|       3| 214.2| 76.3|  4250|        1|[360.0,180.0,290....| 13.15203478337898|
|13.27|       460.0|223| 366|  8.0|  3.0|         4|       3| 228.0| 79.8|  5430|        1|[460.0,223.0,366....|7.8979178887120725|
|19.73|       318.0|140| 255|  8.5| 2.71|         2|       3| 215.3| 76.3|  4370|        1|[318.0,140.0,255....|13.585840873229003|
| 13.9|       351.0|148| 243|  8.0| 3.25|         2|       3| 215.5| 78.5|  4540|        1|[351.0,148.0,243....|13.673274959697096|
|13.27|       351.0|148| 243|  8.0| 3.26|         2|       3| 216.1| 78.5|  4715|        1|[351.0,148.0,243....|12.870382890829859|
|13.77|       360.0|195| 295| 8.25| 3.15|         4|       3| 209.3| 77.4|  4215|        1|[360.0,195.0,295....|14.895915054227537|
+-----+------------+---+------+------+------+----------+--------+------+-----+------+---------+--------------------+------------------+
```

The prediction is not that impressive. There are a couple of reasons for this. There might be quadratic effects or some of the variables might be correlated (for example, length, width, and weight, and we might not need all the three to predict the mpg value). Finally, we might not need all 10 features anyway. I leave it to you to try different combinations of the features.

Model evaluation

Prior to Spark 2.0.0, we had our own code to calculate the error. The spark.ml library has an evaluation class with the required evaluators. The pattern is similar: we create the appropriate object, set the required parameters, and then call the evaluate() method:

```
// Calculate RMSE&MSE
val evaluator = new RegressionEvaluator()
evaluator.setLabelCol("mpg")
valrmse = evaluator.evaluate(predictions)
println("Root Mean Squared Error = "+"%6.3f".format(rmse))
//
evaluator.setMetricName("mse")
valmse = evaluator.evaluate(predictions)
println("Mean Squared Error = "+"%6.3f".format(mse))
//
```

The result is as expected:

```
Root Mean Squared Error =  5.221
Mean Squared Error = 27.260
** That's All Folks **
```

Classification

Classification is very similar to linear regression. The algorithms take vectors, and the algorithm object has various parameters to tweak the algorithm in order to fit the needs of an application. The returned model can be used to predict the class invoking the transform method. We will use the Titanic Dataset and predict who will survive. The Dataset has 15 fields, including age, gender, whether they have siblings/a spouse, parents sailing with them, the class they are in, and so forth.

Loading data

Similar to regression, we load the CSV data using the `read.csv()` method. The code file is `ML02v2.scala`. We load the code and run the `ML02v2` object. The CSV data is loaded and we print the schema to verify:

```
val filePath = "/Users/ksankar/fdps-v3/"
  val passengers = spark.read.option("header","true").
    option("inferSchema","true").
    csv(filePath + "data/titanic3_02.csv")
  println("Passengers has "+passengers.count()+" rows")
  passengers.show(5)
  passengers.printSchema()
  //
```

The output is as expected:

```
scala> ML02v2.main(Array("Hello","World"))
/Users/ksankar
16/07/25 19:14:44 WARN SparkSession$Builder: Use an existing SparkSession, some configuration may not take effect.
Running Spark Version 2.0.0
Passengers has 1309 rows
+------+--------+--------------------+------+------+-----+-----+--------+--------+--------+--------+----+----+--------------------+
|Pclass|Survived|                Name|Gender|   Age|SibSp|Parch|  Ticket|    Fare|   Cabin|Embarked|Boat|Body|            HomeDest|
+------+--------+--------------------+------+------+-----+-----+--------+--------+--------+--------+----+----+--------------------+
|     1|       1|Allen, Miss. Elis...|female|  29.0|    0|    0|   24160|211.3375|      B5|       S|   2|null|        St Louis, MO|
|     1|       1|Allison, Master. ...|  male|0.9167|    1|    2| 113781|  151.55| C22 C26|       S|  11|null|Montreal, PQ / Ch...|
|     1|       0|Allison, Miss. He...|female|   2.0|    1|    2| 113781|  151.55| C22 C26|       S|null|null|Montreal, PQ / Ch...|
|     1|       0|Allison, Mr. Huds...|  male|  30.0|    1|    2| 113781|  151.55| C22 C26|       S|    | 135|Montreal, PQ / Ch...|
|     1|       0|Allison, Mrs. Hud...|female|  25.0|    1|    2| 113781|  151.55| C22 C26|       S|null|null|Montreal, PQ / Ch...|
+------+--------+--------------------+------+------+-----+-----+--------+--------+--------+--------+----+----+--------------------+
only showing top 5 rows
```

The schema is a little more elaborate than the regression example:

```
root
 |-- Pclass: integer (nullable = true)
 |-- Survived: integer (nullable = true)
 |-- Name: string (nullable = true)
 |-- Gender: string (nullable = true)
 |-- Age: double (nullable = true)
 |-- SibSp: integer (nullable = true)
 |-- Parch: integer (nullable = true)
 |-- Ticket: string (nullable = true)
 |-- Fare: double (nullable = true)
 |-- Cabin: string (nullable = true)
 |-- Embarked: string (nullable = true)
 |-- Boat: string (nullable = true)
 |-- Body: integer (nullable = true)
 |-- HomeDest: string (nullable = true)
```

Data transformation and feature extraction

For our model, we extract five attributes. The gender is a string Male/Female, which needs to be converted to 1/0. Here we use the ML transformation function `StringIndexer`. As you can see, `StringIndexer` itself acts as a machine learning algorithm with its own fit and `transform` method. It is this symmetry that makes it easy to create a pipeline.

A couple of records do not have the age criteria on and so we drop the records using the `na.drop()` method.

Even though we drop the records with missing columns, in real life we should try to impute the missing data. Just because data for a column is missing, it doesn't mean that we should toss important data in other columns. There are many strategies we can use in our example:

- We could replace the missing age with the average age
- We could be cleverer and infer the average age from the title in the name (Mr., Mrs., Miss, Jr., Master, and others)

Then, like regression, we use the vector assembler to create a column of vectors called `features`, which will be ready for our algorithms to consume:

```
val passengers1 =
passengers.select(passengers("Pclass"),passengers("Survived").cast(DoubleTy
pe).as("Survived"),passengers("Gender"),passengers("Age"),passengers("SibSp
"),passengers("Parch"),passengers("Fare"))
passengers1.show(5)
    //
    // VectorAssembler does not support the StringType type. So convert
Gender to numeric
    //
val indexer = new StringIndexer()
indexer.setInputCol("Gender")
indexer.setOutputCol("GenderCat")
val passengers2 = indexer.fit(passengers1).transform(passengers1)
passengers2.show(5)
    //
val passengers3 = passengers2.na.drop()
println("Orig = "+passengers2.count()+" Final = "+ passengers3.count() + "
Dropped = "+ (passengers2.count() - passengers3.count()))
    //
val assembler = new VectorAssembler()
assembler.setInputCols(Array("Pclass","GenderCat","Age","SibSp","Parch","Fa
re"))
assembler.setOutputCol("features")
val passengers4 = assembler.transform(passengers3)
passengers4.show(5)
```

The output is as expected, but it's worth a look. The following features get extracted:

Pclass	Survived	Gender	Age	SibSp	Parch	Fare
1	1.0	female	29.0	0	0	211.3375
1	1.0	male	0.9167	1	2	151.55
1	0.0	female	2.0	1	2	151.55
1	0.0	male	30.0	1	2	151.55
1	0.0	female	25.0	1	2	151.55

The `GenderCat` column gets created:

```
+------+--------+------+------+-----+-----+--------+---------+
|Pclass|Survived|Gender|   Age|SibSp|Parch|    Fare|GenderCat|
+------+--------+------+------+-----+-----+--------+---------+
|    1|     1.0|female|  29.0|    0|    0|211.3375|      1.0|
|    1|     1.0|  male|0.9167|    1|    2|  151.55|      0.0|
|    1|     0.0|female|   2.0|    1|    2|  151.55|      1.0|
|    1|     0.0|  male|  30.0|    1|    2|  151.55|      0.0|
|    1|     0.0|female|  25.0|    1|    2|  151.55|      1.0|
+------+--------+------+------+-----+-----+--------+---------+
```

We drop the rows with missing data and create the column with a vector of features. We drop 264 records, 20% of our Dataset! So we should really look at imputing the following strategies:

```
Orig = 1309 Final = 1045 Dropped = 264
+------+--------+------+------+-----+-----+--------+---------+--------------------+
|Pclass|Survived|Gender|   Age|SibSp|Parch|    Fare|GenderCat|            features|
+------+--------+------+------+-----+-----+--------+---------+--------------------+
|    1|     1.0|female|  29.0|    0|    0|211.3375|      1.0|[1.0,1.0,29.0,0.0...|
|    1|     1.0|  male|0.9167|    1|    2|  151.55|      0.0|[1.0,0.0,0.9167,1...|
|    1|     0.0|female|   2.0|    1|    2|  151.55|      1.0|[1.0,1.0,2.0,1.0,...|
|    1|     0.0|  male|  30.0|    1|    2|  151.55|      0.0|[1.0,0.0,30.0,1.0...|
|    1|     0.0|female|  25.0|    1|    2|  151.55|      1.0|[1.0,1.0,25.0,1.0...|
+------+--------+------+------+-----+-----+--------+---------+--------------------+
```

Data split

Unlike the last time, here we will use the `randomSplit()` function, which is part of the Spark framework. Because we have a small Dataset, we will use the 90-10 split between the training and the test Dataset. We have 939 rows in the training set and 106 in the test set:

```
// split data
//
val Array(train, test) = passengers4.randomSplit(Array(0.9, 0.1))
println("Train = "+train.count()+" Test = "+test.count())
```

The regression model

By now, you must have become an expert. For the last time, we will use the same mechanics: create an algorithm object, set the appropriate parameters, fit the training data to the algorithm to get the model, and finally inspect the various attributes of the model:

```
//
// Train a DecisionTree model.
```

```
val algTree = new DecisionTreeClassifier()
algTree.setLabelCol("Survived")
algTree.setImpurity("gini") // could be "entropy"
algTree.setMaxBins(32)algTree.setMaxDepth(5)
    //
val mdlTree = algTree.fit(train)
println("The tree has %d nodes.".format(mdlTree.numNodes))
println(mdlTree.toDebugString)
println(mdlTree.toString)
println(mdlTree.featureImportances)
```

The output is a tree with 57 nodes. We can print the model and inspect the tree. The tree is interesting:

```
Train = 939 Test = 106
The tree has 57 nodes.
DecisionTreeClassificationModel (uid=dtc_574fc58afe7b) of depth 5 with 57 nodes
  If (feature 1 in {0.0})
   If (feature 2 <= 13.0)
    If (feature 3 <= 2.0)
     If (feature 0 <= 2.0)
      Predict: 1.0
     Else (feature 0 > 2.0)
      If (feature 5 <= 12.475)
       Predict: 1.0
      Else (feature 5 > 12.475)
       Predict: 0.0
    Else (feature 3 > 2.0)
     If (feature 4 <= 1.0)
      Predict: 0.0
     Else (feature 4 > 1.0)
      If (feature 2 <= 6.0)
       Predict: 0.0
```

The importance of the attributes is interesting:

```
DecisionTreeClassificationModel (uid=dtc_574fc58afe7b) of depth 5 with 57 nodes
(6,[0,1,2,3,4,5],[0.1992761244807816,0.5657930258461648,0.10452542522610687,0.060509461907802965,0.011152219621042795,0.0587437429181011])
```

This shows the influence of the variables in the prediction. The output shows the variable order and the percentage fraction. The variable Gender explains 57 percent of the survivors (1,0.56579), with the class (0,0.19927) adding another 20%.

Prediction using the model

Again, as before, we use the transform() method and the test Dataset to make a prediction:

```
val predictions = mdlTree.transform(test)
predictions.show(5)
```

We get a new Dataset with the predictions column added:

```
+------+--------+------+----+-----+-----+--------+---------+--------------------+-------------+--------------------+----------+
|Pclass|Survived|Gender| Age|SibSp|Parch|    Fare|GenderCat|            features|rawPrediction|         probability|prediction|
+------+--------+------+----+-----+-----+--------+---------+--------------------+-------------+--------------------+----------+
|     1|     0.0|  male|18.0|    1|    0|   108.9|      0.0|[1.0,0.0,18.0,1.0...|  [24.0,15.0]|[0.61538461538461...|       0.0|
|     1|     0.0|  male|31.0|    0|    0| 50.4958|      0.0|[1.0,0.0,31.0,0.0...|  [24.0,15.0]|[0.61538461538461...|       0.0|
|     1|     0.0|  male|33.0|    0|    0|   26.55|      0.0|[1.0,0.0,33.0,0.0...|  [24.0,15.0]|[0.61538461538461...|       0.0|
|     1|     0.0|  male|37.0|    0|    1|    29.7|      0.0|[1.0,0.0,37.0,0.0...|   [41.0,9.0]|         [0.82,0.18]|       0.0|
|     1|     0.0|  male|39.0|    1|    0| 71.2833|      0.0|[1.0,0.0,39.0,1.0...|  [20.0,11.0]|[0.64516129032258...|       0.0|
+------+--------+------+----+-----+-----+--------+---------+--------------------+-------------+--------------------+----------+
```

Model evaluation

Like regression, we use the evaluator that is available with the ML framework. In this case, we use the `MulticlassClassificationEvaluator` method. We instantiate the object and set the required parameters:

```
val evaluator = new MulticlassClassificationEvaluator()
evaluator.setLabelCol("Survived")
evaluator.setMetricName("accuracy") // could be f1, "weightedPrecision" or
"weightedRecall"
    //
val accuracy = evaluator.evaluate(predictions)
println("Test Accuracy = %.2f%%".format(accuracy*100))
    //
val elapsedTime = (System.nanoTime() - startTime) / 1e9
println("Elapsed time: %.2fseconds".format(elapsedTime))
```

The output is as expected (a test accuracy of 78.3 percent), and we feel good because we have cracked the ML gene and are ready for the clustering algorithm!

Now that we have created a model using the decision tree algorithm, we can follow the same pattern to try out algorithms such as **RandomForests**, **GradientBoosted Trees**, and **Neural Network-based classification**. Create an algorithm object with the appropriate class and set the parameters required for each algorithm. The classes are `org.apache.spark.ml.classification.RandomForestClassifier`, `org.apache.spark.ml.classification,GBTClassifier`, and `org.apache.spark.ml.classification.MultilayerPerceptronClassifier`.

Clustering

Spark MLlib has implemented the K-means clustering algorithm. The model training and prediction interfaces are similar to other machine learning algorithms. Let's see how it works by going through an example.

Let's use a sample data that has two dimensions: x and y. The plot of the points looks like the following screenshot:

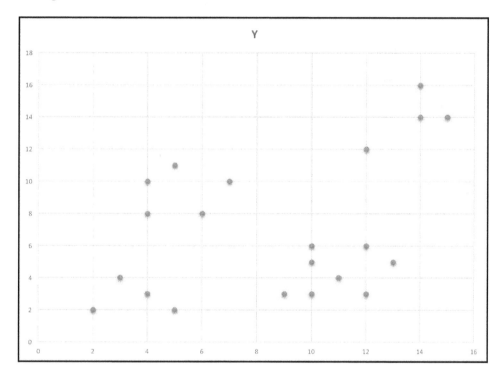

From the preceding graph, we can see that four clusters form one solution. Let's try $k = 2$ and $k=4$. Let's see how the Spark clustering algorithm handles this Dataset and the groupings.

Loading data

By now, we know very well how to load data using the `read.csv()` method. The following code file is `ML03v2.scala`:

```
scala> :load /Users/ksankar/fdps-v3/code/ML03v2.scala
Loading /Users/ksankar/fdps-v3/code/ML03v2.scala...
import org.apache.spark.sql.SparkSession
import org.apache.spark.ml.feature.VectorAssembler
import org.apache.spark.ml.clustering.KMeans
defined object ML03v2
```

We run the `ML03v2` object:

```
scala> :load /Users/ksankar/fdps-v3/code/ML03v2.scala
Loading /Users/ksankar/fdps-v3/code/ML03v2.scala...
import org.apache.spark.sql.SparkSession
import org.apache.spark.ml.feature.VectorAssembler
import org.apache.spark.ml.clustering.KMeans
defined object ML03v2

scala> ML03v2.main(Array("Hello","World"))
/Users/ksankar
16/07/25 21:24:42 WARN SparkSession$Builder: Use an existing SparkSession
Running Spark Version 2.0.0
Data has 21 rows
+---+---+
|  X|  Y|
+---+---+
|  4| 10|
|  7| 10|
|  4|  8|
|  6|  8|
| 12|  3|
+---+---+
only showing top 5 rows

root
 |-- X: integer (nullable = true)
 |-- Y: integer (nullable = true)
```

The code to read data is very similar to the Regression and Classification examples. So we will skip it here; you can look at the source code anyway. After reading the data in, we have the Dataset with two columns: `X` and `Y`.

Data transformation and feature extraction

For this example, the transformation is very simple. Create the features column with the
`VectorAssembler` like this:

```
val assembler = new VectorAssembler()
assembler.setInputCols(Array("X","Y"))
assembler.setOutputCol("features")
valdata1 = assembler.transform(data)
data1.show(5)
```

The output is as expected:

```
+---+---+----------+
|  X|  Y|  features|
+---+---+----------+
|  4| 10|[4.0,10.0]|
|  7| 10|[7.0,10.0]|
|  4|  8| [4.0,8.0]|
|  6|  8| [6.0,8.0]|
| 12|  3|[12.0,3.0]|
+---+---+----------+
```

Data split

Unlike our Regression and Classification models, clustering is not a supervised algorithm.
That is, we have no training data, and we don't need to learn how to cluster data. The
algorithm is unsupervised, which means it applies the K-means algorithm and finds which
cluster each data point belongs to, all on its own. In short, there is no need to split the data.
And there is no measure of accuracy, so a test set is of no use to us in this context. Later, we
will see what all this means for clustering.

In the clustering model, we can use the patterns we learned from Regression and
Classification here as well. We create an algorithm object, set the parameters, and run the
data through. There is one twist: we do need to tell the algorithm how many clusters we
need. This is the k variable we were talking about earlier. In our example here, we will try
with *k=2* and then *k=4*; after the clustering is done, we will discuss the implications.
Following is simple code for this model:

```
var algKMeans = new KMeans().setK(2)
var mdlKMeans = algKMeans.fit(data1)
```

Predicting using the model

The mechanics of predicting are equally simple, but of course the interpretation and evaluation are a little more involved. To predict, we use the `transform()` method and we get the new predictions column:

```
var predictions = mdlKMeans.transform(data1)
predictions.show(3)
    //
predictions.write.mode("overwrite").option("header","true").csv(filePath +
"data/cluster-2K.csv")
```

In this case, we write the data as a CSV file. We will use the data to plot the centers:

```
+---+---+------------+----------+
|  X|  Y|    features|prediction|
+---+---+------------+----------+
|  4| 10| [4.0,10.0]|         0|
|  7| 10| [7.0,10.0]|         0|
|  4|  8|  [4.0,8.0]|         0|
|  6|  8|  [6.0,8.0]|         0|
| 12|  3| [12.0,3.0]|         0|
+---+---+------------+----------+
```

Model evaluation and interpretation

Now we have to face the music and talk about what clustering means and how to make use of the results. First, the metric that we can use to evaluate between models is **WSSE**. This is the sum of errors within a cluster; it is really not an error but the distance of the points in each cluster from its center. Every group has a center (called the **centroid**) and we can calculate the square distance of the points in a group from the group center.

Think of it this way: if we had only one cluster for our data, then there would be one center and there would be one WSSE. Now if we cluster the data around four centers and then calculate the WSSE for each cluster and sum that up, that would be $WSSE_4$. Because we have four centers, the points in each cluster will be closer to its centroid, and the $WSSE_4$ would be smaller than $WSSE_1$. So theoretically, a smaller WSSE means we have better cohesion between the points and k variable.

Calculating WSSE is not that hard; we invoke the `computeCost()` method. Let's compute the WSSE for *k=2* and *k=4* and save the data:

```
var algKMeans = newKMeans().setK(2)
var mdlKMeans = algKMeans.fit(data1)
```

```
    // Evaluate clustering by computing Within Set Sum of Squared Errors.
var WSSSE = mdlKMeans.computeCost(data1)
println(s"Within Set Sum of Squared Errors (K=2) = %.3f".format(WSSSE))
    // Shows the result.
println("Cluster Centers (K=2) : " + mdlKMeans.clusterCenters.mkString("<",
",", ">"))
println("Cluster Sizes (K=2) : " +
mdlKMeans.summary.clusterSizes.mkString("<", ",", ">"))
    //
var predictions = mdlKMeans.transform(data1)
predictions.show(30)
    //
predictions.write.mode("overwrite").option("header","true").csv(filePath +
"data/cluster-2K.csv")
    //
    //
    // Now let us try 4 centers
    //
algKMeans = new KMeans().setK(4)
mdlKMeans = algKMeans.fit(data1)
    // Evaluate clustering by computing Within Set Sum of Squared Errors.
WSSSE = mdlKMeans.computeCost(data1)
println(s"Within Set Sum of Squared Errors (K=4) = %.3f".format(WSSSE))
    // Shows the result.
println("Cluster Centers (K=4) : " + mdlKMeans.clusterCenters.mkString("<",
",", ">"))
println("Cluster Sizes (K=4) : " +
mdlKMeans.summary.clusterSizes.mkString("<", ",", ">"))
    //
predictions = mdlKMeans.transform(data1)
predictions.show(30)
    //
predictions.write.mode("overwrite").option("header","true").csv(filePath +
"data/cluster-4K.csv")
    //
```

The `write.mode.overwrite` library avoids the path file:
`/Users/ksankar/fdps-v3/data/cluster-2K.csv` already exists
exception. But mode is a member of write not CSV, so it has to come first.

The output of the program is as expected:

```
Within Set Sum of Squared Errors (K=2) = 357.221
Cluster Centers (K=2) : <[7.470588235294118,5.470588235294118],[13.75,14.0]>
Cluster Sizes (K=2) : <17,4>
+---+---+--------------+----------+
|  X|  Y|      features|prediction|
+---+---+--------------+----------+
|  4| 10|[4.0,10.0]|            0|
|  7| 10|[7.0,10.0]|            0|
|  4|  8| [4.0,8.0]|            0|
+---+---+--------------+----------+
Within Set Sum of Squared Errors (K=4) = 59.250
Cluster Centers (K=4) : <[10.875,4.375],[13.75,14.0],[3.5,2.75],[5.2,9.4]>
Cluster Sizes (K=4) : <8,4,4,5>
+---+---+--------------+----------+
|  X|  Y|      features|prediction|
+---+---+--------------+----------+
|  4| 10|[4.0,10.0]|            3|
|  7| 10|[7.0,10.0]|            3|
|  4|  8| [4.0,8.0]|            3|
+---+---+--------------+----------+
```

With two clusters (*k=2*), as shown in the following graph, we have WSSE of 357.22 and two centers with points 17 and 4, respectively. We can see that the centers are at the points (7.5,5.5) and (13.75,14.0):

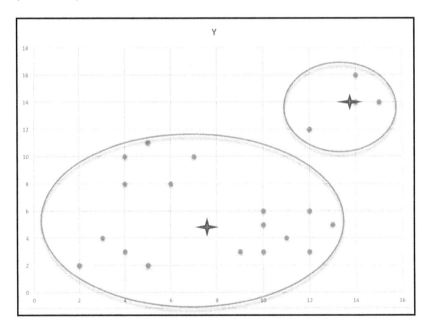

With four clusters (*k=4*), as seen in the following graph, the WSSE is reduced to 59.25. Each center has 8,4,4, and 5 points. The graph shows that the cluster with the center at (13.75,14.0) hasn't changed. The other cluster is now broken into three clusters with appropriate centers:

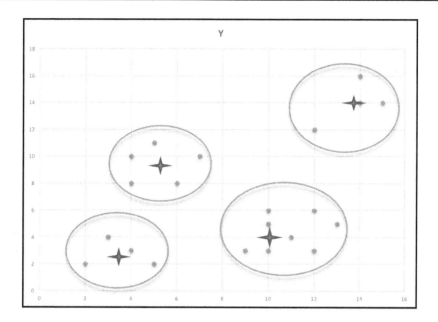

TIP

Bear in mind that the results could vary a little between runs because the clustering algorithm picks the centers randomly and grows from there. With $k=4$, the results are stable; however, with $k=2$, there is room for partitioning the points in different ways. Try it out a few times and see whether the results change. They might not in this case, but can for other Datasets.

Clustering model interpretation

The question remains: how do we select k, especially when we have data with multiple dimensions, that is, 10, 20, or even 100 attributes/columns? The selection of k is also a business question, that is, it depends on the application. For example, if you are an airline and are clustering your frequent flyers based on a set of attributes (say, miles travelled, credit card purchase, bonus miles, and so forth) to market different promotions for different clusters, you would want 5 or 6 clusters; creating 100s of different promotions wouldn't make sense here.

On the other hand, if you are LinkedIn and want to cluster users to recommend potential connections in interesting unexpected ways, even 10 million clusters (thus recommending 50 people per member, that is, 433 million members/10 million clusters ~ 43 per cluster) might be appropriate. Once the clusters are created, you can recommend users in each cluster to each other. Of course, you have to filter members who are already connected, so maybe 5 million or 1 million clusters might be appropriate.

Recommendation

Recommendation systems are one of the most visible and popular machine learning applications on the Web, from Amazon to LinkedIn to Walmart. The algorithms behind recommendations systems are very interesting. Recommendation algorithms fall into roughly five general mechanisms: knowledge-based, demographic-based, content-based, collaborative filtering (item-based or user-based), and latent factor-based. Of these, collaborative filtering is the most widely used and unfortunately very computationally intensive.

Spark implements a scalable variation, the **Alternating Least Square** (**ALS**) algorithm authored by Yehuda Koren, available at `http://dl.acm.org/citation.cfm?id=168614`. It is a user-based collaborative filtering mechanism that uses the *latent factors* method of learning, which can scale to a large Dataset. Let's quickly use the `movielens` medium Dataset to implement a recommendation using Spark. While the model development patterns follow what we have seen so far, there are some interesting waypoints at different stages, as we will see. Apart from that, the code is not that complex.

Loading data

The code file is `ML04v2.scala`. In the Scala shell, we load and run the object `ML04v2`:

```
scala> :load /Users/ksankar/dev/workspace/SparkBook/src/ML04v2.scala
Loading /Users/ksankar/dev/workspace/SparkBook/src/ML04v2.scala...
import org.apache.spark.sql.SparkSession
import org.apache.spark.sql.Row
import org.apache.spark.sql.functions.{split, pow, isnan}
import org.apache.spark.mllib.recommendation.Rating
import org.apache.spark.ml.recommendation.ALS
import org.apache.spark.ml.evaluation.RegressionEvaluator
import org.apache.log4j.{Level, Logger}
defined object ML04v2

scala> ML04v2.main(Array("Hello","World"))
/Users/ksankar
Running Spark Version 2.0.0
+--------------------------------------------------+
|value                                             |
+--------------------------------------------------+
|1::Toy Story (1995)::Animation|Children's|Comedy|
|2::Jumanji (1995)::Adventure|Children's|Fantasy |
|3::Grumpier Old Men (1995)::Comedy|Romance        |
|4::Waiting to Exhale (1995)::Comedy|Drama         |
|5::Father of the Bride Part II (1995)::Comedy     |
+--------------------------------------------------+
only showing top 5 rows
```

The first thing we realize is that the `movielens` data fields are separated by `::` operator, so we can't use `read.csv`. We could of course write a small program to convert the data file into CSV format. Instead, let's take this opportunity to see how we can read text files and process them using RDDs.

One trick is to go down to RDD and use map to parse the files. There are many other ways, but this is good for us as it enables us to see how we can go back and forth between RDDs and Datasets. Once we have this method, the rest is relatively easy to read data in:

```
def parseRating(row:Row) : Rating = {
val aList = row.getList[String](0)
  Rating(aList.get(0).toInt,aList.get(1).toInt,aList.get(2).toDouble)
//.getInt(0), row.getInt(1), row.getDouble(2))
  }
  //
def rowSqDiff(row:Row) : Double = {
  math.pow( (row.getDouble(2) - row.getFloat(3).toDouble),2)
  }
  //
def main(args: Array[String]): Unit = {
println(getCurrentDirectory)
  val spark = SparkSession.builder
      .master("local")
      .appName("Chapter 11")
```

```
        .config("spark.logConf","true")
        .config("spark.logLevel","ERROR")
        .getOrCreate()
    println(s"Running Spark Version ${spark.version}")
        //
        // To turn off INFO messages
        //
    val rootLogger = Logger.getRootLogger()
    rootLogger.setLevel(Level.ERROR)            // INFO, TRACE,...
    val startTime = System.nanoTime()
        //
    val filePath = "/Users/ksankar/fdps-v3/"
    val movies = spark.read.text(filePath + "data/medium/movies.dat")
    movies.show(5,truncate=false)
    movies.printSchema()
    val ratings = spark.read.text(filePath + "data/medium/ratings.dat")
    ratings.show(5,truncate=false)
    val users = spark.read.text(filePath + "data/medium/users.dat")
    users.show(5,truncate=false)
        //
    println("Got %d ratings from %d users on %d
movies.".format(ratings.count(), users.count(), movies.count()))
```

We use a couple of techniques to read the data, parse it to the values, and then get a Dataset back. The results are as expected:

```
+--------------------+
|value               |
+--------------------+
|1::1193::5::978300760|
|1::661::3::978302109 |
|1::914::3::978301968 |
|1::3408::4::978300275|
|1::2355::5::978824291|
+--------------------+
only showing top 5 rows

+-------------------+
|value              |
+-------------------+
|1::F::1::10::48067 |
|2::M::56::16::70072|
|3::M::25::15::55117|
|4::M::45::7::02460 |
|5::M::25::20::55455|
+-------------------+
only showing top 5 rows

Got 1000209 ratings from 6040 users on 3883 movies.
```

While we read in the three files, we will use only the rating data file.

Data transformation and feature extraction

To transform the ratings data, we have to downshift to RDD and then create a DataFrame back. This is one method; there are many other ways:

```
    // Transformation
    // This is a kludge. Let me know if there is a better way
    //
val ratings1 = ratings.select(split(ratings("value"),"::")).as("values")
ratings1.show(5)
val ratings2 = ratings1.rdd.map(row => parseRating(row))
ratings2.take(3).foreach(println)
    //
val ratings3 = spark.createDataFrame(ratings2)
ratings3.show(5)
```

 The map uses the parseRating() method; for it to work in the shell, we need to make our main object serializable.

The following is the output; we can see that the numbers look good:

```
Rating(1,1193,5.0)
Rating(1,661,3.0)
Rating(1,914,3.0)
+----+-------+------+
|user|product|rating|
+----+-------+------+
|   1|   1193|   5.0|
|   1|    661|   3.0|
|   1|    914|   3.0|
|   1|   3408|   4.0|
|   1|   2355|   5.0|
+----+-------+------+
only showing top 5 rows
```

The spark recommendation algorithm takes a Dataset and looks for items and rating; we just need to explain the columns. So we don't need to perform VectorAssembler like we did last time. One of the tasks in the transformation stage is to understand the implementation and the data format it needs before you apply transformations as required.

Data splitting

We will use `RandomSplit` to split the data. Comparing MLlib with the *second edition* of this book, you'll find that, in the second addition, we used the last digit of the timestamp to split the data:

```
val Array(train, test) = ratings3.randomSplit(Array(0.8, 0.2))
println("Train = "+train.count()+" Test = "+test.count())
```

The split works out well. We have training data of 800,625 rows and a test Dataset with 199,584 rows. As we have lots of data, we used the 80-20 split.

In the recommendation model as usual, we create the algorithm object and fit the training data. The algorithm expects a rating column, a user ID column, and an item ID column with the default names `rating`, `user`, and `item`, respectively. In our case, the `item` column is named product, so we use the `setItemCol()` method. We also set parameters such as the regularization parameter, the maximum number of iterations, and the rank:

```
val algALS = new ALS()
algALS.setItemCol("product") // Otherwise will get exception "Field "item"
does not exist"
algALS.setRank(12)
algALS.setRegParam(0.1) // was regularization parameter, was lambda in
MLlib
algALS.setMaxIter(20)
val mdlReco = algALS.fit(train)
```

Predicting using the model

The mechanics of prediction are the same as the other algorithms:

```
val predictions = mdlReco.transform(test)
predictions.show(5)
predictions.printSchema()
```

We get the new predictions column:

```
Train = 800049 Test = 200160
+----+-------+------+----------+
|user|product|rating|prediction|
+----+-------+------+----------+
|4169|    148|   3.0| 2.8510108|
|1069|    148|   2.0| 2.9868996|
| 970|    463|   3.0| 2.7752805|
|4169|    463|   2.0| 2.6649919|
|4277|    463|   4.0|  3.424829|
+----+-------+------+----------+
only showing top 5 rows

root
 |-- user: integer (nullable = false)
 |-- product: integer (nullable = false)
 |-- rating: double (nullable = false)
 |-- prediction: float (nullable = true)
```

Model evaluation and interpretation

As the recommendation algorithm is supervised learning, we can calculate RSME and MSE. But there is one small kink: we might get NaN for either MSE or RMSE. We will run into the issue `RegressionEvaluator` returns NaN for ALS in `Spark.ml`; more information on this is available at https://issues.apache.org/jira/browse/SPARK-14489. What happens is that, when we split training and test data randomly, it might happen that the test data has users that are not in the training data. This is the cold start problem: how can we recommend something to a user who hasn't rated anything before, basically a new user? We have no way of calibrating the tastes of this user and so the recommendation algorithm returns NaN. This is fine as the output of the recommendation, but our RMSE calculation can't work with NaN. The solution, of course, is to drop the test records with NaN. So we need this extra step before we calculate RMSE:

```
// Running into https://issues.apache.org/jira/browse/SPARK-14489 = cold
Start
// So filter them out before calculating MSE et al
//
val pred = predictions.na.drop()
println("Orig = "+predictions.count()+" Final = "+ pred.count() + " Dropped
= "+ (predictions.count() - pred.count()))
// Calculate RMSE&MSE
val evaluator = new RegressionEvaluator()
evaluator.setLabelCol("rating")
var rmse = evaluator.evaluate(pred)
println("Root Mean Squared Error = "+"%.3f".format(rmse))
```

```
//
evaluator.setMetricName("mse")
var mse = evaluator.evaluate(pred)
println("Mean Squared Error = "+"%.3f".format(mse))
mse = pred.rdd.map(r => rowSqDiff(r)).reduce(_+_) /
predictions.count().toDouble
println("Mean Squared Error (Calculated) = "+"%.3f".format(mse))
//
//
val elapsedTime = (System.nanoTime() - startTime) / 1e9
println("Elapsed time: %.2fseconds".format(elapsedTime))
//
println("*** That's All Folks ! ***")
```

Once we drop the NaNs, things are fine. Just to show the calculations, we also calculate MSE by hand:

```
Orig = 200160 Final = 200123 Dropped = 37
Root Mean Squared Error = 0.860
Mean Squared Error = 0.740
Mean Squared Error (Calculated) = 0.740
Elapsed time: 104.42 seconds
```

Hyper parameters

We have glossed over an important aspect: model tuning. As you can see, there are many parameters that can be tuned, depending on the algorithm. And we have been setting the parameters once. For example, in the case of the recommender, we set `rank=12`, `regularizationParameter=0.1`, and `maxIterations=20`. In reality, the rank could be 8 or 12; the regularization parameter 0.1,1.0, or 10; and the iterations 10 or 20. So now we need to try 12 runs with these different values, calculate the accuracy, and then select the one with the best value. This is a simple case; we might have more than 100 runs and many parameters. This is where cross validation comes into the picture. To keep this book within its boundaries, I will leave this part for you to explore. Two places to go are the documentation for `org.apache.spark.ml.tuning` class and the examples code at `https://github.com/apache/spark/tree/master/examples/src/main/java/org/apache/spark/examples/ml`.

The final thing

As we mentioned earlier, one of the interesting additions to spark 2.0.0 is the ML pipeline. A pipeline is nothing but a linear graph of transformers and estimators. If we look at the classes we have been using, they are either transformers or estimators. We had a decent pipeline for our classification example, as follows:

We started with Passengers, which was the Dataset that we read in.

- Passengers1 was after the feature extraction.
- Passenders2 was after `StringIndexer`.
- Passengers3 was after the `na.drop()` function.
- Passengers4 was after the `VectorAssembler()` function.
- The `algTree` object was the algorithm object.

We would have created a pipeline:

```
valtreePipeline = new Pipeline().setStages(Array(indexer, assembler,
algTree))
```

Then, we would have created a model:

```
valmdlTree = treePipeline.fit(trainData)
```

Finally, we would have predicted as usual:

```
val predictions = mdlTree.transform(testData)
```

Of course, our original sequence won't work. We have to do `na.drop()` on `passenger1` and split it into `trainData` and `testData`. But there is no need to do either `StringIndexer` or `VectorAssembler`, as the pipeline has encapsulated those stages. The pipeline will call the `fit()` and `transform()` methods as appropriate.

We will leave this as a topic for you to explore now that you are a master at using the Spark ML classes!

References

During the writing of this chapter, I came across many useful and relevant references. I have listed them here:

- The *GoodbyMapReduce* article from Mahout News (`https://mahout.apache.org/`)
- `https://spark.apache.org/docs/latest/mllib-guide.html`
- The *Collaborative Filtering ALS* paper (`http://dl.acm.org/citation.cfm?id=168614`)
- Good presentation on decision trees (`http://spark-summit.org/wp-content/uploads/214/7/Scalable-Distributed-Decision-Trees-in-Spark-Made-Das-Sparks-Talwalkar.pdf`)
- Recommendation hands-on exercise from Spark Summit 2014 (`https://databricks-training.s3.amazonaws.com/movie-recommendation-with-mllib.html`)
- `https://amplab.cs.berkeley.edu/ml-pipelines/`
- `https://databricks.com/blog/215/1/7/ml-pipelines-a-new-high-level-api-for-mllib.html`
- ML Pipeline Design Doc `https://docs.google.com/document/d/1rVwXRjWKfIb-7PI6b86ipytwbUH7irSNLF1_6dLmh8o/`
- Examples at `https://github.com/apache/spark/tree/master/examples/src/main/scala/org/apache/spark/examples/ml`

Summary

In this chapter, we covered a large surface area of Spark: machine learning with its associated capabilities. We covered core model development and prediction along with feature extraction and model evaluation. Machine learning is a vast subject and requires a lot more study, experimentation, and practical experience with interesting data science problems. Two books that are relevant to Spark Machine Learning are Packt's own book *Machine Learning with Spark*, Nick Pentreath, and O'Reilly's *Advanced Analytics with Spark*, Sandy Ryza, Uri Laserson, Sean Owen, and Josh Wills. Both are excellent books that you can refer to. In the next chapter, we will look at another interesting topic: the processing graphs and graph algorithms using the GraphX APIs.

12
GraphX

In this chapter, we will dive into the graph-processing capabilities of Spark, the GraphX package-very interesting, useful, and relevant. You will see things such as PageRank, connections, and communities. We will start with an introduction to graph processing and then progress to code the GraphX APIs on a simple, yet interesting giraffe graph. We will explore the organization and structure of the APIs and objects and then dive into algorithms that explore the community, PageRank, and so forth. Finally, we will explore the retweet network of the #**alphago** community, exploring the data pipeline, the map attributes of properties, and vertices and edges. We'll then create a graph and run algorithms. Should be an interesting chapter!

Graphs and graph processing – an introduction

Before diving into GraphX, let's take a quick look at the domain of graph processing. Graphs and algorithms on graph structures were always the core of specific industries, such as logistics, transportation, routing, as well as social networking. These industries, among many others, relied on very special algorithms to optimize their businesses, irrespective of whether they were routing trucks or packets. Then came **PageRank** and **social media**, and the domain of graph processing has been growing ever since.

While I was preparing the materials for this book three interesting graph applications crossed my desk, all of which were very representative of the new applications of graph processing. Here's a bit about these applications.

The EU has initiatives such as **fp6** and **fp7**, which consist of projects in multiple domains that are being worked on by a host of companies and educational institutions. And they found that they can measure the impact of a project by applying social network analysis on collaboration structures.

An article an behavioral ecology points out that the infection risk for gastrointestinal helminth parasites is more influenced by weak ties with individuals outside one's clique than by repeated contact with a core set of associates. They talk about a Giraffe graph that ties two cliques and members that are part of the weak tie. We will work with a Giraffe graph in the first example – graph section. Giraffe graphs have interesting properties.

Very recently, an analysis of the graph structures underlying 11.5 million documents in 2.6 TB of Panama papers exposed how celebrities, executives, and politicians invested in questionable tax haven schemes. This 2.6 TB of data (in approximately 4.8 million e-mails, 3 million database-formatted documents, and 2.1 million PDFs) was the largest ever journalistic big data analytics endeavor.

As datasets get larger and graphs become more complex (be they web pages, social networks, structures representing nefarious investments, or social graphs), graph processing becomes more challenging. This is where Spark GraphX and other analytics tools come in handy.

Graph-based systems can be viewed as two major categories: graph processing and graph databases. Graph-processing systems (such as GraphX, **Pregel BSP**, and **GraphLab**) are very good at running complex graph-based algorithms on large datasets, while graph databases (such as **AllegroGraph, Titan, Neo4j**, and **RDF** stores) are better at graph-based queries. Usually, if one has lots of graph-based applications, there would be a graph database as well as a graph-processing stack. Moreover, graph processing would be part of a larger workflow with processing pipelines such as ETL, machine learning, and other processing logic. Graph processing can consist of standalone functions, namely large-scale systems such as the Web or PageRank or high-scale social media applications such as Facebook, where you recommend people whom you may know.

Now let's focus on graph-processing frameworks. What makes them challenging is the nature of their computations—the computations are iterative and recursive, spanning the graph. This makes record-based relational systems unsuitable for running complex graph algorithms. Once the data is large enough to span multiple systems, the partitioning that is normally employed in database systems is not optimal for graph algorithms, especially for long-tail graphs that are the norm in the Internet world. Long-tail graphs have a lot of sparsely connected nodes, where a few of the nodes have most of the edges.

Interestingly, as we were doing AR, Version 0.2 of the graphFrames package was released. Graphframes, as the name implies, leverages Datasets/DataFrames for much easier and powerful graph queries.

Even with frameworks such as MapReduce, data parallelism-based on disk-based partition schemes-has an impedance-related mismatch with graph representations. The processing of graphs is proportional to the edge cuts, that is, the number of edges cut by a partition scheme. Remember that with long-tail graphs, there will be lots of edge cuts for popular nodes because all the nodes won't fit in one system; therefore, the nodes would be stored in a distributed fashion.

This is where Spark GraphX comes into the picture. Spark offers graph parallelism over data parallelism and data-distributed RDD mechanism, almost the best of both the worlds! As we will see later, Graph offers different partition and storage schemes that can optimize complex graph algorithms. Of course, Spark can't eliminate the domain complexity, and some of the graph processing would need tuning and careful selection of partitioning and algorithms. Spark does provide enough primitives in terms of representing and processing APIs such that it makes many of the complex algorithms possible and fast and that too in most of the cases.

Spark GraphX

GraphX is a layer over Spark, thus it leverages all the interesting things about Spark-distributed processing, the algorithms, the versioned computation graph, and so forth. Interestingly, a couple of ML algorithms are written using GraphX APIs. Now refer to the following figure:

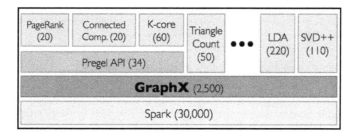

This diagram shows the layers and the relationships between GraphX, Spark, and the algorithms. GraphX is truly a distributed graph-processing component at scale with powerful partitioning mechanisms, and of course, the in-memory representation that makes iterative processing faster than normal. The programming is much more succinct and very powerful. I went back to the source code and counted the lines of implementations of graph-related algorithms. PageRank is composed of 60 lines using the aggregateMessages API (which, as you will see later, is a very powerful abstraction) and 60 lines for `runUntilConvergence` using the Pregel API. The triangle count is 50 lines of code, and SVD++ is 150 lines of code. The Pregel API itself is approximately 35 lines of code. The LDA, which is part of the ML library, is approximately 400 lines of GraphX APIs, where the documents and terms are represented as vertices and the document-term matrix is captured as GraphX edges. There is some very elegant and compact code here—it's worth investing your time in trying to understand the code.

Spark GraphX has a rich computational model, built-in algorithms, as well as APIs for implementing powerful algorithms on your own. The current focus is on computation rather than query, and the new GraphFrames API combines the DataFrame and the graph to offer a rich query interface. The GraphX APIs include graph creation, structure queries, attribute transformers, structure transformers, connection mining primitives, and algorithms. In this chapter, we will focus on GraphX, and you will work with the APIs.

There are lots of interesting graph Datasets one can work with. Airline data, co-occurrence and co-citation from papers, and Wikipedia PageRank Analysis are all types of data that one can use to learn graph processing. We will use an example from social media, particularly the retweet network of the AlphaGo community, as a case study for this chapter.

As of Spark 2.0, GraphX has only Scala APIs, so we will do all of our programming via the Spark Shell and Scala. Actually, this is good; you will get a chance to work with Scala in the context of this book.

GraphX – computational model

Before we dive into creating a graph and applying algorithms, we need to understand the computational model. Needless to say, GraphX has a rich yet simple computational model:

1. It consists of vertices connected by edges.
2. It is a property graph, which means the vertices and edges can have arbitrary objects as properties, and most importantly, these properties are visible to the APIs.

It is also a directed multigraph, meaning the edges have a direction and there can be any number of edges between the vertices. This is important to note down, because some of the algorithms can be tricky when faced with loops and cyclic graphs. GraphX has APIs that will come in handy, for example, the `removeSelfEdges` method will be helpful when you want to remove loops.

With this model, many kinds of graphs can be created, including bipartite and tripartite graphs (for example, the Users-Tags-Web pages). The following diagram illustrates the computational model of GraphX:

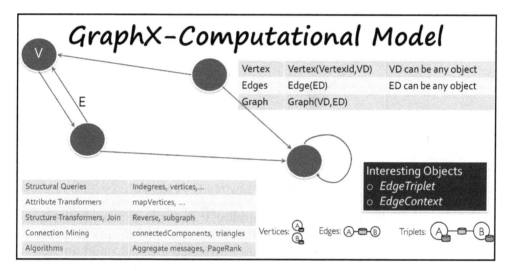

A vertex consists of a vertexID(64-bit long int) and a property object. The property object Is required, but you can always have an arbitrary value if you are not using the property. An edge consists of a source vertexID, a destination vertexID, and a property object. The APIs, as you will see, have the vertex and edge parameterized over object types. You can think of the properties as methods that help you attach user-defined objects to edges and vertices (ED/VD).

The first example – graph

As our first example, let's create a simple graph. Remember the Giraffe Graph we talked about? Let's create one that is shown in the following figure:

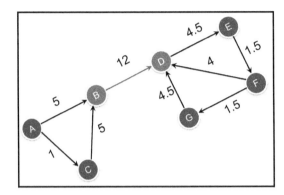

This is a graph from the lecture given by Prof. Jeffrey D. Ullman at Stanford University on graphs and social Networks (http://web.stanford.edu/class/cs246/handouts.html). It is a giraffe graph with two strong cliques connected by a weak edge. The numbers are the *betweenness centrality* of each node, as calculated by the **G-N** algorithm.

Fun facts about betweenness centrality: It shows how many paths an edge is part of; that is, its relevancy. High betweenness centrality is the sign of a bottleneck, a point of single failure; such edges need HA and probably alternate paths for rerouting, and they are susceptible to parasite infections and good candidates for a cut!

From the GraphX computational model, you can see that betweenness centrality would be represented as an edge property.

The nodes **A**, **B**,… are people, and we will have the age as the vertex property. That way, we have an interesting, realistic graph to apply GraphX APIs to.

In designing graph apps, a lot of work goes in to figuring out the vertices, the edges, and their properties. These are not abstract; they depend on the application. For example, if you are looking at a PageRank type of application, then the vertices would be people, topics, or web pages and edges would be followers/followees or links. The directions are important. You should also consider what attributes you want to work on, such as locations, hashtags, retweets, categories, and so on.

Our node table and the edge table is as follows. Later, when we work on the retweet use case, you will see how we figure out the vertices and edges, then extract the appropriate data and apply transformations.

vertexID	Property-Name	Property-Age		Source ID	Destination ID	Property
1	Alice	18		1	2	5
2	Bernie	17		1	3	1
3	Cruz	15		3	2	5
4	Donald	12		2	4	12
5	Ed	15		4	5	4
6	Fran	10		5	6	2
7	Genghis	854		6	7	2
				7	4	5
				6	4	4

Building graphs

Now that we have our data, the next step is to create a graph. Let's fire up the Spark Shell. Run it from the directory where you have installed Spark:

```
USS-Defiant:~ ksankar$ /Volumes/sdxc-01/spark-2.0.0-preview/bin/spark-shell
Using Spark's default log4j profile: org/apache/spark/log4j-defaults.properties
Setting default log level to "WARN".
To adjust logging level use sc.setLogLevel(newLevel).
16/06/14 13:33:59 WARN NativeCodeLoader: Unable to load native-hadoop library for your p
16/06/14 13:34:01 WARN AbstractHandler: No Server set for org.spark_project.jetty.server
Spark context Web UI available at http://10.39.81.150:4040
Spark context available as 'sc' (master = local[*], app id = local-1465936441227).
Spark session available as 'spark'.
Welcome to
      ____              __
     / __/__  ___ _____/ /__
    _\ \/ _ \/ _ `/ __/  '_/
   /___/ .__/\_,_/_/ /_/\_\   version 2.0.0-preview
      /_/

Using Scala version 2.11.8 (Java HotSpot(TM) 64-Bit Server VM, Java 1.7.0_60)
Type in expressions to have them evaluated.
Type :help for more information.

scala>
```

We create the graph in two steps: first we create an RDD list of the vertices and edges, then we create RDDs and eventually the graph. You don't need to type the code; the graphx-0x.scala files have the programs to create a graph and do the rest of the API stuff.

First we create the lists:

```
scala> :load /Users/ksankar/fdps-v3/code/graphX-01.scala
Loading /Users/ksankar/fdps-v3/code/graphX-01.scala...
import org.apache.spark.graphx._
import org.apache.spark.rdd.RDD
2.0.0-preview
defined class Person
defaultPerson: Person = Person(NA,0)
vertexList: List[(Long, Person)] = List((1,Person(Alice,18)), (2,Person(Bernie,17)), (3,Person(Cruz,15)),
(4,Person(Donald,12)), (5,Person(Ed,15)), (6,Person(Fran,10)), (7,Person(Genghis,854)))
edgeList: List[org.apache.spark.graphx.Edge[Int]] = List(Edge(1,2,5), Edge(1,3,1), Edge(3,2,5), Edge(2,4,1
2), Edge(4,5,4), Edge(5,6,2), Edge(6,7,2), Edge(7,4,5), Edge(6,4,4))

scala>
```

Let's quickly run through the code:

```
case class Person(name:String,age:Int)

val defaultPerson = Person("NA",0)

val vertexList = List( (1L, Person("Alice", 18)), (2L, Person("Bernie",
17)), (3L, Person("Cruz", 15)), (4L, Person("Donald", 12)), (5L,
Person("Ed", 15)), (6L, Person("Fran", 10)), (7L, Person("Genghis",854)) )

val edgeList = List( Edge(1L, 2L, 5), Edge(1L, 3L, 1), Edge(3L, 2L, 5),
Edge(2L, 4L, 12), Edge(4L, 5L, 4), Edge(5L, 6L, 2), Edge(6L, 7L, 2),
Edge(7L, 4L, 5), Edge(6L, 4L, 4) )
```

Remember the GraphX vertex is a vertexID plus a user-defined object as the property; the edge is the sourceID and destinationID plus a user-defined object as an edge property. In addition, as you will see later, the graph will create a default object for vertices that are not defined in the vertex list but are present in the edge list.

Our vertex object is a person with a name and an age. Our edge object is the inbetweenness of an integer. So the vertex list consists of elements that have an ID (integer) and a person object with a name (string) and age (integer). The edge list is actually three Integers, the ID of the source vertex, the destination vertexID and the inbetweenness centrality. As you can see from the output, Spark creates two lists, as expected.

As we discussed earlier, the property object for the vertex and edge is an important design consideration. How they would look, what attributes would they contain, and the object hierarchy are all determined by your app and the algorithms you use.

The next step is to create RDDs, and the graph-`fdps-v3/code/graphX-02.scala` helps you do that:

```
scala> :load /Users/ksankar/fdps-v3/code/graphX-02.scala
Loading /Users/ksankar/fdps-v3/code/graphX-02.scala...
vertexRDD: org.apache.spark.rdd.RDD[(Long, Person)] = ParallelCollectionRDD[0] at parallelize at <console>:32
edgeRDD: org.apache.spark.rdd.RDD[org.apache.spark.graphx.Edge[Int]] = ParallelCollectionRDD[1] at parallelize at <console>:30
graph: org.apache.spark.graphx.Graph[Person,Int] = org.apache.spark.graphx.impl.GraphImpl@2d358e4f

scala>
```

The code is deceptively simple. It is so, because we have done all the background work to architect the data and the objects:

```
val vertexRDD = sc.parallelize(vertexList)
val edgeRDD = sc.parallelize(edgeList)
val graph = Graph(vertexRDD, edgeRDD, defaultPerson)
```

We create two RDDs, which have the required structure and elements, and create a graph with them. Note that we also give the default object, that is, `defaultPerson` to the object creator code. Then, if it finds a new vertexID in the edge list, it will automatically create a vertex with `defaultPerson` as the user-defined property of the vertex.

In GraphX, there are four ways to create a graph. You can load an edge list file using the `GraphLoader.edgeListFile(...)` call. The file would be of the form source id <tab> target id. You can also load the file using RDDs, a set of edge tuples of IDs using the `fromEdgeTuples()` call, and a list of edges using the `fromEdges()` call, all in the similar fashion.
I like to create it using the edge and vertex RDDs because they are flexible and very powerful, especially when it comes to manipulating the user-defined objects for the vertices and edges.

The GraphX API landscape

The next task in our to-do list is to take a quick look at the GraphX APIs. For the most part, the organization is the same, except for a couple of twists. The following figure shows the organization and categories of the APIs:

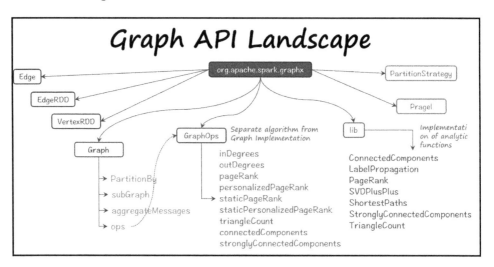

Objects such as Edge, EdgeRDD, and others are under `org.apache.spark.graphx`. The graph object has APIs such as triplets, persist, subgraph and so on. But the graph algorithms are separated under ops, which is a GraphOps object, to separate the algorithms from the graph implementation. Another quirk is `lib`, which has analytic functions such as SVD++, ShortestPath, and others. So navigate around the GraphX classes and you will find all the methods and classes.

One interesting thing to note is that the objects have a few methods that the class might not have. So take a look at the object methods if you cannot find them under the class:

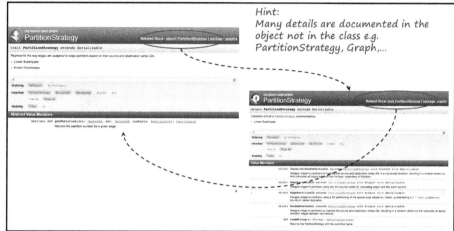

Hint:
Many details are documented in the object not in the class e.g. PartitionStrategy, Graph,...

Structural APIs

Armed with the knowledge of how to create a graph and the knowledge of how to navigate the APIs, let's focus on the structural APIs. The code is available in `graph-03.scala`, `graph-04.scala`, and `graph-05.scala` files:

```
scala> :load /Users/ksankar/fdps-v3/code/graphX-03.scala
Loading /Users/ksankar/fdps-v3/code/graphX-03.scala...
res1: Long = 9
res2: Long = 7
```

```
res5: Array[org.apache.spark.graphx.EdgeTriplet[Person,Int]] = Array(((1,Person(Alice,18)),(2,Person(Bernie,17)),5), ((1,Person
(Alice,18)),(3,Person(Cruz,15)),1), ((2,Person(Bernie,17)),(4,Person(Donald,12)),12))
((1,Person(Alice,18)),(2,Person(Bernie,17)),5)
((1,Person(Alice,18)),(3,Person(Cruz,15)),1)
((2,Person(Bernie,17)),(4,Person(Donald,12)),12)
((3,Person(Cruz,15)),(2,Person(Bernie,17)),5)
((4,Person(Donald,12)),(5,Person(Ed,15)),4)
((5,Person(Ed,15)),(6,Person(Fran,10)),2)
((6,Person(Fran,10)),(4,Person(Donald,12)),4)
((6,Person(Fran,10)),(7,Person(Genghis,854)),2)
((7,Person(Genghis,854)),(4,Person(Donald,12)),5)
```

You can get the number of edges and vertices by `numEdges` and `numVertices`.

```
graph.numEdges
graph.numVertices
//
val vertices = graph.vertices
vertices.collect.foreach(println)
//
val edges = graph.edges
edges.collect.foreach(println)
//
val triplets = graph.triplets
triplets.take(3)
triplets.map(t=>t.toString).collect().foreach(println)
```

The triplets are interesting. They actually encompass an edge and two vertices that the edge connects to and all the user-defined objects in one neat object. They are very useful when we want to write algorithms:

```
scala> :load /Users/ksankar/fdps-v3/code/graphX-04.scala
Loading /Users/ksankar/fdps-v3/code/graphX-04.scala...
inDeg: org.apache.spark.graphx.VertexRDD[Int] = VertexRDDImpl[26] at RDD at
VertexRDD.scala:57
res7: Array[(org.apache.spark.graphx.VertexId, Int)] = Array((4,3), (5,1), (6,1), (2,2),
(3,1), (7,1))
outDeg: org.apache.spark.graphx.VertexRDD[Int] = VertexRDDImpl[30] at RDD at
VertexRDD.scala:57
res8: Array[(org.apache.spark.graphx.VertexId, Int)] = Array((4,1), (1,2), (5,1), (6,2),
(2,1), (3,1), (7,1))
allDeg: org.apache.spark.graphx.VertexRDD[Int] = VertexRDDImpl[34] at RDD at
VertexRDD.scala:57
res9: Array[(org.apache.spark.graphx.VertexId, Int)] = Array((4,4), (1,2), (5,2), (6,3),
(2,3), (3,2), (7,2))
g1: org.apache.spark.graphx.Graph[Person,Int] =
org.apache.spark.graphx.impl.GraphImpl@67183d3f
((1,Person(Alice,18)),(2,Person(Bernie,17)),5)
((2,Person(Bernie,17)),(4,Person(Donald,12)),12)
((3,Person(Cruz,15)),(2,Person(Bernie,17)),5)
((7,Person(Genghis,854)),(4,Person(Donald,12)),5)
g2: org.apache.spark.graphx.Graph[Person,Int] =
org.apache.spark.graphx.impl.GraphImpl@3d5d0af5
```

Let's look at the code. It is not that complex:

```
val inDeg = graph.inDegrees // Followers
inDeg.collect()
val outDeg = graph.outDegrees // Follows
outDeg.collect()
val allDeg = graph.degrees
allDeg.collect()
//
val g1 = graph.subgraph(epred = (edge) => edge.attr > 4)
g1.triplets.collect.foreach(println)
```

```
//
// What is wrong ?
//
val g2 = graph.subgraph(vpred = (id, person) => person.age > 21)
g2.triplets.collect.foreach(println)
```

The `inDegrees` are the edges pointing toward the vertices (followers, links referring to a web page, and others) and `outDegrees` are outward edges (things one follows, links that a web page has to other pages, and others). We extract a `subgraph` by giving a filter predicate on the property object of the edge (the edge predicate) or the property object of the vertices (the vertex predicate). This is where the versatility of GraphX shines. As we saw earlier, we can attach user-defined objects and use them in our graph-processing algorithms. In this code, for `g1`, we filtered edges that have more than four centralities.

What's wrong with the output?

When we do a subgraph `g2`, filtering the vertices with age > 21, and then print the triplets of the subgraph, we get nothing. Is there something wrong? Actually, things are fine, as we can see from running `graph-05.scala` file:

```
scala> :load /Users/ksankar/fdps-v3/code/graphX-05.scala
Loading /Users/ksankar/fdps-v3/code/graphX-05.scala...
(7,Person(Genghis,854))
g3: org.apache.spark.graphx.Graph[Person,Int] =
org.apache.spark.graphx.impl.GraphImpl@7c2650ae
res14: Array[org.apache.spark.graphx.EdgeTriplet[Person,Int]] = Array()
(1,Person(Alice,18))
(7,Person(Genghis,854))
```

As earlier, the code is simple. The subgraph query takes a predicate, in our case, age >= 18:

```
// Look ma, no edges !
g2.vertices.collect.foreach(println)
g2.edges.collect.foreach(println)
//
val g3 = graph.subgraph(vpred = (id, person) => person.age >= 18)
g3.triplets.collect
//
// Just two disjoint vertices
// If there are no edges, is it really a graph ?
g3.vertices.collect.foreach(println)
//
```

The reason the triplets do not print anything is because there are no edges in g2, just one vertex. A similar issue arises in g3: this has two vertices, but they are not joined by an edge. (you can check the results by looking at our Giraffe graph and correlating with the data table.) So again, no triplets are printed. The reason we were looking at these situations is to show that at times, graph processing can be a little tricky and our algorithms need to consider all the corner cases.

Community, affiliation, and strengths

Let's now look at the network connections and others. These algorithms are applied widely for fraud detection and security applications. Triangular spamming is a well-known technique that can be detected using the triangle count and community algorithms. Another interesting application of the triangle count is to estimate and rank communities. The age of a community is related to the density of the triangles; new communities will have fewer triangles, and as the communities mature, triangles start to form. Another interesting application is the concept of a heavy hitter in a community, defined as any vertex that has more than sqrt(n) degrees. Finding heavy hitter triangles would be like finding influential people in a community. Connected communities and strongly connected communities expose the structure in an underlying graph, akin to the Panama papers. And all these are APIs in GraphX. No wonder GraphX is part of the processing stack for Linkedin:

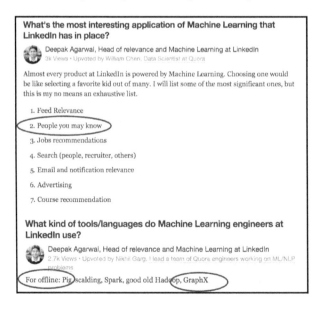

Let's apply some of the connection and community algorithms to our graph and explore the results:

```
scala> :load /Users/ksankar/fdps-v3/code/graphX-06.scala
Loading /Users/ksankar/fdps-v3/code/graphX-06.scala...
cc: org.apache.spark.graphx.Graph[org.apache.spark.graphx.VertexId,Int] =
org.apache.spark.graphx.impl.GraphImpl@796b45
res16: Array[org.apache.spark.graphx.EdgeTriplet[org.apache.spark.graphx.VertexId,Int]] =
Array(((1,1),(2,1),5), ((1,1),(3,1),1), ((2,1),(4,1),12), ((3,1),(2,1),5),
((4,1),(5,1),4), ((5,1),(6,1),2), ((6,1),(4,1),4), ((6,1),(7,1),2), ((7,1),(4,1),5))
res17: Array[Iterable[org.apache.spark.graphx.VertexId]] = Array(CompactBuffer(4, 1, 5, 6,
2, 3, 7))
res18: Int = 1
res19: Array[(org.apache.spark.graphx.VertexId, Int)] = Array((1,7))
ccS: org.apache.spark.graphx.Graph[org.apache.spark.graphx.VertexId,Int] =
org.apache.spark.graphx.impl.GraphImpl@851f257
res20: Array[org.apache.spark.graphx.EdgeTriplet[org.apache.spark.graphx.VertexId,Int]] =
Array(((1,1),(2,2),5), ((1,1),(3,3),1), ((2,2),(4,4),12), ((3,3),(2,2),5),
((4,4),(5,4),4), ((5,4),(6,4),2), ((6,4),(4,4),4), ((6,4),(7,4),2), ((7,4),(4,4),5))
res21: Array[Iterable[org.apache.spark.graphx.VertexId]] = Array(CompactBuffer(4, 5, 6,
7), CompactBuffer(1), CompactBuffer(2), CompactBuffer(3))
res22: Int = 4
triCounts: org.apache.spark.graphx.Graph[Int,Int] =
org.apache.spark.graphx.impl.GraphImpl@65c35fd4
triangleCounts: Array[(org.apache.spark.graphx.VertexId, Int)] = Array((4,2), (1,1),
(5,1), (6,2), (2,1), (3,1), (7,1))
```

The APIs are relatively simple, but the results are semantically richer and we can get interesting inferences:

```
val cc = graph.connectedComponents() // returns another graph; costly
operation
cc.triplets.collect
graph.connectedComponents.vertices.map(_.swap).groupByKey.map(_._2).collect
cc.vertices.map(_._2).collect.distinct.size // No. of connected components
//
// list the components and its number of nodes in the descending order
cc.vertices.groupBy(_._2).map(p=>(p._1,p._2.size)).
   sortBy(x=>x._2,false). // sortBy(keyFunc,ascending)
   collect()
//
// stronglyConnectedComponents
//     Compute the strongly connected component (SCC) of each vertex and
//     return a graph with the vertex value containing the lowest vertex id
//     in the SCC containing that vertex.
//
val ccS = graph.stronglyConnectedComponents(10)
ccS.triplets.collect
ccS.vertices.map(_.swap).groupByKey.map(_._2).collect
ccS.vertices.map(_._2).collect.distinct.size // No. of connected components
//
val triCounts = graph.triangleCount()
val triangleCounts = triCounts.vertices.collect
//
```

The `connectedComponents` call returns an interesting graph structure: the node IDs and the ID of the community that it belongs to. Looking at the graph, we can see that all the nodes are part of a single connected community. But if we apply `stronglyConnectedComponents`, we get four communities. This makes sense as strong connection requires bi-directed edges, and we can see that that is there only in the D-E-F-G network, and A, B, and C are strong communities by themselves. The triangle count shows that 4/D and 6/F are part of two triangles, and the others are part of one triangle. This can be verified by a visual analysis of our Giraffe graph. Algorithms such as `connectedComponents` and `stronglyConnectedComponents` are iterative and would take time and computing resources, depending on the size and complexity of the graph that you are processing.

Algorithms

Now we dive into the most interesting part of GraphX: algorithms and the graph parallel computation APIs to implement more algorithms. The following table shows a bird's eye view of the algorithms:

Type	GraphX method/example
Graph-Parallel Computation	The method is `aggregateMessages()`, Function `Pregel()`. Refer to https://issues.apache.org/jira/browse/SPARK-5062 for examples.
PageRank	The method is `PageRank()`. As an example, refer to the influential papers in a citation network, Influencer in retweet. You can specifically check out the following: **staticPageRank()**: This provides a static no of iterations and dynamic tolerance; see the parameters (tol versus numIter) **personalizedPageRank()**: This is a variation of PageRank that gives a rank relative to a specified "source" vertex in the graph-People
You May Know ShortestPaths and SVD++	The methods are `ShortestPaths()` and SVD++. As an example, consider the fact that SDV++ takes an RDD of edges.
LabelPropagation (LPA)	The method is `LabelPropagation()`.

PageRank is probably the most talked about algorithm available in GraphX. In fact, it has three flavors: first, the PageRank algorithm, which is a dynamic version that takes a tolerance and runs until it converges to that tolerance. Second, there is a `staticPageRank` algorithm that takes a number of iterations and runs that many times, rather than seeking convergence. Finally, there is `personalizedPageRank`, which calculates PageRank with respect to a given vertex, probably a good algorithm to implement the "people you may know" or "find popular people in a specified subcommunity" functions.

Other interesting algorithms are `LabelPropogation` to find communities, `ShortestPaths`, and `SVD++`.

Calling the algorithms is straightforward. Let's see how we can run the page rank in our small graph. We will run `fdps-v3/code/graphX-07.scala` and inspect the output step by step, comparing with the program code:

```
scala> :load /Users/ksankar/fdps-v3/code/graphX-07.scala
Loading /Users/ksankar/fdps-v3/code/graphX-07.scala...
ranks: org.apache.spark.graphx.VertexRDD[Double] = VertexRDDImpl[949] at RDD at VertexRDD.scala:57
(4,0.89599134375)
(1,0.15)
(5,0.732675)
(6,0.7727737499999999)
(2,0.34124999999999994)
(3,0.21375)
(7,0.47842884375)

(4,0.89599134375)
(6,0.7727737499999999)
(5,0.732675)
(7,0.47842884375)
(2,0.34124999999999994)
(3,0.21375)
(1,0.15)
topVertices: Unit = ()
```

Getting PageRank is very straightforward. We call it for the graph like this:

```
val ranks = graph.pageRank(0.1).vertices
ranks.collect().foreach(println)
val topVertices = ranks.sortBy(_._2,false).collect.foreach(println)
```

This returns the vertexID and the PageRank. We can then sort it and print the array or even print only the first few. Looking at our Giraffe graph, it makes sense that 4/D has the highest PageRank. We would have expected 5/E to be next (as 4/D points to 5/E), but for some reason, 6/F has a larger PageRank than 5/E. Note that 1/A has the lowest PageRank (0.15), which is the default damping factor, even though nothing points to it.

PageRank is an algorithm that determines the importance/popularity of a web page based on the number of links that are pointing to it. So the PageRank of a page being pointed to by 100 web pages would normally be higher than one that is pointed to by only 10 pages. It also considers the popularity of the web pages that are pointing to it. For example, if you have a page that is linked by Google, the PageRank would be much higher.

Graph parallel computation APIs

Now let's switch gears and look at the APIs available for implementing algorithms: `aggregateMessages()` and `Pregel()`. These are basic graph parallel computation primitives that can be used to implement all kinds of interesting algorithms. We will dig deeper into `aggregateMessages()` in this chapter and will leave the `Pregel()` API for you to explore. Interestingly, the Pregel API is a superset of `aggregateMessages()`, and it is in fact implemented using the `aggregateMessages()` API. Now it will probably make more sense to read the second section and appreciate the elegance of the GraphX APIs—the `staticPageRank` API consists of 60 lines of code and uses the `aggregateMessages()` call, while `pageRank()` (the converging version) consists of 60 lines and uses the `Pregel()` call.

The aggregateMessages() API

The `aggregateMessages()` API is somewhat daunting if you just look at the signature, but it gets easier as one works with the API. So in this section, let's work on a few simple problems using the API to really understand the mechanism. The signature is as follows:

```
def aggregateMessages[A](sendMsg: (EdgeContext[VD, ED, A]) ⇒ Unit,
mergeMsg: (A, A) ⇒ A, tripletFields: TripletFields =
TripletFields.All)(implicit arg0: ClassTag[A]): VertexRDD[A]
```

Aggregates values from the neighboring edges and vertices of each vertex. The user-supplied `sendMsg` function is invoked on each edge of the graph, generating 0 or more messages to be sent to either vertex in the edge. The `mergeMsg` function is then used to combine all messages destined to the same vertex.

Let's parse the call signature and then apply it to a few situations. It has four elements, as follows:

- **Message type**: Note that `aggregateMessages()` is parameterized by the message type [A]. It is the value that gets passed around. It will be an integer in our examples.
- **EdgeContext**: This is an interesting one. It is a superset of `EdgeTriplet`, which we have seen earlier (that is, the source and destination vertices, the edge, and all the user objects attached to the vertices and the edge). Plus, it also has the capability to send a message to the destination vertex or the source vertex. Remember that our graph is directed, which means the edges have a source vertex and a destination vertex. And the message would be the `messageType` object we saw just a moment ago.
- **sendMsg**: This basically means a message sent in the context of EdgeContext, either to the source vertex or to the destination vertex, and as we discussed, it contains an object of the message type.
- **mergeMsg**: A routine/code run at each vertex that will aggregate all the messages received by that vertex.

You can also look at `aggregateMessages()` as a MapReduce paradigm over the graph, the map being `sendMsg` and reduce being `mergeMsg`. Interestingly, in its previous incarnation, `aggregateMessages()` was called `mapReduceTriplets()`—you can still see it in the Pregel implementation code. JIRA has an interesting diagram on this, which will appear soon.

Of course, our abstract discussion wouldn't be complete without a few pragmatic examples.

The first example – the oldest follower

In our Giraffe graph, let's find the oldest follower. Remember that the edges are directed and we have the age as a property. Use the template for the four elements of the `aggregateMessages()` signature as follows:

- **messageType**: Because we are working with age, we'll use an integer.
- **edgeContext**: From all the pieces of information available, we will use the age and send it to the source through `sendToDst`.

As A is following B, A is the source and B is the destination; A sends its age to B. This might take a little thinking, but make sure you internalize the direction. Don't worry! We have more examples to practice this.

- **sendMsg**: This is `sendtoSrc`, the age at each vertex.
- **mergeMsg**: We want the oldest follower, so the reduce operation must be max.

In fact, our code nicely translates from what we just discussed:

```
val oldestFollower = graph.aggregateMessages[Int](
edgeContext => edgeContext.sendToDst(edgeContext.srcAttr.age),//sendMsg
(x,y) => math.max(x,y) //mergeMsg
)
oldestFollower.collect()
```

And the output looks fine:

```
oldestFollower: org.apache.spark.graphx.VertexRDD[Int] = VertexRDDImpl[960] at RDD at VertexRDD.scala:57
res35: Array[(org.apache.spark.graphx.VertexId, Int)] = Array((4,854), (5,12), (6,15), (2,18), (3,18), (7,10))
```

We can compare the output with the following graph:

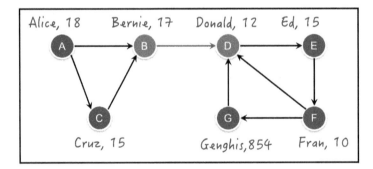

The second example – the oldest followee

Now what if we want to find the oldest followee, that is, the oldest person a vertex is following? Everything else remains the same: the age as the message, integer as the message type, and max as the reduce operation; the only difference is that `sendToSrc` should be changed to `dstAttr`.

As A is following B, A is the source and B is the destination; as we want to get the age of the followee (which B knows), B sends its age to A, that is, `sendtoSrc` the `dstAttr`. An easy way to understand this is to see who has the information; find that in the `edgeContext` object and the direction to send to.

Our code looks very similar to the first example, except the direction:

```
//  How do we get the oldest followee ?
val oldestFollowee = graph.aggregateMessages[Int](
    edgeContext => edgeContext.sendToSrc(edgeContext.dstAttr.age),//sendMsg
    (x,y) => math.max(x,y) //mergeMsg
    )
oldestFollowee.collect()
```

And the output is as expected:

```
oldestFollowee: org.apache.spark.graphx.VertexRDD[Int] = VertexRDDImpl[964] at RDD at VertexRDD.scala:57
res36: Array[(org.apache.spark.graphx.VertexId, Int)] = Array((4,15), (1,17), (5,10), (6,854), (2,12), (3,17), (7,12))
```

The third example – the youngest follower/followee

Now it is easier. Our signature template (from the first and second examples) remains the same, except for the reduce operation, that is, `mergeMsg`. It will become `min (x,y)` instead of `max (x,y)`.

We make the changes in both of the code and run it:

```
// #1 : What if we want the youngest follower?
val youngestFollower = graph.aggregateMessages[Int](
  edgeContext => edgeContext.sendToDst(edgeContext.srcAttr.age),//sendMsg
  (x,y) => math.min(x,y) //mergeMsg
  )
youngestFollower.collect()
//
// #2 : What if we want the youngest of the nodes folowee ?
val youngestFollowee = graph.aggregateMessages[Int](
  edgeContext => edgeContext.sendToSrc(edgeContext.dstAttr.age),//sendMsg
  (x,y) => math.min(x,y) //mergeMsg
  )
youngestFollowee.collect()
```

The output looks fine. You should check the graph and convince yourself that it is right:

```
youngestFollower: org.apache.spark.graphx.VertexRDD[Int] = VertexRDDImpl[968] at RDD at VertexRDD.scala:57
res37: Array[(org.apache.spark.graphx.VertexId, Int)] = Array((4,10), (5,12), (6,15), (2,15), (3,18), (7,10))

youngestFollowee: org.apache.spark.graphx.VertexRDD[Int] = VertexRDDImpl[972] at RDD at VertexRDD.scala:57
res38: Array[(org.apache.spark.graphx.VertexId, Int)] = Array((4,15), (1,15), (5,10), (6,12), (2,12), (3,17), (7,12))
```

The fourth example – inDegree/outDegree

Remember the `inDegree` and `outDegree` methods? Let's see whether we can implement them using our favorite call, `aggregateMessages()`.

 Thinking about the `inDegree` operation as a MapReduce reminds us of the `count` in the map reduce, where we send a tuple with the word and the number 1. In our case, we do the reduce at each vertex, so we only need the 1.

With that tip in mind, our signature template becomes easier:

- **MessageType** – This is just the number 1, which is an integer.
- **edgeContext**: We really don't need anything from `edgeContext`. Just the presense of a vertex is enough. So our message is just the number 1, as we do in the mapReduce word count.
- **sendMsg**: For `inDegree`, this is `sendToDst`, and for `outDegree`, it is `sendToSrc`.
- **mergeMsg**: Our reduce operation is the classic "add" we use in the word count.

In fact, our code exactly looks like this, and the output values are the same as the inDegrees and `outDegrees` call:

```
// #3 : Can we get inDegree with aggregateMessages ?
var iDegree = graph.aggregateMessages[Int](
edgeContext => edgeContext.sendToDst(1),//sendMsg
(x,y) => x+y //mergeMsg
)
iDegree.collect()
graph.inDegrees.collect()
//
val oDegree = graph.aggregateMessages[Int](
edgeContext => edgeContext.sendToSrc(1),//sendMsg
(x,y) => x+y //mergeMsg
)
oDegree.collect()
```

```
graph.outDegrees.collect()
```

The output values are as expected:

```
iDegree: org.apache.spark.graphx.VertexRDD[Int] = VertexRDDImpl[980] at RDD at VertexRDD.scala:57
res41: Array[(org.apache.spark.graphx.VertexId, Int)] = Array((4,3), (5,1), (6,1), (2,2), (3,1), (7,1))
res42: Array[(org.apache.spark.graphx.VertexId, Int)] = Array((4,3), (5,1), (6,1), (2,2), (3,1), (7,1))

oDegree: org.apache.spark.graphx.VertexRDD[Int] = VertexRDDImpl[984] at RDD at VertexRDD.scala:57
res43: Array[(org.apache.spark.graphx.VertexId, Int)] = Array((4,1), (1,2), (5,1), (6,2), (2,1), (3,1), (7,1))
res44: Array[(org.apache.spark.graphx.VertexId, Int)] = Array((4,1), (1,2), (5,1), (6,2), (2,1), (3,1), (7,1))
```

The preceding discussions are summarized in the following diagram for clarity:

```
val oldestFollower = graph.aggregateMessages[Int](
    edgeContext => edgeContext.sendToDst(edgeContext.srcAttr.age),//sendMsg
    (x,y) => math.max(x,y) //mergeMsg
    )
oldestFollower.collect()                                              sendToDst vs sendToSrc

oldestFollower: org.apache.spark.graphx.VertexRDD[Int] = VertexRDDImpl[2056] at RDD at VertexRDD.scala:57
res79: Array[(org.apache.spark.graphx.VertexId, Int)] = Array((4,854), (5,12), (6,15), (2,18), (3,18), (7,10))

val oldestFollowee = graph.aggregateMessages[Int](
    edgeContext => edgeContext.sendToSrc(edgeContext.srcAttr.age),//sendMsg
    (x,y) => math.max(x,y) //mergeMsg
    )
oldestFollowee.collect()

oldestFollowee: org.apache.spark.graphx.VertexRDD[Int] = VertexRDDImpl[2092] at RDD at VertexRDD.scala:57
res99: Array[(org.apache.spark.graphx.VertexId, Int)] = Array((4,12), (1,18), (5,15), (6,10), (2,17), (3,15), (7,854))

                                                val oDegree = graph.aggregateMessages[Int](
                                                    edgeContext => edgeContext.sendToSrc(1),//sendMsg
                                                    (x,y) => x+y //mergeMsg
                                                    )
                                                oDegree.collect()
                                                graph.outDegrees.collect()
val iDegree = graph.aggregateMessages[Int](
    edgeContext => edgeContext.sendToDst(1),//sendMsg    oDegree: org.apache.spark.graphx.VertexRDD[Int] = VertexRDDImpl[2100] at RDD at VertexRDD.scala:57
    (x,y) => x+y //mergeMsg                              res104: Array[(org.apache.spark.graphx.VertexId, Int)] = Array((4,1), (1,2), (5,1), (6,2), (2,1), (3,1), (7,1))
    )                                                    res105: Array[(org.apache.spark.graphx.VertexId, Int)] = Array((4,1), (1,2), (5,1), (6,2), (2,1), (3,1), (7,1))
iDegree.collect()
graph.inDegrees.collect()

iDegree: org.apache.spark.graphx.VertexRDD[Int] = VertexRDDImpl[2096] at RDD at VertexRDD.scala:57
res101: Array[(org.apache.spark.graphx.VertexId, Int)] = Array((4,3), (5,1), (6,1), (2,2), (3,1), (7,1))
res102: Array[(org.apache.spark.graphx.VertexId, Int)] = Array((4,3), (5,1), (6,1), (2,2), (3,1), (7,1))
```

Interestingly, `inDegrees` and `outDegrees` are actually implemented using `aggregateMessages()`. You can see the code in the Spark source file, namely `src/main/scala/org/apache/spark/graphx/GraphOps.scala`, method `private def degreesRDD`.

Partition strategy

As we had mentioned earlier, graph processing becomes challenging when we use disk-partitioning strategies employed in MapReduce and others. Let's elaborate on this topic a little; we won't go into too much detail.

The problem is when we have millions of vertices and edges that do not fit into one machine, which means we need a distributed storage scheme. Naturally, we will have to store vertices and edges in many machines. Then the challenge is running iterative algorithms that would need back and forth communication between the machines. Interestingly, a Giraffe graph lends itself to efficient partitioning—one can cut the graph at the neck. So in our example, we can store the vertices A, B, and C in one machine and D, E, F, and G in another machine and still have optimum communication. This is called the edge cut. Unfortunately, the large graphs we encounter are all long-tail-based, that is, a few vertices are very popular and have lots of connections. In such cases, the communication when performing graph algorithms is not divided equally among all the nodes.

In short, unlike a relational table, graph processing is contextual with regard to a neighborhood; therefore, maintaining the locality and equal-sized partitioning becomes a challenge. Check out the following diagram:

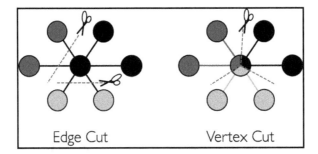

The diagram illustrates two schemes: the Edge cut and Vertex cut. Following is the description for both:

- **Edge cut**: The scheme partitions the vertices into different machines. The communication and storage overhead of an edge cut is directly proportional to the number of edges that are cut. For vertices that are very popular, this will be high.
- **Vertex cut**: The scheme partitions the edges, which means there would be duplication of the vertices. The communication and storage overhead of a vertex cut is directly proportional to the sum of the number of machines spanned by each vertex. The more the duplication, the higher the cost.

In GraphX, the vertex cut strategy is set by default (to balance the hotspot issue due to the power law / Zipf's Law) with min replication of edges. But you can select a different scheme, depending on your application and characteristics of data. The `org.apache.spark.graphx.Graph` file has the partition API to repartition a graph. It takes a partition strategy, and optionally, the number of partitions:

```
partitionBy(partitionStrategy: PartitionStrategy, numPartitions: Int)
partitionBy(partitionStrategy: PartitionStrategy)
```

The GraphX has four partition strategies, described as following:

- **RandomVertexCut:**(usually the best) This collocates all the edges with the same direction edges between two vertices (hashing the source and destination vertex IDs).
- **CanonicalRandomVertexCut**: This is a random vertex cut that collocates all the edges between two vertices, regardless of the direction (hashing the source and destination vertex IDs in a canonical direction). ... *remember GraphX is multi graph*
- **EdgePartition1D**: This assigns edges to partitions using only the source vertex ID, collocating edges with the same source.
- **EdgePartition2D**: This provides 2D partitioning of the sparse edge adjacency matrix.

An in-depth discussion is outside the scope of this book, but it is important to know that GraphX has a partition strategy. In fact, some of the algorithms require a partition strategy to run. For example, **groupEdges** mention that the graph must have a partition strategy:

```
groupEdges(merge: (ED, ED) ⇒ ED): Graph[VD, ED]
```
Merges multiple edges between two vertices into a single edge. For correct results, the graph must have been partitioned using partitionBy.

Case study – AlphaGo tweets analytics

Now that we have a good understanding of GraphX, let's apply our newly gained knowledge to analyze a retweet network. Like any big data project, the first task is to define a pipeline, figure out the data elements, the source, transformations, mapping, and processing.

Data pipeline

For this case study, I collected Twitter data pertaining to the AlphaGo project:

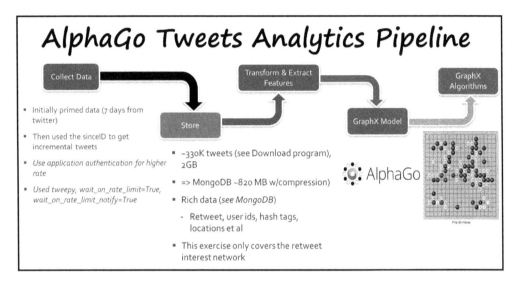

While the full mechanics of data collection from Twitter is out of scope, I will quickly mention the main steps:

1. Using Python and the **tweepy** framework, you can download the tweets mentioning the hashtag #alphago. Initially, pull all the tweets that Twitter will give and then use the since ID to incrementally get the tweets.

2. Then use application authentication for a higher rate. Twitter implements rate limiting, so the amount of tweets one can get without their firehose subscription is limited. Even then, I had collected approximately 300K tweets and 2 GB worth of data.

3. Store the data in **MongoDB**. Twitter has a very rich Dataset with hundreds of attributes.

4. I wanted to create a graph model of the retweet network. So the transformations and feature extraction was aimed at that smaller task.

5. Lastly, store the extracted data in the `reTweetNetwork-small.psv` file.

GraphX modeling

The interesting and challenging part is to model the vertices, edges, and objects. In this case, we want to find out the rank of users based on their retweet characteristics. We also want to understand the locations, time zones, and also the follower-followee characteristics. In this chapter, we will work up to PageRank calculation, but I have the location and time zone data for you to play with on your own. The following figure shows the data model and how it is created from the tweet record. The `tweetID`, count, and text go as part of the edge object; the details of the person who is tweeting go to the destination vertex, and the details of the person who is retweeting go to the source vertex:

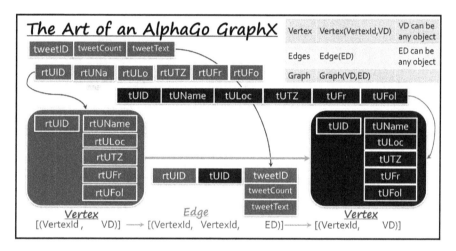

Let's look at the data model:

- Our vertices are the users. Interestingly, Twitter has a 64-bit user ID, which we can use as the vertex ID. As you will see in a minute, this makes our mapping easier.
- As we are modeling the retweet domain, the edges represent the retweets, the source being the person who is retweeting, and the destination being the person who wrote the original tweet.
- Once we have the vertices and edges, defining the objects becomes a little easier:
- We store the username, location, time zone, and the number of friends and followers as the user object
- The **tweetID**, **tweet text**, and others become the object that is associated with each edge

- Interestingly, the **PSV** file is inverted, that is, each record has the **tweetID**, text, the details of the retweet user, and the details of the person who wrote the original tweet
- The preceding figure shows how the elements map to the graph.

GraphX processing and algorithms

Now we will start going through the code (`AlphaGo-01.scala`) and running it. The first step is to construct the vertex list and the edge list. To read the file, we use the **spark-csv** package. So the Spark Shell needs to be started with the package option as shown here:

```
/Volumes/sdxc-01/spark-1.6.0/bin/spark-shell --packages
com.databricks:spark-csv_2.10:1.4.0
```

Refer to the following figure:

```
USS-Defiant:~ ksankar$ /Volumes/sdxc-01/spark-1.6.0/bin/spark-shell --packages com.databricks:spark-csv_2.10:1.4.0
Ivy Default Cache set to: /Users/ksankar/.ivy2/cache
The jars for the packages stored in: /Users/ksankar/.ivy2/jars
:: loading settings :: url = jar:file:/Volumes/sdxc-01/spark-1.6.0/assembly/target/scala-2.10/spark-assembly-1.6.0-hadoop
ngs/ivysettings.xml
com.databricks#spark-csv_2.10 added as a dependency
:: resolving dependencies :: org.apache.spark#spark-submit-parent;1.0
        confs: [default]
        found com.databricks#spark-csv_2.10;1.4.0 in central
        found org.apache.commons#commons-csv;1.1 in list
        found com.univocity#univocity-parsers;1.5.1 in list
:: resolution report :: resolve 325ms :: artifacts dl 14ms
        :: modules in use:
        com.databricks#spark-csv_2.10;1.4.0 from central in [default]
        com.univocity#univocity-parsers;1.5.1 from list in [default]
        org.apache.commons#commons-csv;1.1 from list in [default]
        ---------------------------------------------------------------------
        |                  |            modules            ||   artifacts   |
        |       conf       | number| search|dwnlded|evicted|| number|dwnlded|
        ---------------------------------------------------------------------
        |      default     |   3   |   0   |   0   |   0   ||   3   |   0   |
        ---------------------------------------------------------------------
:: retrieving :: org.apache.spark#spark-submit-parent
        confs: [default]
        0 artifacts copied, 3 already retrieved (0kB/8ms)
log4j:WARN No appenders could be found for logger (org.apache.hadoop.metrics2.lib.MutableMetricsFactory).
log4j:WARN Please initialize the log4j system properly.
log4j:WARN See http://logging.apache.org/log4j/1.2/faq.html#noconfig for more info.
Using Spark's repl log4j profile: org/apache/spark/log4j-defaults-repl.properties
To adjust logging level use sc.setLogLevel("INFO")
Welcome to
      ____              __
     / __/__  ___ _____/ /__
    _\ \/ _ \/ _ `/ __/  '_/
   /___/ .__/\_,_/_/ /_/\_\   version 1.6.0
      /_/

Using Scala version 2.10.5 (Java HotSpot(TM) 64-Bit Server VM, Java 1.7.0_60)
Type in expressions to have them evaluated.
Type :help for more information.
Spark context available as sc.
SQL context available as sqlContext.
```

First we load the data and create a DataFrame:

```scala
import org.apache.spark.SparkContext
import org.apache.spark.SparkConf
import org.apache.spark.graphx._

println(new java.io.File( "." ).getCanonicalPath)
println(s"Running Spark Version ${sc.version}")
//
val sqlContext = new org.apache.spark.sql.SQLContext(sc)
val df =
sqlContext.read.format("com.databricks.spark.csv").option("header",
"false").option("inferSchema",
"true").option("delimiter","|").load("file:/Users/ksankar/fdps-
v3/data/reTweetNetwork-small.psv")
df.show(5)
df.count()
//
case class User(name:String, location:String, tz : String, fr:Int,fol:Int)
case class Tweet(id:String,count:Int)

val graphData = df.rdd
println("--- The Graph Data ---")
graphData.take(2).foreach(println)
```

We run the code by loading the file: `scala> :load /Users/ksankar/fdps-v3/code/AlphaGo-01.scala`.

The DataFrame corresponds closely to the data model in the preceding figure. The run output shows the rows with 14 fields:

```
scala> :load /Users/ksankar/fdps-v3/code/AlphaGo-01.scala
Loading /Users/ksankar/fdps-v3/code/AlphaGo-01.scala...
import org.apache.spark.SparkContext
import org.apache.spark.SparkConf
import org.apache.spark.graphx._
/Users/ksankar
Running Spark Version 1.6.0
sqlContext: org.apache.spark.sql.SQLContext = org.apache.spark.sql.SQLContext@14f9a04e
df: org.apache.spark.sql.DataFrame = [C0: bigint, C1: int, C2: string, C3: bigint, C4: string, C5: string, C6: string, C7: int, C8: int, C9: bigint, C10: string, C11: string, C12: string, C13: int, C14: int]
+--------------------+---+---+---------+-------------+------------------+-----------+---+---+---------+--------------------+-----------+---
--------------------+---+---+-------+
|                  C0| C1| C2|       C3|           C4|                C5|         C6| C7| C8|       C9|                 C10|        C11|
             C12| C13|   C14|
+--------------------+---+---+---------+-------------+------------------+-----------+---+---+---------+--------------------+-----------+---
--------------------+---+---+-------+
|709210987015114752|  2| NA| 589277295| Unsigned Heroes|          Seattle WA|    Arizona| 919|2703|127984521|Erick Schonfeld|         New York|Cen
tral Time (US ...|1292|  776571|
|709210994875039744| 25| NA| 271007340|  Johnny Apuan|                NA|         NA|1252|  99| 134495511|           WIRED|San Francisco/New...|Pac
ific Time (US ...| 264|57147631|
|709210924714672641| 39| NA| 166001040|       Nedpool|Canterbury New Ze...|Wellington|1033| 572| 89171421| Dan Kaminsky|Chief Scientist, ...|Pac
ific Time (US ...| 401|  502291|
|709210923928559616| 25| NA|3244208187|Deen over Duniya|            Mars|         NA|  93| 223| 134495511|           WIRED|San Francisco/New...|Pac
ific Time (US ...| 264|57147631|
|709210919729963008| 25| NA|2749754251|  Farzan Sabet|                NA|Eastern Time (US ...| 373| 862| 134495511|           WIRED|San Francisco/New...|Pac
ific Time (US ...| 264|57147631|
+--------------------+---+---+---------+-------------+------------------+-----------+---+---+---------+--------------------+-----------+---
--------------------+---+---+-------+
only showing top 5 rows
```

The next step is to map each row to the vertex and edge, with appropriate data elements in the objects:

```
val vert1 = graphData.map(row =>
(row(3).toString.toLong,User(row(4).toString,row(5).toString,row(6).toStrin
g,row(7).toString.toInt,row(8).toString.toInt)))
println("--- Vertices-1 ---")
vert1.count()
vert1.take(3).foreach(println)

val vert2 = graphData.map(row =>
(row(9).toString.toLong,User(row(10).toString,row(11).toString,row(12).toSt
ring,row(13).toString.toInt,row(14).toString.toInt)))
println("--- Vertices-2 ---")
vert2.count()
vert2.take(3).foreach(println)

val vertX = vert1.++(vert2)
println("--- Vertices-combined ---")
vertX.count()

val edgX = graphData.map(row =>
(Edge(row(3).toString.toLong,row(9).toString.toLong,Tweet(row(0).toString,r
ow(1).toString.toInt)))))
println("--- Edges ---")
edgX.take(3).foreach(println)
```

The output is as expected. We can see that we have 10001 vertices for each group, that is, the users who tweeted and the users who retweeted:

```
res3: Long = 10001
defined class User
defined class Tweet
graphData: org.apache.spark.rdd.RDD[org.apache.spark.sql.Row] = MapPartitionsRDD[27] at rdd at <console>:36
--- The Graph Data ---
[709210987015114752,2,NA,589277295,Unsigned Heroes,Seattle WA,Arizona,919,2703,12798452,Erick Schonfeld,New York,Central Time (US & Canada),1292,77657]
[709210994875039744,25,NA,271007340,Johnny Apuan,NA,NA,1252,99,1344951,WIRED,San Francisco/New York,Pacific Time (US & Canada),264,5714763]
vert1: org.apache.spark.rdd.RDD[(Long, User)] = MapPartitionsRDD[28] at map at <console>:40
--- Vertices-1 ---
res7: Long = 10001
(589277295,User(Unsigned Heroes,Seattle WA,Arizona,919,2703))
(271007340,User(Johnny Apuan,NA,NA,1252,99))
(166001040,User(Nedpool,Canterbury New Zealand,Wellington,1033,572))
vert2: org.apache.spark.rdd.RDD[(Long, User)] = MapPartitionsRDD[29] at map at <console>:40
--- Vertices-2 ---
res10: Long = 10001
(12798452,User(Erick Schonfeld,New York,Central Time (US & Canada),1292,77657))
(1344951,User(WIRED,San Francisco/New York,Pacific Time (US & Canada),264,5714763))
(8917142,User(Dan Kaminsky,Chief Scientist, whiteops.com,Pacific Time (US & Canada),401,50229))
vertX: org.apache.spark.rdd.RDD[(Long, User)] = UnionRDD[30] at $plus$plus at <console>:44
--- Vertices-combined ---
res13: Long = 20002
edgX: org.apache.spark.rdd.RDD[org.apache.spark.graphx.Edge[Tweet]] = MapPartitionsRDD[31] at map at <console>:40
--- Edges ---
Edge(589277295,12798452,Tweet(709210987015114752,2))
Edge(271007340,1344951,Tweet(709210994875039744,25))
Edge(166001040,8917142,Tweet(709210924771467264,39))
rtGraph: org.apache.spark.graphx.Graph[User,Tweet] = org.apache.spark.graphx.impl.GraphImpl@27737937
ranks: org.apache.spark.graphx.VertexRDD[Double] = VertexRDDImpl[199] at RDD at VertexRDD.scala:57
```

Once we have the vertices and the edges in place, creating the graph and running the algorithms is easier:

```
val rtGraph = Graph(vertX,edgX)
//
val ranks = rtGraph.pageRank(0.1).vertices
println("--- Page Rank ---")
ranks.take(2)
println("--- Top Users ---")
val topUsers = ranks.sortBy(_._2,false).take(3).foreach(println)
val topUsersWNames =
ranks.join(rtGraph.vertices).sortBy(_._2._1,false).take(3).foreach(println)
//
//How big ?
println("--- How Big ? ---")
rtGraph.vertices.count
rtGraph.edges.count
//
// How many retweets ?
//
println("--- How many retweets ? ---")
val iDeg = rtGraph.inDegrees
val oDeg = rtGraph.outDegrees
//
iDeg.take(3)
iDeg.sortBy(_._2,false).take(3).foreach(println)
//
oDeg.take(3)
oDeg.sortBy(_._2,false).take(3).foreach(println)
//
// max retweets
println("--- Max retweets ---")
val topRT =
iDeg.join(rtGraph.vertices).sortBy(_._2._1,false).take(3).foreach(println)
val topRT1 =
oDeg.join(rtGraph.vertices).sortBy(_._2._1,false).take(3).foreach(println)
```

The output is interesting to study:

```
--- Page Rank ---
res17: Array[(org.apache.spark.graphx.VertexId, Double)] = Array((144366820,0.15), (9734132,0.15))
--- Top Users ---
(11821362,322.9447926136434)
(1482581556,84.29509874154466)
(14497118,43.956874999999826)
topUsers: Unit = ()
(11821362,(322.9447926136434,User(Statsman Bruno,Stockholm,Stockholm,53,79094)))
(1482581556,(84.29509874154466,User(Demis Hassabis,NA,NA,11,22637)))
(14497118,(43.956874999999826,User(Ken Kawamoto,Kokubunji, Tokyo,Tokyo,549,5675)))
topUsersWNames: Unit = ()
--- How Big ? ---
res20: Long = 9743
res21: Long = 10001
--- How many retweets ? ---
iDeg: org.apache.spark.graphx.VertexRDD[Int] = VertexRDDImpl[220] at RDD at VertexRDD.scala:57
oDeg: org.apache.spark.graphx.VertexRDD[Int] = VertexRDDImpl[47] at RDD at VertexRDD.scala:57
res23: Array[(org.apache.spark.graphx.VertexId, Int)] = Array((630222308,1), (149925820,11), (169630984,2))
(11821362,2574)
(1482581556,863)
(14497118,360)
res25: Array[(org.apache.spark.graphx.VertexId, Int)] = Array((144366820,1), (9734132,1), (764148504,1))
(2214694938,40)
(52500519,25)
(156263005,12)
--- Max retweets ---
(11821362,(2574,User(Statsman Bruno,Stockholm,Stockholm,53,79094)))
(1482581556,(863,User(Demis Hassabis,NA,NA,11,22637)))
(14497118,(360,User(Ken Kawamoto,Kokubunji, Tokyo,Tokyo,549,5675)))
topRT: Unit = ()
(2214694938,(40,User(Brain Bot,NA,NA,104,1327)))
(52500519,(25,User(Tech XB,London,London,2977,5066)))
(156263005,(12,User(NA,NA,NA,288,2543)))
topRT1: Unit = ()
```

The top retweeted users are Bruno, Hassabis, and Ken. Hassabis is the CEO of DeepMind, the company that created the AlphaGo program. Our data has 20,002 vertices, but the resulting graph has only 9,743 vertices and 10,001 edges. This makes sense as duplicate vertices are collapsed.

References

For more information, refer to the following links. They will further add to your knowledge:

- http://neo4j.com/blog/icij-neo4j-unravel-panama-papers/
- The GraphX paper at https://www.usenix.org/system/files/conference/osdi14/osdi14-paper-gonzalez.pdf
- The Pragel paper at http://kowshik.github.io/JPregel/pregel_paper.pdf

- Scala/Python support at `https://issues.apache.org/jira/browse/SPARK-3789`
- The Java API for GraphX at `https://issues.apache.org/jira/browse/SPARK-3665`
- LDA at `https://issues.apache.org/jira/browse/SPARK-1405`
- Some good exercises at
  `https://www.sics.se/~amir/files/download/dic/answers6.pdf`
- `http://ampcamp.berkeley.edu/big-data-mini-course/graph-analytics-with-graphx.html`
- `https://www.quora.com/What-are-the-main-concepts-behind-Googles-Pregel`
- `http://www.istc-cc.cmu.edu/publications/papers/2013/grades-graphx_with_fonts.pdf`
- `https://www.sics.se/~amir/files/download/papers/jabeja-vc.pdf`
- Paco Nathan, Scala Days 2015, `https://www.youtube.com/watch?v=P_V71n-gtDs`
- Apache Spark Graph Processing by Packt at
  `https://www.packtpub.com/big-data-and-business-intelligence/apache-spark-graph-processing`
- `http://hortonworks.com/blog/introduction-to-data-science-with-apache-spark/`
- `http://stanford.edu/~rezab/nips2014workshop/slides/ankur.pdf`
- Mining Massive Datasets book v2,
  `http://infolab.stanford.edu/~ullman/mmds/ch10.pdf`
- `http://web.stanford.edu/class/cs246/handouts.html`
- `http://www.cs.princeton.edu/~chazelle/courses/BIB/pagerank.htm`
- `http://kukuruku.co/hub/algorithms/social-network-analysis-spark-graphx`
- `http://sparktutorials.net/setup-your-zeppelin-notebook-for-data-science-in-apache-spark`
- `http://www.transtats.bts.gov/DL_SelectFields.asp?Table_ID=236&DB_Short_Name=On-Time`
- `http://openflights.org/data.html`

Summary

This was a slightly longer chapter, but I am sure you have progressed to be experts in Spark by now. We started by looking at graph processing and then moved on to GraphX APIs and finally to a case study. Keep a look out for more GraphX APIs and also the new GraphFrame API, which is being developed for querying. We also have come to the end of this book. You started by installing Spark and understanding Spark from the basics, then you progressed to RDDs, Datasets, SQL, big data, and machine learning. In the process, we also discussed how Spark has matured from 1.x to 2.x, what data scientists would look for in a framework such as Spark, and the Spark architecture. We (the authors, editors, reviewers, and the rest of the gang at Packt) enjoyed writing this book, and we hope you were able to get a good start on your journey to distributed computing with Apache Spark.

Index

www.ingramcontent.com/pod-product-compliance
Lightning Source LLC
Chambersburg PA
CBHW060530060326
40690CB00017B/3441